NATURALIZATION OF THE SOUL

'...an exceptionally rich and stimulating work... this is a splendid book full of fascinating information and insights, and it deserves a wide readership.'

Philosophical Books

'...at every turn they seek to reassure the reader that some feature or other of the texts they discuss finds an echo in present-day debate... a price worth paying if *Naturalization of the Soul* helps to awaken some interest in neglected figures from the past.'

Times Literary Supplement

'...a solid piece of scholarship, based on a careful examination of an impressive number of primary tests... I found their accounts consistently thoughtful and intelligent.'

Mind

Naturalization of the Soul charts the evolution of theories of self and personal identity from John Locke to William Hazlitt in the nineteenth century. The authors also explore two critical transitions which marked the eighteenth century: the move from religious conception of soul to a philosophical conception of self, to the scientific conception of mind. This rigorous and erudite study becomes even more compelling when it argues that theories of self, thought to be discussed for the first time in the 1960s, were in fact widely debated in the eighteenth century – including the implications of fission examples for personal identity theory and the thesis that personal identity is not what matters primarily in survival. Martin and Barresi also break new ground by recognising William Hazlitt as perhaps the most significant personal identity theorist of the English Enlightenment, after Locke and Hume, for his direct relevance to contemporary thinking.

Naturalization of the Soul makes a major contribution to one of the most radical transformations in the history of thought and is essential reading for all who are interested in issues which lie at the core of the Western philosophical tradition.

'This is an excellent book, with an original and interesting approach to its topic.' Stephen Gaukroger, University of Sydney.

Raymond Martin is Professor of Philosophy, Union College, and Emeritus Professor of Philosophy at the University of Maryland College Park. **John Barresi** is Professor of Psychology at Dalhousie University.

ROUTLEDGE STUDIES IN EIGHTEENTH CENTURY PHILOSOPHY

NATURALIZATION OF THE SOUL

Self and personal identity in the eighteenth century

Raymond Martin and John Barresi

Routledge
Taylor & Francis Group

LONDON AND NEW YORK

First published 2000
by Routledge
2 Park Square, Milton Park, Abingdon, Oxon OX14 4RN

Simultaneously published in the USA and Canada
by Routledge
711 Third Avenue, New York, NY 10017

First published in paperback 2004

Routledge is an imprint of the Taylor & Francis Group, an informa business

Typeset in Times by
BOOK NOW Ltd

British Library Cataloguing in Publication Data
A catalogue record for this book is available
from the British Library

Library of Congress Cataloging-in-Publication Data
Martin, Raymond, 1914
Naturalization of the soul: self and personal identity in the eighteenth century/
Raymond Martin and John Barresi.
Xi, 203 p. ; 25 cm (Routledge studies in eighteenth century philosophy)
Includes bibliographical references and index
1. Self (Philosophy) – Great Britain – History – 17th century. 2. Identity
(Psychology) – Great Britain – History – 17th century 3. Self (Philosophy) –
Great Britain – History – 18th century. 4. Identity (Psychology) – Great Britain
– History – 18th century
BD438.5 .M37   2000
126/.09 21

ISBN 978-0-415-21645-6 (hbk)
ISBN 978-0-415-33355-9 (pbk)

CONTENTS

PREFACE

In the eighteenth century in Britain, there was a revolution in personal identity theory. In our own times, beginning in the early 1970s, there has been another. It is well known that in the earlier revolution, the self as immaterial soul was replaced with the self as mind. This replacement involved movement away from substance accounts of personal identity, according to which the self is a simple persisting thing, toward relational accounts, according to which the self consists essentially of physical and/or psychological relations among different temporal stages of an organism or person.

At the heart of the revolution in our own times has been the emergence of two questions where previously, it seemed, there had been only one. The traditional question is: What are the necessary and sufficient conditions for personal identity over time? That is, what must obtain in order for the same person to persist, and what, if it does obtain, guarantees that the same person persists? The new question is: What matters fundamentally in a person's apparently self-interested concern to survive? That is, from the perspective of what, in normal circumstances, would count as a person's self-interested concern to survive, is it fundamentally personal identity that matters – does the person fundamentally want to persist – or is what matters other ways of continuing that do not themselves suffice for identity? Readers unfamiliar with the contemporary debate may want to read the section entitled, 'Contemporary philosophy of self and personal identity,' in Chapter 6, before reading the rest of the present book.

Probably, most philosophers who are engaged in the post-1970 debate over self and personal identity suppose that the emergence of their 'new question' – what matters fundamentally in a person's apparently self-interested concern to survive – is a recent philosophical development. We too used to make this assumption. Then we discovered William Hazlitt's little-known, first book, *An Essay on the Principles of Human Action* (1805), in which he addressed many of the core questions that were being hotly debated, as if for the first time, in the 1970s. He even made important use of a kind of example – what has come to be known as a *fission example* – that had been primarily responsible for ushering in the recent revolution in personal identity theory.

Our discovery of Hazlitt's early book quickly led to an even more surprising discovery. It was that Hazlitt had neither invented fission examples nor been the first to see their relevance to personal identity theory. Throughout the eighteenth century in Britain, fission examples had been close to the center of a continuing and vigorous debate over self and personal identity. In this debate, many of the core issues had been discussed that since the 1970s have been discussed again, as if for the first time. Eventually we were forced to the realization that it is only a slight exaggeration to say that in the late twentieth century, personal identity theorists were to a large extent merely replaying the unresolved concerns of eighteenth century thinkers.

Although key elements of the eighteenth century debate over personal identity and the debate in our own times are remarkably similar, the larger contexts in which the two debates occurred is radically different. The eighteenth century debate occurred in the context of a larger debate over the naturalization of the soul. In our own times, the debate occurred against the backdrop of an intellectual view in which the 'soul' had already been naturalized. Central to the larger context in which the eighteenth century debate took place were certain issues, such as whether matter can think, which were thought to be highly relevant to views of self and personal identity. Also central was intense concern over the fate of religion, and in particular Christianity, in an era of increasing secularism. To understand the evolution of the eighteenth century debate over self and personal identity, one must keep one eye on its connections to the emerging science of human nature and the other on its perceived relevance to religious concerns. We try to do this.

Almost all of the theoretical action with which we shall be concerned took place in Britain. In the eighteenth century, at least prior to Kant, this is where the main action took place. However, in a fuller study, non-British thinkers, especially Diderot and Rousseau in France, and Leibniz, Wolff, and of course, Kant, in Germany, would have to be taken into account. Our reason for ignoring these non-British thinkers is that, for the most part, until at least the end of the eighteenth century, their views did not impinge much on developments in Britain. Where their views may have had some influence, such as in the case of Leibniz's early views on metaphysics and Rousseau's on education, we consider them briefly. Eventually, of course, Kant's influence on English-speaking philosophy was enormous, but his influence did not begin to be felt seriously in Britain until the nineteenth century. And when his influence was finally felt, its effect was not primarily to continue the tradition of debate over self and personal identity that had flourished in Britain throughout the eighteenth century but, rather, to terminate that debate in favor of another, rather different way, of framing questions about the self. With the exception of a few nineteenth century philosophers and psychologists, such as William Hazlitt, Thomas Brown, James Mill, John Stuart Mill and then eventually F. H. Bradley, it was not until the twentieth century, in what became the analytic tradition in philosophy, that the most conspicuous themes in the earlier eighteenth century British controversy were rediscovered and debated anew.

The Introduction is a development of material, some of which is included in Raymond Martin's *Self-Concern: An Experiential Approach to What Matters in Survival* (1998) and some in his 'Personal Identity from Plato to Parfit', in *The Experience of Philosophy*, 4th edn, Daniel Kolak and Raymond Martin (eds) (1999). Chapter 1 is based on Martin's paper, 'Locke's Psychology of Personal Identity', *Journal of the History of Philosophy* (2000). Chapters 2, 5 and 6 draw on Raymond Martin, John Barresi, and Alessandro Giovannelli's, 'Fission Examples in the Eighteenth and Early Nineteenth Century Personal Identity Debate', *History of Philosophy Quarterly* (1998) and Raymond Martin and John Barresi's, 'Hazlitt on the Future of the Self', *Journal of the History of Ideas* (1995). An addendum to our account in the present book may be found in John Barresi and Raymond Martin, 'Self-Concern from Priestley to Hazlitt', *The British Journal for the History of Philosophy* (2003).

During 1996, while doing research at the Huntington Library, of San Marino, California, John Barresi discovered *A System of Pneumatology In A Series of Lectures by the late Rev'd Mr. Henry Grove*, 1786 (Huntington Manuscript HM46326). Grove's views are discussed in Chapters 2 and 3. The portions of Grove's manuscript that we have reproduced are by permission of The Huntington Library, San Marino, California. We wish to thank the Huntington for allowing us to quote from this manuscript.

For their support of research that contributed to writing this book, we thank the Research Development Fund of Dalhousie University, the Social Science and Humanities Research Council of Canada, and the General Research Board of the University of Maryland.

Finally, we thank James Clark and Alessandro Giovannelli, each of whom read the penultimate draft of this book and made many perceptive criticisms and helpful suggestions. And John Barresi thanks his wife, Jolien, for her extraordinary patience during the writing of this book, as well as for over thirty years of support and encouragement.

INTRODUCTION

At the beginning of the seventeenth century, European philosophers were still thinking about the self pretty much as philosophers had been thinking about it for the previous two thousand years. The self was the soul, an immaterial substance. But in Europe the seventeenth century was a time of momentous and soul-shattering intellectual transformation. By the end of that century, Newton had shown that there could be a natural philosophy of the external world. Progressive eighteenth century thinkers were intent on showing that there could also be a natural philosophy of the internal world. As a consequence of their attempts to develop one, by the end of the eighteenth century the self had become the mind, a dynamic natural system subject to general laws of growth and development.

In trying to be scientific, the new natural philosophers of human nature turned away from dogmatic assertions about the essence of the soul in favor of investigating the mind's activities as found in experience. In attempting to explain how conscious activities connected to each other over time, they confronted new possibilities about the nature of self. The religious self, or soul, was an immaterial substance, naturally immortal. Hence, there was never any question about its persisting into an afterlife. In contrast, the empirical self, or mind, as discovered in conscious mental activity, had all the appearances of a conceptual artifact. As a consequence, the debate over how to understand ourselves, over what it is essentially that each of us is, provoked not only intellectual controversy but existential terror.

To many important thinkers of the time it seemed that what could not possibly be a question – whether we even exist as selves that persist from moment to moment, let alone into an afterlife – had suddenly become one. It was as if these thinkers had been forced against their wills to walk to the edge of a steep cliff and peer over into the abyss. What they saw – that the self may be merely imaginary – caused them to draw back in horror. As a consequence, at the end of the eighteenth century, and even well into the nineteenth, many who contributed significantly to the new empirical philosophy of human nature still thought that each human being had an immaterial soul that was above nature. And even those who accepted the new vision never came to

1

terms with how they should feel about the self's possibly having only an imaginary or pragmatic status. In sum, whereas throughout most of the seventeenth century the self had been a soul, by the end of the eighteenth century it had become a mind, albeit one whose status as a real entity was obscure. One mystery, the immaterial soul, had been dropped. Another, the self as material mind, had emerged to take its place.

Early seventeenth century views of selves and their persistence were the direct decedents of classical theories. However, in classical times, there had not really been a philosophical problem about selves or their persistence. Rather, there had been a problem of death. The question of interest was not what accounts for the fact that we persist from moment to moment, day to day, and so on through various changes, but whether bodily death is the end. The topics of self and personal identity entered the discussion through the back door, in the service of answering this more pressing question. The decisive moment occurred in Plato's *Phaedo*, in which Socrates claimed that humans survive their bodily deaths. Socrates' claim was not unusual. What was unusual is that he then went on to explain, in a way that no one had ever explained before, what *accounts* for the fact that humans survive. In his view, what accounts for it is that humans have (or, are) immaterial souls.

In ancient times (and still today) almost everyone assumed that if humans survive their bodily deaths, then there must be a vehicle (or medium) for their survivals. However, even before anyone had thought of the idea of an immaterial (unextended) soul, there was a ready vehicle available: 'fine matter'. When Socrates was alive, many Greeks thought that the soul leaves the body when the person who dies expels his last breath; they also thought that at least at that moment the soul *is* that last breath. It was Plato's genius (or perversity) to have suggested a *radical* alternative.

Although Plato never quite got the whole idea out, Socrates, in *Phaedo*, suggested that the vehicle for survival is not any sort of physical object, not even breath, but an unextended thing. So far as is known, this suggestion was original to Plato (or Socrates). Previously, when others had talked of immaterial souls, they usually meant invisible (though still extended) matter. Even Socrates, in *Phaedo*, did not always distinguish sharply between something's being immaterial and its being invisible. But sometimes he did distinguish between these. Subsequently, in the third century CE, the pagan philosopher, Plotinus, as well as certain Church fathers, including Clement, Origen and Gregory of Nyssa, developed Plato's idea that, essentially, each of us is (or has) an immaterial, naturally indivisible soul. Then, throughout the middle ages, Christian philosophers relied on this originally pagan view to explain how people survived their bodily deaths.

How, then, if he did, did Plato arrive at the idea of an immaterial, unextended soul? No one knows. In *Phaedo*, Socrates is concerned with the sources of generation and corruption, that is, with how things come to be and pass away. In his view, the corruption of a thing is brought about by its coming apart, that is, by its breaking into pieces or decomposing. Plato *may* have reasoned that any extended thing, merely in virtue of its being extended, is potentially divisible and, hence, potentially corruptible. So, if people are immortal, not only by accident but necessarily, then they have to be un-extended and therefore immaterial.

But why suppose that people are immortal? Along with others of the time, Plato may have thought he had evidence that people survive the demise of their gross physical bodies. In *Phaedo*, Socrates remarks that in graveyards people sometimes see ghosts. But people would not have to be immortal to survive for a time the demise of their gross physical bodies. It is not clear why Plato thought that people are immortal. Nor is it clear why Aristotle, in spite of his more scientific turn of mind, followed Plato in assuming that people (or, at least, *nous*, the rational part of the human soul) are immortal. Of course, in *Phaedo* Socrates does not just assert the immortality of the soul, he argues for it. So, in a sense we know why Plato may have believed that souls are immortal. But Socrates' arguments are murky and unconvincing. In any case, it was not his arguments for immortality but later ones, mainly deriving from Plotinus, that became the main source of support for the Platonic view that the soul is an unextended, indivisible, immaterial substance and, as such, incorruptible and naturally immortal.

It is a little clearer why Plato (or Socrates) thought it mattered whether people survive the demise of their gross physical bodies. He thought that in trying to understand the nature of reality, one's body is a distraction. In his view, if thinkers could discard their bodies, it would help them to discover eternal truths. In addition, Plato tells us that in one of Socrates' last thoughts, he mused about the joys of conversing with the dead. If Plato thought that after peoples' bodily deaths, they can converse with other people who have also died, then he must have supposed that souls carry with them through the process of bodily death at least some of their associated mental dispositions, such as their memories. Since Plato (or Socrates) looked forward to con-versing with the dead, he must have also thought that people are entitled to anticipate having the experiences of their post-mortem selves.

A few centuries later, Lucretius questioned this latter assumption. As a materialist, he did not believe that humans have immaterial souls but, rather, that they have minds or 'spirits' that are composed of fine matter. Even so, he took the view that the persistence of one's spirit, were this to occur, would *not* entitle a person to anticipate having future experiences. In the context of his making the point that we have nothing to fear from bodily death, he said that 'if any feeling remains in mind or spirit after it has been torn from body, that is nothing to us, who are brought into being by the wedlock of body and spirit, conjoined and coalesced'. He then considered the possibility that 'the matter that composes us should be reassembled by time after our death and brought back into its present state'. It may seem that in Lucretius' materialistic view, the matter's being brought into its present state would ensure not only that it would exactly resemble one's own current body but also that the body replicated would be attended with a mentality exactly like one's own current mentality. So, among other things, it may seem that this happening would ensure that whatever one likes or dislikes now, one's replica also would like or dislike, whatever one intends to do now, one's replica (at least at the moment of its creation) also would intend to do, whatever one remembers now, one's replica also would seem to remember, and so on. This may or may not have been Lucretius' view. In any event, he clearly thought that one's replica would not *truly* remember having been oneself now. Thus, he claimed that even if after bodily death, one were to be replicated, the replica would 'be no concern of ours once the chain of our identity [*repetentia*] had been snapped' (Lucretius 1951: 121).

Why would the replica be of no concern to the person who was replicated? Lucretius answers, in effect, by making two points. First, since at our bodily deaths our memories are dissipated *we* cease at our bodily deaths. Second, our continuing as the same persons we now are is a precondition of any rational egoistic concern we might have in the experiences of anyone who might exist in the future, including (except for the difference in memories) an exact replica of ourselves. He said, 'If the future holds travail and anguish in store, the self [that is, a unique union of body and spirit that is continuous with one's current body and spirit and has a normal pattern of memories] must be in existence, when that time comes, in order to experience it.' 'From this fate', Lucretius continued, 'we are redeemed by death, which denies existence to the self that might have suffered these tribulations'. The moral of these reflections, he thought, is 'that we have nothing to fear in death' since 'one who no longer is cannot suffer, or differ in any way from one who has never been born, when once this mortal life has been usurped by death the immortal' (Lucretius 1951: 122).[1]

Lucretius immediately followed this passage with the reflection that, for all we know, the very arrangement of matter which, in his view, each of us currently consists in, may in the limitless past have already existed, and that if it did exist, then that past person too is of no concern to us. Thus, in the context of arguing that we have nothing to fear from death, Lucretius acknowledged the existence of what today we would call *self-concern*, that is, a special way of caring about persons who existed in the past or will exist in the future that ordinarily occurs only if the persons cared about are ourselves. In articulating what he took to be the prerequisites for rational self-concern, Lucretius employed thought-experiments in which he imagined that something that is currently part of us survives bodily death and is capable of having experiences and of performing actions. However, he then insisted that since this part of ourselves would neither be continuous with us nor have normal memory access to our lives – for it to be continuous, our bodies would have to persist through death as integrated, functioning entities, in which case we never would have died in the first place – this surviving part of ourselves would neither be us nor any concern of ours. He concluded that, since this surviving part of ourselves would not be us, its experiences and actions are not something we can look forward to having and performing. In other words, in the case of post-mortem 'replicas' of ourselves, Lucretius' reason for saying that death is of no concern is that for it to be of concern we would have to be rationally entitled to anticipate having the experiences of these replicas and we are not rationally entitled to anticipate this because any such replicas would not literally be ourselves. Unfortunately, Lucretius did not then further defend this view. He merely asserted it. Even so, his discussion is impressive, not so much because he *answered* the question of what matters primarily in survival by saying that it is personal identity, that is, our continuous existence as integrated bodily, spiritual, and remembering entities, but because he thought to *ask* this question. No one previously, at least in the West, had thought to ask it.

As we shall see in Chapter 5, in the late eighteenth and early nineteenth centuries, the question of whether identity or something else matters primarily in survival resurfaced again, at the heart of the theoretical transformation in which the immaterial soul became naturalized. In our own times, as we shall see in Chapter 6, this same question of whether identity matters primarily resurfaced once again, even more dramatically. In this latest incarnation of the question, the issue arose especially in connection with the work of Derek Parfit and other theorists sympathetic to his views (Parfit 1984).

Suppose Lucretius had thought to *argue* for his view that personal identity, or continuous existence of a sort that requires the unity of body and spirit, is what matters primarily in survival. How might he have argued for it? A natural move for him to have made would have been, first, to have distinguished between personal unity at a time and personal unity over time and, then, to have argued that whatever explains one of these unities should also explain the other. In his view, it is the union of body and spirit that explains both unities. Consequently, since nothing but the union of body and spirit could preserve personal unity after bodily death, and necessarily (it would seem) at bodily death body and spirit come apart (since the body, at least, decays), then necessarily at bodily death the person perishes.

In contrast to this way in which Lucretius may have viewed survival, in Plato's earlier view, it is enough if peoples' souls persist, along with many of their mental dispositions. In fact, in Plato's view, the soul without the body is actually preferable to the soul with the body. Plato may also have assumed that before bodily death it is the soul alone that explains the unity in people that matters, which for him, at least when he wrote *Phaedo*, probably was simply mental unity. If this is right, Plato would have agreed with Lucretius that in bodily death the union of soul (spirit) and body dissolves, but he would have disagreed with Lucretius that what at bodily death dissolves – the union of soul (spirit) and body – matters. In Plato's view, the body is a useless appendage, which the person is better off having discarded.

What, though, in Plato's view, accounts for the unity, at a time, of our souls? What accounts for the unity, at a time, of our mental lives? Plato did not raise these questions. Had he raised them, presumably his answer would have had to do with the soul's immateriality and, hence, with its indivisibility. About six centuries later, Plotinus did raise these questions. He argued that unity of either sort, that is, of either the soul or the mind, would be impossible if the soul were matter, because matter is inherently divisible in a way that would destroy its own and also the mind's unity. While conceding that the soul also is divisible, he argued that it is divisible in a way that does not interfere with unity. 'The nature, at once divisible and indivisible, which we affirm to be soul has not the unity of an extended thing: it does not consist of separate sections; its divisibility lies in its presence at every point in the recipient, but it is indivisible as dwelling entire in any part'. Plotinus then observed that if the soul 'had the nature of body, it would consist of isolated members each unaware of the conditions of each other'. In that case, he continued, 'there would be a particular soul – say, a soul of the finger – answering as a distinct and independent entity to every local experience' and, hence, 'there would be a multiplicity of souls administering each individual'. But the mental lives of such individuals, he pointed out, would be unlike our mental lives, so each of us cannot be administered by a multiplicity of (equal) souls. 'Without a dominant unity', he concluded, 'our lives would be "meaningless"' (Plotinus 1952: 140).

In what in our own times has come to be known as a fission example, a person's consciousness divides into two parts, each of which is mentally complete in itself and neither of which is conscious, from the inside, of the other's mental states. Probably Plotinus was not thinking directly about fission. But fission was not far from his thoughts.[2] Nevertheless, as we shall see in Chapter 1, the passage last quoted from Plotinus is similar to one in which Locke introduced fission examples to the eighteenth century. Locke even used the image of a finger's retaining an independent consciousness after it had been separated from the rest of the body. Probably Locke had read Plotinus; if not, he was at least familiar with Plotinus' views through the Cambridge Platonists.[3] In any case, among the questions that eighteenth century philosophers (but not Locke) soon asked about fission examples, two are crucial: What becomes of the identity of the person (or mind) that divides – does he (or it) persist? And, regardless of how that question is answered, in a fission scenario could the pre-fission person obtain after fission what prior to fission mattered primarily to him in survival?

The Platonic conception of self, especially in its neo-Platonic form, was congenial to Christian theology. Largely but not exclusively for that reason it survived in Europe more or less intact until modern times. In the late middle ages, particularly in the work of Thomas Aquinas, the Platonic conception became integrated with an Aristotelian view. According to this view the living person is composed of a material body informed by an immaterial soul; in the initial stage of the afterlife, the individual is merely a soul; and at the resurrection, when the individual is again reunited with the body, there is once again a complete person. However, even in this integrated account, the essential core of the Platonic view, belief in an immaterial soul-substance that because it is immaterial is also indivisible and, hence, naturally immortal, remained intact.

This Platonic view was thought to be crucial to defending the Christian dogma of life after bodily death. It would not be abandoned without a struggle. The decisive phase of this struggle occurred in the eighteenth century. However, the view persisted, even among intellectuals, well into the nineteenth century and has resurfaced again in our own times. To the extent that it ever fell into disrepute, it did so only after the general acceptance among educated people of evolutionary theory. In the end, it was Darwin who fully naturalized the connection between humans and other animals and, thus, made humans an integrated part of the natural world.

Descartes, in the early seventeenth century, was the first influential modern philosopher to free up the Platonic view from its Aristotelian accretions. The main question for Descartes, so far as immaterial souls were concerned, is how they fit into an otherwise wholly material world, governed by mechanistic laws. In his view, individual souls of living humans are in a one-to-one relationship with individual human bodies. So, for him, the immediate question was how each person's own soul is related to his own body. The answer, he thought, is that each soul exists in a relation of mutual influence with its body and that this influence is exerted through the pineal gland.

Although Descartes was a dualist as extreme as Plato, in claiming that thinking is the essence of mind and extension the essence of body, he distinguished between mind and body more clearly than had Plato. Descartes also expressed more adequately the intimacy of the connection between mind and body. Specifically, he rejected the idea, which may well have been congenial to Plato, that the relationship of oneself as a thinking thing to one's body is like that of a pilot to his ship:

> Nature also teaches me, by these sensations of pain, hunger, thirst and so on, that I am not merely present in my body as a sailor is present in a ship [in the French version: 'as a pilot in his ship'] but that I am very closely joined and, as it were, intermingled with it, so that I and the body form a unit. If this were not so, I, who am nothing but a thinking thing, would not feel pain when the body was hurt, but would perceive the damage purely by the intellect, just as a sailor perceives by sight if anything in his ship is broken. Similarly, when the body needed food or drink, I should have an explicit understanding of the fact, instead of having confused sensations of hunger and thirst. For

these sensations of hunger, thirst, pain and so on are nothing but confused modes of thinking which arise from the union and, as it were, intermingling of the mind with the body.

(Descartes 1984: 56)

Here, Descartes drew attention to the importance of what today we might call *self-concern*. The aspect of self-concern that particularly interested him in these remarks is an ingredient of sensations. Presumably it consists, at least in part, in a kind of identification people make with the content of their sensations, as a consequence of which they *feel* that something has happened to *them*, rather than merely *think* that it has happened to *their bodies*. In Descartes' view, this feeling is due to the way oneself as a thinking thing is causally connected to one's body. Descartes' dualism prevented him from saying much that is informative about the nature of these causal connections, but what is interesting in his account is the suggestion that the unity of the person – mind and body – is due to the person's being a causally integrated system. In acknowledging this unity, and suggesting this explanation of its source, Descartes initiated exploration of the psychological mechanisms of self-constitution.

As we shall see in Chapter 1, Locke, perhaps as a consequence of taking these remarks of Descartes seriously, returned to the theme of identification and elevated it to a central position in his own theory of personal identity. Locke's word for the form of identification that interested him is *appropriation*, a notion he used to put together the first ever, fully-fledged empirical account of self-constitution. This aspect of Locke's account was then mostly ignored by subsequent eighteenth century philosophers. However, Bishop Butler, one of Locke's keenest critics, picked up on it in drawing the consequence, which Butler abhorred, that if Locke's account of self-constitution were correct, the self would be fictional. Butler then reasserted the Platonic view that our relations to our bodies are like those of a pilot to his ship.

Descartes had an additional view about consciousness which was at least as influential as the one just mentioned. It is that all thought is intrinsically reflexive; that is, necessarily if a person is aware, then he is also aware that he is aware. In reply to Hobbes and in the context of explaining what he meant by *idea*, Descartes said, 'When I want something, or am afraid of something, I *simultaneously* perceive that I want, or am afraid'; and 'It is certain that we cannot will anything without thereby perceiving that we are willing it' (Descartes 1984: 127). However, the clearest statement of his commitment to the necessarily reflexive character of thought comes in his reply to the seventh set of objections to the *Meditations*. In these objections, Bourdin complained that in holding that for a substance to be superior to matter and wholly spiritual, it is 'not sufficient for it to think' but 'is further required that it should think that it is thinking, by means of a reflexive act', Descartes was multiplying entities beyond necessity. Descartes replied that 'the initial thought by means of which we become aware of something *does not differ from* the second thought by means of which we become aware that we were aware of it, anymore than this second thought differs from a third thought by which we become aware that we were aware that we were aware' (Descartes 1984: 382). Thus, in Descartes' view, each thought not only encapsulates perhaps infinitely many reflexive mental acts but also necessarily incorporates a self-reference. This latter view, as we shall see, thwarted the emergence of a developmental psychology of the acquisition of self-concepts. For if people cannot think at all without also thinking that they think, then it is impossible to trace in the pattern of the ways people learn to think the gradual development of the ability to think of themselves.

Even so, Descartes sometimes teetered on the brink of discussing self-concepts developmentally, particularly in distinguishing between the consciousness of infants and adults. For instance, in a letter to Arnauld, written seven years after the *Meditations*, Descartes made a distinction between 'direct and reflective thoughts'. As an example of the former, he cites 'the first and simple thoughts of infants', such as 'the pleasure they feel when nourished by sweet blood'. On the other hand, he continued, 'when an adult feels something, and simultaneously perceives that he has not felt it before', we should call this 'second perception *reflection*' and attribute it 'to the intellect alone, in spite of its being so linked to sensation that the two occur together and appear to be indistinguishable from each other' (Descartes 1991, v. 3: 357).[4]

So far as theories of identity, in general, and personal identity, in particular, are concerned, both Hobbes and Spinoza, by championing their own relational views, set the stage for Locke's relational view of personal identity.[5] Of the two, Hobbes was more influential, primarily for introducing the idea that the form of a thing, that is, its organizational structure, rather than the stuff of which it is composed, can be used as a criterion of its identity:

> If the name be given for such form as is the beginning of motion, then, as long as that motion remains, it will be the same individual thing; as that man will be always the same, whose actions and thoughts proceed all from the same beginning of motion, namely, that which was in his generation; and that will be the same river which flows from one and the same fountain, whether the same water, or other water, or something else than water, flow from thence; and that the same city, whose acts proceed continually from the same institution, whether the men be the same or no.
>
> (Hobbes 1656: 137)

In Locke's hands, this idea would be used to construct a powerful rival to the Platonic conception of the person.

In 1690, just four years before Locke added his chapter on identity to the second edition of *An Essay Concerning Human Understanding*, William

Sherlock promulgated a view about the Trinity which Locke was aware of and which may have influenced him.[6] Sherlock's innovation was to use consciousness, rather than substance, as a criterion of personhood. In his view, what distinguishes the three divine Persons, each of whom share the same substance, is consciousness, and what unites the three Persons as one God is also consciousness, albeit of a different kind. In other words, the Divine Substance has two different sorts of consciousness, one of which makes the three Persons three and another of which makes them One. Sherlock – like Locke and perhaps even because of Locke, who had recently published the first edition of the *Essay* – began his account of the Trinity by confessing our human inability to know the essence of substance:

> It is agreed by all Men whoever considered this matter, that the essences of things cannot be known, but only their properties and qualities: The World is divided into Matter, and Spirit, and we know no more, what the substance of Matter, than what the substance of a Spirit is, though we think we know one, much better than the other.
> (Sherlock 1690: 7)

Then, Sherlock explained what 'makes any Substance numerically One' by, first, describing identity conditions for unorganized Matter and, then, for living organisms. Subsequently, in the second edition of the *Essay*, Locke would follow this same order of exposition.

Sherlock then said that a different account was required for 'finite created Spirits which have neither parts nor extension', and that this account depends essentially on the notion of consciousness. In his view, the 'numerical Oneness [of created Spirits] can be nothing else, but every Spirit's Unity with itself, and distinct and separate subsistence from all other created Spirits', which consists of its 'Self-consciousness'. By a Spirit's self-consciousness, Sherlock meant the fact that each Spirit feels 'only its own Thoughts and Passions, but is not conscious to the Thoughts and Passions of any other Spirit'. (Sherlock 1690: 48–9).

The same holds for the Divine Spirit: 'As far as consciousness reaches, so far the unity of a Spirit extends, for we know no other unity of a Mind or Spirit, but consciousness.' Sherlock added that:

> In a created Spirit this consciousness extends only to itself, and therefore self-consciousness makes it One with itself, and divides and separates it from all other Spirits; but could this consciousness extend to other Spirits, as it does to itself, all these Spirits, which were mutually conscious to each other, as they are to themselves, though they were distinct Persons, would be essentially One: And this is that essential unity, which is between Father, Son, and Holy Ghost, who are essentially united by mutual consciousness to whatever is in each

other, and do by an internal sensation (I want other words to express it in) feel each other, as they do themselves; and therefore are as essentially One, as a Mind and Spirit is One with itself.

(Sherlock 1690: 68)

Although unified by mutual consciousness into One God, the Divine Persons are also distinguished from each other by Self-consciousness:

The distinction between these Three Infinite Minds is plain according to this Notion; for they are distinguished, just as Three finite, and created Minds are, by Self-consciousness: . . . each Divine Person has a Self-consciousness of its own, and knows and feels itself (if I may so speak) as distinct for the other Divine Persons; the Father has a Self-consciousness of his own, whereby he knows and feels himself to be the Father, and not the Son, nor the Holy Ghost . . . as *James* feels himself to be *James*, and not *Peter*, nor *John;* which proves them to be distinct Persons: . . . Here is no confounding of Persons .

(Sherlock 1690: 67)

In sum, in Sherlock's view, what distinguishes the three Divine Persons is 'self-consciousness' and what unites them is 'mutual consciousness'. Sherlock never succeeded in explaining how these two are different. For present purposes, this deficiency in his account is not important. What is important is that he used consciousness, not substance, to unite the disparate parts of persons and to mark the boundaries between persons. It was this idea that may have influenced Locke and through Locke modern personal identity theory.

In spite of these ways in which Hobbes, Spinoza, and Sherlock anticipated his views, Locke deserves his title as father of modern personal identity theory. Locke integrated ideas he borrowed from others with ones which were wholly his own, weaving both together into a highly influential general theory of identity. In the case of personal identity, he had two fundamental doctrines, one negative and one positive. The negative doctrine is that the persistence of persons cannot be understood as parasitic upon the persistence of *any* underlying substance(s) out of which humans (or persons) may be composed. The positive doctrine is that the persistence of persons has to be understood in terms of the unifying role of consciousness. Prior to Locke there had been mostly *a priori philosophies* of personal identity. Locke was the first to propose an empirically grounded *psychology* of personal identity.

1

PERSONAL IDENTITY

The first edition of Locke's *An Essay Concerning Human Understanding* appeared in December of 1689. In his 'Epistle to the Reader', Locke says that his book was prompted by a philosophical discussion among he and 'five or six Friends' that came 'quickly at a stand, by the Difficulties that rose on every side'. It seemed to Locke that he and his friends 'took a wrong course' and that before setting 'ourselves upon Enquiries of that Nature, it was necessary to examine our own Abilities, and see, what Objects our Understandings were, or were not fitted to deal with' (Locke 1975: 7). His goal was to determine the limits of human understanding. He resolved to follow what he called a 'Historical, plain Method', by which he meant an account not of how the Mind *actually* comes to be furnished with its Ideas but rather of how through experience it could have acquired them. That is, Locke analyzed complex and abstract ideas into simple components, all of which, in his view, easily could have come from experience. He thought that by such means 'we can find out, how far the Understanding can extend its view; how far it has Faculties to attain Certainty; and in what Cases it can only judge and guess' (Locke 1975: 44–5).

Locke abjured making contributions to 'the Physical Consideration of the Mind'. Instead, he set himself the modest task of toiling merely 'as an Under-Labourer in clearing Ground a little, and removing some of the Rubbish, that lies in the way to Knowledge', so that others who were engaged in what later would be regarded as properly scientific pursuits could work unobstructed (Locke 1975:10). Locke's self-characterization of his project is largely accurate. In later terms, he was not doing scientific psychology, but, rather, a quasi-historical, empirical investigation of the origins of knowledge, from which he claimed to derive empirical epistemological results.

Locke argued against two philosophical traditions: the Aristotelian Scholasticism of his day, in which he was educated and for which he had no respect, and Cartesian Rationalism, which he regarded as his real competition. To oppose the latter, Locke began the *Essay* with a long, repetitive diatribe against the doctrine of innate ideas, in which he assumed that if anyone ever has innate ideas, then everyone always has them; in particular, if anyone ever has them, then idiots and savages have them, and normal, civilized people have them from birth.

Even at the beginning of the first edition of the *Essay*, in his critique of innate ideas, Locke seized the opportunity to express his concern and puzzlement over the issue of human or personal identity. For example, to illustrate how utterly absurd it is to suppose that anyone has from birth an innate idea of identity, he remarked, that 'if *Identity* (to instance in that alone) be a native Impression; and consequently so clear and obvious to us, that we must needs know it even from our Cradles, I would gladly be resolved, by one of Seven, or Seventy Years old, Whether a Man, being a Creature, consisting of Soul and Body, be the same Man, when his Body is changed', for instance, 'Whether *Euphorbus* and *Pythagoras*, having had the same Soul, were the same Man, though they lived several Ages asunder?' (Ibid.: I.iv.4; 86).

As Locke continued it became clear that he was not worried just about whether people have an innate idea of identity but about the theological implications of any proper theory of identity: 'Nor let anyone think, that the Questions, I have here proposed, about the *Identity* of Man, are bare, empty Speculations; which if they were, would [still] be enough to shew, That there was in the Understandings of Men *no innate* Idea *of* Identity'.

> He, that shall, with a little Attention, reflect on the Resurrection, and consider, that Divine Justice shall bring to Judgment, at the last Day, the very same Persons, to be happy or miserable in the other, who did well in This Life, will find it, perhaps, not easy to resolve with himself, what makes the same Man, or wherein *Identity* consists: And will not be forward to think he, and every one, even Children themselves, have naturally a clear *Idea* of it.
>
> (Ibid.: I.iv.5; 86)

What Locke is saying here is that if the reader thinks he has a clear understanding of these matters even now, in his maturity, let alone in his childhood, that shows that he has never really thought about it. The context suggests that Locke thinks the issue is so profoundly puzzling that this example by itself all but decisively refutes the doctrine of innate ideas, at least in its application to the idea of identity.

Four years later, in the second edition of the *Essay* (1694), Locke addressed in its own separate chapter the issue of identity and diversity. The heart of this chapter is his account of personal identity. In 1694, Cartesians, Neo-Platonists, and even Aristoteleans had been taking the identity of a person to depend essentially on the continuity of an immaterial soul, which was thought to be indivisible and, hence, naturally immortal. These theorists differed on how matter could combine with soul to form a person. But virtually all of them accepted the doctrine of the resurrection and so were concerned to provide an account that would explain how the same persons who had lived on Earth

13

could live again in the afterlife. They relied in their accounts of this on the idea that during the interim between bodily death and the resurrection the soul persists. Most thought that for the soul to persist, it had to be mentally active continuously. They hotly debated whether the soul would join again with the same or with different matter. Then, onto the stage of this rather scholastic debate, Locke burst forth with the genuinely radical and progressive thesis that persons are distinct from humans and do not depend for their persistence on retaining either the same soul or the same material body, but on having the same consciousness.[1]

Almost all views of self and personal identity prior to Locke's were pre-modern in that they relied on the notion of an immaterial soul. The self is the soul, a simple immaterial substance that by its very nature maintains unity both at a time and over time, and is naturally immortal. The basis of the self's unity with matter to form a living human being was a source of unbounded debate, virtually all of which was purely scholastic in that it rested on *a priori* metaphysics, rather than on issues open to empirical investigation.[2] Aristotelians maintained that the soul informed matter, providing it with life and, in the case of humans, also with rationality and immortality.[3] Cartesians maintained that all living things except humans are just biological machines, whereas humans are machines made conscious by their connection somehow with an immaterial soul. Both groups, largely because of their reliance on the soul, were predisposed to give, and actually gave, static, non-developmental accounts of human mentality on the basis of which the distinction between self and other is unproblematic.

Locke's account, while not fully modern (he retained his belief in the immaterial soul and in the refexive nature of consciousness), was the point of departure for the subsequent development of modern theories. Unlike previous theories, Locke's theory was grounded in experience and open to empirical investigation. Thus, it became the point of departure for the subsequent development of modern theories. By the end of the eighteenth century the transition to modern theories of the self and personal identity had been completed, at least in the views of some thinkers. Our purpose is to explain not so much every nuance in Locke's account, particularly in his metaphysics, but rather to show how Locke sowed the seeds for this transition to modern theories. For this purpose, it is more important to determine what ideas others could find in Locke's account than what ideas Locke intended them to find.

In Britain, every significant eighteenth century thinker took Locke's account of personal identity seriously. Most of them struggled, as anyone who grapples with Locke' account must, even to understand what his view was. Yet, as we shall see, his account, while chaotic, is so rich in potent ideas that the struggle to understand it inevitably brought thinkers face to face with most of what they needed to make the transition to modern views. Ironically, had Locke expressed himself more coherently, his account of personal identity may well have been less influential than it was.

Inanimate objects, plants, and animals

Fortunately, some things about Locke's account are relatively clear. He proposed separate accounts of the identity conditions for inanimate objects, animate objects, and persons. Setting aside, for a moment, his account of the identity conditions for artifacts, in the case of inanimate objects, Locke's view was that an individual at one time and one at another are the same just if they are composed of exactly the same matter. A heap of sand remains the same heap so long as it does not either gain or lose a grain, even if the grains are rearranged. Apparently, Locke thought of composite inanimate objects, implausibly in our view, as if they were sets, rather than wholes composed of parts.[4]

In the case of plants and animals, Locke held that an individual at one time and one at another are the same just if each has the kind of shape appropriate to that sort of plant or animal and sustains the same life. The shape of an animal, not its mentality, determines what biological kind of thing it is. Unless one recognizes this, Locke thought, one might be tempted to say of a rational parrot, if there were one, that it is a human. The life of a thing is simply a way in which its (perhaps exclusively) material parts are organized so as to promote its functioning in a manner appropriate to the sort of thing it is. And a plant or animal can so function even if the matter (and/or spirit) out of which it is composed at any given time is replaced by different matter (and/or spirit). In sum, still leaving the question of artifacts to one side, in Locke's view, in the case of inanimate objects, composition but not organization matters and, in the case of animate objects, shape and organization but not composition or mentality matters. In the case of artifacts, Locke acknowledged the importance of function and allowed for replacement of matter, but he did this not in his chapter on identity and not systematically, but intermittently, in different parts of the *Essay* (Ibid.: III.vi.40; 464. Also, III.vi.41; 465).

Persons

In the case of persons, Locke is unequivocal: consciousness and only consciousness matters. Thus, although biological kind, in virtue of its relation to shape and life, is essential to *human*hood, it is not essential to *person*hood. In Locke's view, a rational parrot could not be *a* human and, hence, *a fortiori*, could not be the *same* human as an individual at another time. But a rational parrot could be the same person as an individual at another time.

On one interpretation of Locke's account, an individual at one time and one at a later time are the same *person* only if the individual at the later time is conscious of having experienced or done what the individual at the earlier time experienced or did. On what is possibly another interpretation, an additional requirement is that the individual at the later time has the 'same consciousness' as the individual at the earlier time. Whether these seemingly different interpretations collapse into one depends on whether satisfying the requirement of the first guarantees that the individuals in question have the same consciousness. A reason why it might not guarantee this is that, in Locke's view, qualitative *similarity* of consciousness, especially in cases in which the later consciousness simply takes up where the earlier left off, might not guarantee numerical *identity* of consciousness. For instance, when the later individual 'wakes up' from a period of unconsciousness, the mere replication in him of a previous consciousness may not guarantee sameness of consciousness, but only mere similarity of consciousness.

In general, when Locke used the phrase 'is conscious of', in the context of talking about personal identity over time, he meant 'remembers', which is also ambiguous as between the two interpretations just distinguished. In any case, there is a textual basis for supposing that Locke, in his capacity as a theorist of personal identity over time, was a memory theorist, and a rather simple-minded one at that; that is, there is a basis for supposing that Locke proposed to define or analyze personal identity in terms of memory. For the most part, this is how Locke has been interpreted ever since the publication of the second edition of the *Essay*, but particularly by his eighteenth-century critics.

As far as it goes, the simple memory interpretation of Locke's account of personal identity over time is almost, but not quite, correct. As we shall see, Locke made some allowances for forgetfulness. More importantly, Locke may not have been trying, in the first place, to present a non-circular analysis of personal identity over time. Even aside from such qualifications, however, the simple memory interpretation of Locke is, at best, radically incomplete. For central to Locke's account of the self is the idea that consciousness is reflexive and that it plays a dual role in self-constitution: it is what unifies a person not only *over* time but also *at* a time. Memory interpretations, whether simple or not, do not explain how consciousness plays this dual role.

Even so, it is clear that an important part of what Locke meant by *consciousness* has to do with memory. Most of his eighteenth-century critics seized upon this aspect of his account, while basically ignoring the rest, in order to attribute to Locke the simple memory view. According to that view, a person at one time and one at another have the same consciousness, and hence are the same person, just in case the person at the later time *remembers* having had experiences or having performed actions that were had or performed by the person at the earlier time. As we shall see in a moment, these critics were right in thinking that this simple memory view of personal identity is vulnerable to decisive objections. However, in the eighteenth century almost all of Locke's critics wanted to defeat the simple memory view in order to retain the (immaterial) soul view. But even the simple memory view of personal identity which they attributed to Locke is, in important respects, an advance on the soul view.

According to the soul view, personal identity depends on sameness of soul. As simple, immaterial substances, souls are not part of the natural world.

Whatever exists or obtains, but not as part of the natural world, is inherently mysterious. Other peoples' souls cannot be observed either directly or indirectly. And since only the activities and not the substance of the soul is open to empirical investigation, there is no way to detect by observing an individual whether his soul remains the same. Hence, on the soul view, personal identity is inherently mysterious.

On the simple memory interpretation of Locke's account, by contrast, personal identity depends on the presence of a psychological relationship – remembering – that binds together earlier and later stages of a person. Other peoples' rememberings, unlike their souls, can be observed indirectly. For instance, by listening to another talk one may be able to determine that they remember having experienced or done various things. In the case of oneself, each person may observe directly, via introspection, that he or she remembers having experienced and done various things. Only by explaining personal identity in terms of things or relations that are observable can an account of it be developed on the basis of which one can determine empirically whether a person at one time and one at another are the same.

For this reason, Locke's account of personal identity was not just another in a long tradition of such accounts that began with Plato. Rather, his account was an idea whose time had come. As Locke seems to have recognized, the *kind* of view that he was proposing was irresistible. By contrast, his critics, though right in thinking that the simple memory view that they attributed to Locke is deeply flawed, failed to notice that their own views were more deeply flawed. So far as the verdict of history is concerned, the soul view was not just a wrong account of personal identity, it was the wrong kind of account. The simple memory view of personal identity, by contrast, was the right kind of account, even if it was not the right account. In short, Locke's critics failed to see that even the simple memory view was riding on the crest of a wave of naturalization that was about to engulf them.

Consciousness

In Locke's actual view of personal identity, as opposed to the one most of his critics attributed to him, consciousness is more inclusive than memory; it is, he said, 'inseparable from thinking' and 'essential to it: It being impossible for any one to perceive, without perceiving that he does perceive'. Locke added that 'When we see, hear, smell, taste, feel, meditate, or will any thing, we know that we do so' (Ibid.: II.xxvii.9; 335). It is in, and by, knowing that we 'do so', that is, that we perform one of these typically first-order mental operations, that we are conscious. Hence, consciousness is *any* sort of reflexive awareness (or reflexive knowledge).

It is an implication of this view of consciousness that when you *remember* having had an experience or having performed an action, a reflexivity is involved which is similar to that which is involved when you are merely aware that, in the present, you are having an experience or performing an action. But in the case of memory, it would seem, the reflexivity happens twice over. That is, when you remember having had the experience, say, of being anxious, you are aware that it is you who, in the present, is having the experience of *remembering* and also that it was you who, in the past, had the experience of *being anxious*.

In other words, in Locke's view, if right now you are remembering having experienced being anxious, you are not just aware that an experience of being anxious occurred, you are also aware that it was *you* who had the experience; that is, an ingredient of your remembering of 'the having of an experience' is that it was you who had it. Thereby, you *appropriate* (claim *ownership* of) the having of the experience. It is as if you were to claim of the *experience remembered*, 'That was mine' and of the *current having* of the memory experience, 'And this too is mine'. Of course, normally you do not explicitly claim ownership of either experience; rather, your double claim of ownership is implicit in your remembering having had the original experience.

In adopting from Descartes this view of the self-reflexive nature of consciousness and then wedding it to his own memory analysis of personal identity over time, Locke himself, in effect, originated that objection to the memory analysis for which Bishop Butler is famous but which had surfaced earlier in criticisms of Locke by John Sergeant and Samuel Clarke.[5] The objection is that one cannot analyze personal identity non-circularly in terms of memory because the notion of memory includes the notion of personal identity. That Locke was aware of this, indeed that in his unquestioning, explicit, and up-front commitment to the view that all consciousness is reflexive, he all but insisted on the point, is evidence that, contrary to what is often said, he was not, in fact, trying to analyze personal identity non-circularly in terms of memory.

Locke's objectives were different. Primary among them were his developing an account of personal identity that would satisfy two criteria: first, persons had to be capable of persisting through change of substance (or else it would be impossible to determine observationally whether an individual remained the same person over time, and post-mortem persons might not be identifiable with anyone who had lived on Earth); and, second, persons had to be *accountable* for their thoughts and deeds and, hence, appropriate subjects for the just distribution of rewards and punishments (or else the Christian dogmas of the resurrection and divine judgment would not make sense). These objectives were thrust upon Locke by his epistemology and his religious convictions. That is, since Locke was *officially* agnostic about the soul, the fate of persons could not be tied to that of souls; since he accepted that people survive their bodily deaths and that subsequently they are either justly rewarded or punished for what they had done prior to bodily death the fate of persons could not, then, be tied to material bodies (since after bodily death people may not have them, or at least may not have the same ones they had prior to bodily death); and persons, in Locke's view, had to be entities which after bodily death could be rewarded or punished justly for deeds performed before bodily death.

What sort of entity could possibly satisfy such criteria? Only one that could span the migration from being constituted, prior to bodily death, just of matter, to being constituted, after bodily death, of matter or spirit, or both; and only one so linked throughout its duration to its earlier phases that it is transparently accountable for the thoughts and deeds of its earlier phases. To show that there is such an entity, or at least that there is one prior to bodily death, Locke had to show how persons originate in the process of normal human development. And to show how persons could have originated, he had to show how consciousness could unify a person both over time and at a time, regardless of whether there was a change in the person's underlying substance. Locke did this by explaining how *persons* are by-products of the development in at least normal *humans* of reflexive consciousness.

Humans and persons

Locke distinguished between humans and persons in the first place for two reasons: first, he thought that we have different ideas of *man* (= human) and *person* and, so, need different identity conditions for them. In saying that we have different ideas of human and person, Locke was not making a point about ordinary language.[6] In commenting on his prince and cobbler example, in which overnight the 'souls' (= minds) of a prince and cobbler switch bodies, Locke admitted that 'in the ordinary way of speaking, the same Person, and the same Man, stand for one and the same thing' (Ibid.: II.xxvii.15; 340). Locke's point, rather, was that there is one *idea* corresponding to what *he* wants to understand by *man* and another corresponding to what *he* wants to understand by *person*. The word *man*, when it corresponds to Locke's idea of man, is what *we* might call a scientific term. It means, or refers to, a certain biological kind. We assume that individual humans are instances of this kind. The word, *person*, on the other hand, when it corresponds to Locke's idea of person, is, he says, 'a Forensick Term appropriating Actions and their Merit; and so belongs only to intelligent Agents capable of a Law, and Happiness and Misery' (Ibid.: II.xxvii.26; 346). What that forensic term means is a separate question, to which we shall return.

Whether Locke thought persons were substances and, if so, how and why, are questions that have been discussed endlessly by commentators.[7] In our opinion, it is impossible to determine what Locke's views on the status of persons as substances actually were. But for present purposes, it does not really matter. What matters, rather, is that as Locke was interpreted by some of his most famous critics and followers, persons, as he accounts for them, could not be genuine substances. Rather, since the nominal essence of person is based on a mode, persons, as we might say, are merely virtual (that is, fictional) substances. In saying of a putative substance that it is virtual, rather than real, we mean, first, that, it is not a substance and, second, that for pragmatic reasons one nevertheless continues to speak of it as if it were a substance.

A second reason Locke distinguished between humans and persons has to do with survival and accountability. As already noted, he was interested that his theory of persons somehow reflect or express the circumstances under which humans should be held responsible for their thoughts and deeds; and he was interested in framing a theory of human and personal identity that would be adequate to the Christian doctrine of the resurrection. Although Locke never said so explicitly, his principal worry in connection with the doctrine of the resurrection may well have been that it is implausible to suppose that the same *humans* who acted on Earth will, on the Day of Judgment, be available to be judged. The reasons Locke may have thought this are, first, that there cannot be more than one beginning to a thing, second, that we do not know whether humans have immaterial souls, and, third, that humans obviously decompose soon after their bodily deaths, the material of which they are made becoming parts of other entities.

In Locke's day, many thinkers believed that the matter out of which (some phase or other of) one's body was composed on Earth would be reassembled in the afterlife. But to Locke, this proposal may have been objectionably speculative. And unless one's body were reassembled immediately, bodily continuity, and perhaps also one's persistence as a human, has been broken. Persons, as Locke proposed that we conceive of them, are free of such obstacles to their potential survival. Yet, to make the trick work, persons have to be connected to their associated humans closely enough and in the right ways so as to make persons appropriate recipients of Divine rewards and punishments.

Persons and selves

Locke's idea of *person* may be the same as his idea of *self*. Sometimes he uses the words interchangeably. However, often he seems to use *self* to refer to a momentary entity and *person* to refer to a temporally extended one. And, seemingly for other reasons, he defines the two terms differently. A *person*, he says, 'is a thinking intelligent Being, that has reason and reflection, and can consider it self as it self, the same thinking thing in different times and places' (Ibid.: II.xxvii.9; 335). A *self*, on the other hand 'is that conscious thinking thing, (whatever Substance, made up of whether Spiritual, or Material, Simple, or Compounded, it matters not) which is sensible, or conscious of Pleasure and Pain, capable of Happiness or Misery, and so is concern'd for it *self*, as far as that consciousness extends' (Ibid.: II.xxvii.17; 341). There are important differences, at least in emphasis, between these two definitions. Locke's definition of *person* highlights that persons are *thinkers* and, as such, have reason, reflection, intelligence, and whatever else may be required for trans-temporal self-reference. His definition of *self*, on the other hand, highlights that selves are *sensors* and as such feel pleasure and pain, and are capable of happiness, misery and self-concern.

Such differences reflect disparate concerns that Locke expressed throughout his discussion of personal identity. Primary among these are that persons be appropriately subject both to moral and civil law and that they be things that naturally constitute themselves. Locke's concern that persons be appropriately subject to law raises the possibility that persons might simply be artifacts of theory – like *legal property*, or *legal persons* (where, say, corporations count as persons); however, his concern that persons be things that naturally constitute themselves counts against the idea that persons are merely creatures of theory. It is debatable how this tension in Locke's theory should be resolved.

The origin of selves

We know how, in Locke's view, humans come into being. It is a biological process. How do selves (or persons) come into being? It would seem, in some such way as this: first, a human organism's experience of pleasure and pain gives rise to the idea of a self – its own self – that is the experiencer of pleasure and pain. Second, a human organism's experience of pleasure and pain also gives rise to concern with the quality of that self's experience (each of us wants more pleasure, less pain). In thus constituting itself as a self, the organism, in effect, creates what initially is 'a momentary self'. In creating this self, the organism does not create any new matter or spirit. Third, the momentary self thus constituted (or perhaps the organism) thinks of itself (or its self) as extended over brief periods of time (say, the specious present). Then, through memory and the appropriation ingredient in self-consciousness, it thinks of itself as extended over longer periods of time:

> This personality extends it *self* beyond present Existence to what is past, only by consciousness, whereby it becomes concerned and accountable, owns and imputes to it *self* past Actions, just upon the same ground, and for the same reason, that it does the present. All which is founded in a concern for Happiness, the unavoidable concomitant of consciousness, that which is conscious of Pleasure and Pain, desiring, that that *self*, that is conscious, should be happy. And therefore whatever past Actions it cannot reconcile or appropriate to that present *self* by consciousness, it can be no more concerned in, than if they had never been done.
>
> (Ibid.: II.xxvii.26; 346)[8]

Thus, Locke thought of the constitution of the self as an ordered, multi-step process. It is unclear, however, whether he thought of this process as one in which prior phases temporally preceded subsequent phases. While he seems to have thought this, as evidenced by the quotation above, it is possible that he thought of selves (or persons) as significantly temporally extended from their inception.

Whatever Locke's view, if any, on this issue, he clearly seems to have thought that the self (or, the organism) appropriates on behalf of itself (or, its self) not only whatever it is in it that does its thinking (he is agnostic about what this is) but also, in so far as the self (or, the organism) is conscious of them: pleasures, pains, bodily parts and actions, both current and past. And he thought that the self (or, the organism) does this appropriating not in a separate mental act but, rather, as an integral part of what is involved simply in being conscious.

In sum, according to Locke, the original motive for self-constitution is provided by pleasure and pain. In normal humans, at least, these arouse 'concernment' and the assignment of the pleasure or pain to a self, which then is, or soon becomes, one's own self. If we think of this concernment and assignment as the 'glue' in self-constitution, then what gets glued together, are, first, whatever it is in the human organism that is conscious; second, mental states; third, actions; and, fourth, non-conscious bodily parts. Via consciousness, first, of present experiences and actions and, second, of memories of past ones, the ultimate product of this gluing together of disparate elements is the temporally extended self.

There is an analogous account to be given of how one should understand Locke on the topic of the origins of reflexive consciousness. One might say that when a human organism becomes aware (of something), necessarily it is also aware that *it*, the human organism, is aware. Or, instead, one might say that when a human organism becomes aware (of something), necessarily the *self*, whose organism it is, is also aware that *it*, that is, the *self*, is aware. For example, in Locke's view, if right now you are experiencing anxiety or intellectual puzzlement, or lust, you are not just aware that an experience of anxiety, puzzlement, or lust, is occurring, you are also aware that *you* are having the experience. That is, it is an ingredient of your awareness that an experience is occurring and that the experience is yours. And in having that awareness you thereby *appropriate* (declare *ownership* of) the experience, as if you were to claim of the experience, 'This too is part of me'.

But, what in such a (typically implicit) claim is the referent of the word *me*? The referent might be you, the human organism, or you, the self, or both. One possibility is that, in claiming ownership of experience through reflexive self-consciousness, you, the human organism, elevate yourself above the status of human organism, in the process creating yourself as a person. That is, when the organism says implicitly, 'This too is part of me', the *me* is not the human organism but the *person* whose human organism it is. On such an interpretation, 'This too is part of me' would, in effect, be equivalent to 'This too is part of the self that is *my*self and that owns this human organism'.

Mental development

In Locke's day, thinkers tended in their theories to overlook that people *develop* mentally. Included in this development is, that over time, people acquire progressively more sophisticated concepts and also that the functioning of those parts of their brains or minds, that is, their so-called 'faculties', which operate on their concepts, mature. In modern times, it was not until the last quarter of the eighteenth century that the idea of such mental development began to take hold. Rousseau and Locke, however, were partial exceptions to the rule, perhaps because both of them were interested in education. And in holding that the mind at birth is a *tabula rasa*, Locke had an additional motive for attending to mental development. Thus, there are intimations throughout the *Essay* that, in Locke's view, over time people acquire progressively more sophisticated ideas and principles. For example, 'The Senses *at first* let in particular *Ideas*, and furnish the yet empty Cabinet: And the Mind *by degrees* growing familiar with some of them, they are lodged in the Memory, and Names got to them'. *'Afterwards'* Locke continues, 'the Mind proceeding farther, abstracts them, and *by Degrees* learns the use of general Names. In this manner the Mind *comes to be* furnish'd with *Ideas* and Language, the Materials about which to exercise its discursive Faculty: And the use of Reason *becomes daily more visible'*, and so on (Ibid.: I.ii.15; 55, emphasis added).

There are also in the *Essay* indications that, those parts of peoples' brains or minds which operate on their concepts, that is, their 'faculties' of thinking, function over time in progressively more sophisticated ways. For example, Locke says of the 'soul' that 'it comes, by Exercise, to improve its Faculty of thinking in the several parts of it, as well as afterwards, by compounding those *Ideas*, and reflecting on its own Operations, it increases its Stock as well as Facility in remembering, imagining, reasoning, and other modes of thinking' (Ibid.: II.1.20; 116). And, somewhat more ambiguously, he says, 'These, I think, are the first Faculties and Operations of the Mind, which it makes use of in Understanding; . . . several of these *Faculties* being exercised at first principally about simple *Ideas*, we might, by following Nature in its ordinary method, trace and discover *them* in their rise, progress, and gradual improvements' (Ibid.: II.xi.14; 161, emphasis added).[9] Although the point is debatable, it seems to us that in the last quoted sentence Locke intended that the word *them* refer to faculties, rather than Ideas.

Appropriation and accountability

While Locke's views on mental development are likely to remain murky, he clearly thought that appropriation and accountability go hand in hand. His view was that a person is 'justly accountable for any Action' just if it is appropriated to that person by their self-consciousness (Ibid.: II.xxvii.16;

341). It is via this view of his that the appropriation ingredient in reflexive self-consciousness, which is a natural relation between the organism and her present and past, becomes the basis for a non-natural relation of moral ownership. That is, it is primarily this view – not any vague association between consciousness and conscience, or equivocation on the notion of ownership – that connects the natural appropriation that is part of human psychology with the non-natural appropriation that is the concern of both ethics and the law.[10]

Why did Locke think that appropriation and accountability go hand in hand? There is an admittedly speculative but still, we think, plausible reason why Locke might have thought this. He might have thought that, analogous to the way in which people come under the rule of their government by constituting themselves as a body-politic, and hence accepting civil responsibility for what they do, humans become subject to ethical norms by constituting themselves as persons, and hence accepting ethical responsibility for what they do. That is to say, humans, merely by virtue of being *alive*, and, hence, by virtue of being humans, do not, as it were, accept accountability for their pasts. But humans (or, persons) do accept accountability for their pasts, or at least for those parts of their pasts that they remember, when, *through consciousness*, they declare ownership of the various parts that collectively constitute themselves.

Are persons genuine or only virtual substances?

One of the most puzzling aspects of Locke's account of personal identity is that of determining his view of the ontological status of persons. There are two aspects to the puzzle. One is that of determining his view of the status of humans, the other that of determining his view of the status of persons. Many commentators assume that there is only one puzzle; that is, they assume that humans are substances, and the puzzle is that of determining whether persons are also substances. However, there is some reason to believe that in Book II, Chapter 27 Locke may have used the term *substance* in a more restricted way than he did in the rest of the *Essay*.[11] In this more restricted sense of *substance*, only God, immaterial thinking things, and individual atoms would be *particular substances*. Cohesive collections of atoms – a lump of gold – would be *collective substances*. Other things that Locke elsewhere speaks of, in a more expansive sense of *substance*, as particular substances – oak trees, horses and persons – are, in this more restricted sense of *substance*, not substances at all but, rather, *particular mixed modes*, that is, functional organizations of particular substances. If this interpretation is correct, then Locke was at least ambivalent about the substantial status of living things, including humans, and perhaps also of such inanimate but macroscopic objects as rocks and chairs.[12]

Elsewhere, however, Locke talks of living things as if they were substances. But it is never clear whether he means by such talk that they are substances in the same primary way as 'Particles of Matter' are substances or, rather, that they are substances only in some second-class way and, hence, strictly speaking not really substances at all. Whatever Locke's intention, he laid the groundwork for others to claim that selves are not really substances. As we shall see, this became a major issue among subsequent eighteenth century thinkers. However, even though Locke, perhaps unintentionally, encouraged the view that the self is a fiction, he certainly did not mean to encourage the view that the self is created explicitly by the philosopher, for purposes of ethical theory, or by judicial thinkers, for purposes of law. Rather, in Locke's view, whether or not the self is a fiction it is created implicitly by human mentality, via processes of appropriation and the application of self-concepts that are ingredient in reflexive consciousness.

Real and nominal essences

In Locke's view, we do not sort substances on the basis of their real constitutions, which are unknown but, rather, on the basis of our ideas of them, which are derived from gross sensible appearances. That is, we sort substances on the basis of their nominal, rather than their real, essences. Because of this Locke doubts whether the ways we ordinarily sort among substances are appropriate. He says, for instance, that our ideas of substances are 'inadequate' because they are referred to unknown 'patterns' (Ibid.: II.xxxi.3; 377). He is not skeptical just of the ways in which ordinary people sort among substances, but is almost as skeptical of the ways in which scientists do so. He says, for instance, that 'Chymists' often discover 'by sad experience' that things supposedly of the same sort are more different from each other than they are from things supposedly of different sorts (Ibid.: III.vi.8; 443). And 'our faculties carry us no farther towards the knowledge and distinction of Substances, than a Collection of those sensible *Ideas*, which we observe in them; which however made with the greatest diligence and exactness, we are capable of, yet is more remote from the true internal Constitution, from which those Qualities flow, than, as I said, a Countryman's *Idea* is from the inward contrivance of that famous Clock at *Strasburg* whereof he only sees the outward Figure and Motions'. Locke continues: 'There is not so contemptible a Plant or Animal, that does not confound the most inlarged Understanding. Though the familiar use of Things about us, take off our Wonder; yet it cures not our Ignorance' (Ibid.: III.vi.9; 444). His skepticism extends also to 'Spirits': 'For the Mind getting, only by reflecting on its own Operations, those simple *Ideas* which it attributes to *Spirits*, it hath, or can have no other Notion of *Spirit*, but by attributing all those Operations, it finds in it self, to a sort of Beings, without Consideration of Matter' (Ibid.: III.vi.11; 445). Apparently, the worry in such remarks is that, for all we know, 'Spirits' might just consist of matter. And since we form our ideas of Spirits introspectively, without regard to their possible material constitution, the nominal essences we attribute to

Spirits may be far removed from their real essences. This problem is compounded, Locke thought, by the fact that while in our ideas we make sharp distinctions among kinds of things, nature is gradual: '[W]e shall find everywhere, that the several *Species* are linked together, and differ but in almost insensible degrees' (Ibid.: III.vi.12; 447).

Then, after talking about several different actual individuals or sorts of individuals, whose status as humans is questionable, he said: 'Wherein, then, would I gladly know, consists the precise and *unmovable Boundaries of* that *Species* [that is, "Man"]? 'Tis plain, if we examine, there is *no* such thing *made by Nature*, and established by Her amongst Men' (Ibid.: III.vi.27; 454).[13] As a consequence, Locke thought, there may well, in a certain respect, be fewer substances in nature than we think there are:

> If therefore, any one will think, that a *Man*, and a *Horse*, and an Animal, and a Plant, *etc.* are distinguished by real Essences made by Nature, he must think Nature to be very liberal of these real Essences, making one for Body, another for Animal, and another for a Horse; and all these Essences liberally bestowed upon *Bucephalus*. But if we would rightly consider . . . we should find, that there is no new Thing made, but only more or less comprehensive signs whereby we may be enabled to express, in a few syllables, great numbers of particular Things, as they agree in more or less general conceptions, which we have framed to that purpose.
>
> (Ibid.: III.vi.32; 460)

So, it is not just a matter of fuzzy boundaries between sorts of things but also of their not being any real things of those *sorts* in the first place; instead, there are only, as it were, fictions ('more or less comprehensive signs'), which people make for the purpose of 'convenience' (Ibid.: III.vi. 36; 462).

Pathologies of memory

As Locke's critics saw, in his analysis of personal identity there is a problem about his use of the notion of memory. Ironically, though, there is a problem not primarily, as they tended to think, because memory is useless for the purpose of providing a non-circular analysis (or definition) of personal identity but for two other reasons. One of these has to do with forgetfulness, the other with delusions of memory. Locke responded to both problems. However, his responses seem incompatible with his theory of personal identity and, hence, constitute an embarrassment to virtually every interpretation of his theory.

Consider, first, the case in which people are (forgetfully) not conscious of having done things they did do. There are three parts to Locke's response to this seeming possibility. First, he denied that people who are awake and thinking about it ever are not conscious of having done anything they did do since if they are not conscious of having done something, they did not do it. In making this point, Locke first recounted that someone he knew thought he had Socrates' soul. Locke then considered the analogous case of someone who thinks he has the soul either of Nestor or Thersites. Locke asked rhetorically, 'Now having no consciousness of any of the Actions either of *Nestor* or *Thersites*, does, or can he, conceive himself the same Person with either of them? Can he be concerned in either of their Actions? Attribute them to himself, or think them his own more than the Actions of any other Man, that ever existed?' (Ibid.: II.xxvii.14; 339). The answer, which Locke apparently thought is too obvious to need saying, is, no. Locke continued, 'But let him [someone who claims to be Nestor] once find himself conscious of any of the Actions of *Nestor*, he then finds himself the same Person with *Nestor*' (Ibid.: II.xxvii.14; 340). By implication, we think, Locke also must have been saying of the person he knows who claims to have Socrates' soul, that whatever he might *say* he thinks, he does not *really* think he is Socrates, since if he did think that, he would be 'concerned' in the actions of Socrates, that is, he would own them and hold himself accountable for them, and he does not own them or hold himself accountable for them. Locke's point, then, may have been that if the person in question thinks he is concerned in the actions of Socrates, he is deceiving himself.

If this was Locke's point, then far from its being a blunder or symptom of incoherence in his view, as commentators often suppose, it is quite insightful. For what Locke was saying is that whether we appropriate the actions of someone in the past is *not* a matter of what theories we may have about who we are but, rather, of the nature of our experience. In other words, Locke was making two points: first, that our appropriating the experiences and actions of someone in the past depends on our being actually concerned, in the right way, with those experiences and actions, and not on whether we think we are that person or even on whether we think we are concerned in the right way with that person's experiences and actions; and, second, that whether we are actually concerned, in the right way, with someone's past experiences and actions is determined by our phenomenology.

And what sort of phenomenologically expressed concernment is the right sort of concernment to forge identity between ourselves and people who lived in the past? Why, of course, the sort of concernment that is ingredient in reflexive self-consciousness. And, in order to have that sort of concernment, Locke is saying, at least normally, if not always, I must remember in a first-personal way, that is, 'from the inside', the having of the experiences of someone in the past and the performing of his actions. If I do that, Locke thought, then I not only remember, say, the having of the experiences, but I remember that *I* had them, and in remembering that I had them, I appropriate – that is, declare ownership of – them. It is such acts of appropriation, not any theory I may have about who I am or what I am concerned about, that makes the previous experiences and actions mine.

The second part of Locke's response to the possibility that some people may not be conscious of having done things they did do was to the supposition that he might wholly lose all memories of some parts of his life, with no possibility of retrieving them. 'Yet', Locke asked, 'am I not the same person, that did those Actions, had those Thoughts, that I was once conscious of, though I have now forgot them?' His answer was that 'we must here take notice what the Word *I* is applied to, which in this case is the Man only'. Locke conceded that since, in common language, the man is presumed to be the person, '*I* is easily here supposed to stand also for the same Person'. But, he continued, 'if it be possible for the same Man to have distinct incommunicable consciousness [*sic*] at different times, it is past doubt the same Man would at different times make different Persons'. Locke said that what he is suggesting here is in accord with 'the Sense of Mankind in the solemnest Declaration of their Opinions, Humane Laws not punishing the *Mad Man* for the *Sober Man's* Actions, nor the *Sober Man* for what the *Mad Man* did, thereby making them two Persons'. He also cited in support of his view 'our way of speaking in *English*, when we say such an one *is not himself*, or is *besides himself*; in which Phrases it is insinuated, as if those who now, or, at least, first used them, thought, that *self* was changed, the *self* same Person was no longer in that Man' (Ibid.: II.xxvii.20; 342–3). On a charitable reading, Locke's point here, seemingly about ambiguous self-reference, is just his way of saying that while the man performed the actions, the person, who now does not remember having performed them, did not.

The final part of Locke's answer to the problem that some people may not be conscious of having done something they did is that, if it serves Justice, then eventually they will be conscious of it 'when every one shall *receive according to his doing*' and '*the secrets of all hearts shall be laid open*' (Ibid.: II.xxvii.26; 347). There is an obvious problem with this answer. In so far as reward and punishment is accorded to a person only for what the person does, and God on the day of judgment arranges it so that a person is conscious of everything he does, then there must be some standard by which God determines what a person has done other than that of what the person is conscious of having done. Many commentators think that here also Locke lapses into irretrievable incoherence. However, Locke may here simply be betraying the fact that except for a benign skepticism, he is indifferent to mundane metaphysics. He did not think that we can know the real essences of any substances, either persons or anything else. But he also did not think that it matters. At least he did not think that it matters for the practical conduct of our lives, which for Locke is all that really matters. And, as we shall see in more detail when we consider his response to the next pathology of memory to be considered, one of the reasons that Locke was relatively unconcerned about whether he got the metaphysics right was his belief that if he were to get it wrong, God would set it right (Ibid.: I.i.5; 45).

Consider next, people who are (delusionally) conscious of having done things they did not do. Locke's answer to the problem of 'delusions of identity' is in two parts. He began by conceding that, without bringing theology into the picture, there is no way to know that delusions of identity do not occur: '[W]hy one intellectual Substance may not have represented to it, as done by it self, what it never did, and was perhaps done by some other Agent, why I say such a representation may not possibly be without reality of Matter of Fact, as well as several representations in Dreams are, which yet, whilst dreaming, we take for true, will be difficult to conclude from the Nature of things'. Then, Locke brought theology into the picture: 'And that it [such delusions] never is so, will by us, till we have clearer views of the Nature of thinking Substances be best resolv'd into the Goodness of God, who as far as the Happiness or Misery of any of his sensible Creatures is concerned in it, will not by a fatal Error of theirs transfer from one to another, that consciousness, which draws Reward or Punishment with it' (Ibid.: II.xxvii.13; 338). So, in effect, Locke, first, conceded that temporarily and on Earth delusions of identity may occur but, then, denied that in the final analysis there will be any. This would seem to be a problem for Locke, since the view of personal identity he had been developing seems to leave no room for delusions of identity. From Locke's point of view, we suspect, it was much less of a problem.

In our view, to a greater degree than is usually acknowledged by commentators, Locke, in the *Essay*, was a 'theological pragmatist', that is, a pragmatist for whom other-worldly consequences were paramount. Surprising as it may seem, with the exception of three theses – that God exists, that the Self exists, and that there is an external world with the power to cause our ideas of it – Locke was not nearly as interested in *positive* metaphysics as he is usually portrayed as having been. He had a *negative* interest in metaphysics that grew out of his desire to set strict limits on the possibilities of human knowledge. And he had a *positive* interest in establishing theological pragmatism. But except for a few views about the details of corpuscular mechanism, that is about it. Recognizing this becomes important in understanding Locke's response to the problem of forgetfulness.

As a theological pragmatist, Locke's attitude toward problems to his theory of personal identity posed by faulty memory may well have been this: Based on what we (humans) know, the view I (Locke) am expounding is at least as reasonable as any competing view; perhaps even it is the most reasonable view. However, there is no way to know whether it is the true view. On the day of judgment, God will judge on the basis of the true view. While we do not know what that view will be, we know it will be close enough to maximally reasonable views that our view will have been an adequate basis for conduct. Otherwise God would be a deceiver, and God is not a deceiver. And, insofar as personal identity (or anything else) is concerned, all we really need to know is that our view is an adequate basis for conduct.[14]

2

FISSION

In our own times, the introduction of fission examples into the personal identity debate provoked a fierce controversy, still raging, over the seemingly new question of whether personal identity is what matters primarily in survival.[1] In Chapter 6, we return briefly to this contemporary controversy. In the present chapter, we want to consider the first half of a curious phenomenon. It is that neither fission examples nor the recognition of their importance to the question of what matters in survival are late twentieth century discoveries.[2] Throughout the eighteenth century, personal identity theorists were aware of fission examples. By the end of the century, Priestley had raised the 'new question' about personal identity's importance, and may even have suggested in response to it that personal identity is *not* what matters primarily in survival. At the beginning of the nineteenth century, Hazlitt, using fission examples, suggested that the distinction between self and other is not nearly as important as had traditionally been supposed. Then, hard as it may be to believe, throughout the rest of the nineteenth and most of the twentieth centuries, the discussion of fission examples and their implications for personal identity theory fell almost (but not completely) out of sight! In the present chapter, our story is about how fission first came into view. As usual, we begin with Locke.

Locke on unity of consciousness

In his chapter on identity, Locke was preoccupied with the implications of *fission-like* examples: 'Could we suppose two distinct incommunicable consciousnesses acting the same Body, the one constantly by Day, the other by Night; and on the other side the same consciousness, acting by Intervals two distinct Bodies'. Regarding these, Locke said, 'I ask in the first case, Whether the *Day-* and the *Night-man* would not be two as distinct Persons, as Socrates and Plato; and whether in the second case, there would not be one Person in two distinct Bodies, as much as one Man is the same in two distinct clothings' (Locke 1975: II.xxvii.23; 344).

The first of these examples, the day/night case, is like a case of multiple personality disorder with amnesiac barriers between the personas; there are two consciousnesses in one body and these consciousnesses are 'incommunicable' (i.e., not co-conscious). In Locke's view, the day-person and night-person, in spite of their sharing the same body, are different people.

In the second example, one consciousness is in two bodies. Locke's use of the expression, 'acting by intervals' suggests that he meant that the consciousness was first in one body and then in the other, but never in both at the same time. If this is what he meant, then neither of these examples is a genuine fission example since neither involves (i) one consciousness dividing into two, each of which is then (ii) continuous with the original, (iii) contemporaneous with the other, and yet (iv) independent of the other. Unless all four of these conditions are satisfied, as they are only in what we are calling genuine fission examples, one lacks a compelling motive to regard fission-descendants as different people from each other, and to regard the original person as different from each of the fission-descendants.

In a third example, Locke said, 'It must be allowed, That if the same consciousness' can be 'transferr'd from one thinking Substance to another it will be possible, that two thinking Substances may make but one Person. For the same consciousness being preserv'd, whether in the same or different Substances, the personal Identity is preserv'd' (Ibid.: II.xxvii.13; 338). It is unclear whether Locke here was considering the possibility of the same consciousness being transferred first to one thinking substance and then to another, but never to both at once, or whether he was considering the possibility of its being transferred at the same time to two independently conscious thinking substances. Only in the latter case would he have presented what we are calling a genuine fission example.

Locke then went on to consider a case in which one's little finger is cut off and consciousness, rather than staying with the main part of the body, goes with the little finger. He concludes, 'Upon separation of this little Finger, should this consciousness go along with the little Finger, and leave the rest of the Body, 'tis evident the little Finger would be the *Person*, the *same Person*; and *self* then would have nothing to do with the rest of the Body'. In the section immediately following, Locke returns to this example, at least amplifying it and possibly turning it into a case of what we are calling a genuine fission example: 'Though if the same Body should still live, and immediately from the separation of the little Finger have its own peculiar consciousness, whereof the little Finger knew nothing, it would not at all be concerned for it, as a part of it *self*, or could own any of its Actions, or have any of them imputed to him' (Ibid.: II.xxvii.18; 342). In this version of the example, it is unclear what Locke meant to be suggesting. One possibility is that he meant that the original consciousness went with the finger and the rest of the body acquired a new consciousness; another is that the original consciousness split into two parts, one part in the finger and one in the rest of the body, each part a whole consciousness qualitatively identical to the original. Although it is debatable what Locke had in mind, the latter reading seems the more natural one to us. On it, Locke's case is a genuine fission example, the first fission example to be considered explicitly in the context of personal identity theory. Whatever he may have had in mind, Locke did not explore the implications of his example. But once he published his new theory, the fission-example cat was out of the bag.

Disputes with Locke over the resurrection

In the *Essay*, Locke suggested diplomatically that it is highly probable that the soul is an immaterial substance to which consciousness is annexed. He also said that, in principle, God could have 'superadded' the power of thought to matter. His advancing of this latter possibility together with his new theory of personal identity provoked a storm of immediate criticism, to most of which Locke refused to respond (in 1702, Catharine Trotter replied on his behalf to Burnet's extended critique).[3] However, Locke could not avoid an engagement with Bishop Stillingfleet, who drew Locke into debate by linking his view with Toland's infamous, deist tract, *Christianity Not Mysterious* (1696). From 1696 to 1698, there was an exchange of letters between Locke and Stillingfleet, which on Locke's side alone is half as long as the *Essay*! (Locke 1963: v.4). Subsequently, some of the material in these letters was included in footnotes to the fifth edition of the *Essay*, which was published after Locke's death.

On the issue of the resurrection, Stillingfleet defended the traditional view that to be resurrected one's body must include the very matter it had at the end of one's life. Locke argued, first, that this view is incoherent and, then, that St. Paul's idea that the resurrected body could be composed of entirely new, 'spiritualized' matter is consistent with his own view. Late in the century, Priestley, in defense of his materialistic view of the resurrection, would appeal in a similar way to St. Paul. On the issue of thinking matter, Locke vigorously defended the idea that thought – perhaps like life, sensibility, and even gravity – could be 'superadded' to matter. Stillingfleet died before he could respond to Locke's third letter. Others soon entered the lists.

Isaac Watts was a dissenting minister whose philosophical, religious, and literary works were much admired during the eighteenth century both in England and America. He wrote several philosophical works that criticized Locke from a Cartesian perspective, while also adopting several of Locke's empirical and logical methods. Like many others, Watts was more concerned over Locke's apparent tolerance of discontinuity than over whether the same matter would be involved in the resurrection. Watts felt that any discontinuity whatsoever in the thinking activity of the spirit or soul implied a cessation of existence, and thus that any 'resurrection' after such a discontinuity was not a resurrection of the same person, but rather the beginning of a new one. He conceded that God could create such a new person with a consciousness qualitatively similar to that of the old, but he thought that if such a newly created being 'should suppose itself to remember things done in a former state, before it had any existence' this 'would be properly a false apprehension, and error and not a real memory of what was done before, and would lay no just foundation for the recompenses of vice or virtue' (Watts 1789: 265–6). In making this point, Watts, in effect, made the distinction between genuine and mere seeming memory that in our own times, through Martin and Deutscher's influential paper (1966), has been used to support a physical criterion of personal identity.

Philip Doddridge, another dissenting minister, in lecture notes on personal identity that would be used to teach the young Priestley at Daventry, sided with Watts against Locke: 'If God should utterly destroy the soul and body of any man whom we know, and afterwards create a new spirit, united to a new body, and in form resembling the other, and give to it the exact consciousness of the man whose body and soul was destroyed, and should reveal to us what he had done, *we could not converse with this new produced man as the same man we formerly knew*, or approve that as an equitable conduct, by which he should be rewarded or punished for the actions of the annihilated man'. Doddridge concluded that 'this abundantly shows the impropriety of Mr. Locke's manner of stating the question, and how much Dr. Watts's is to be preferred to it' (Doddridge 1763: 23–4, emphasis added). Doddridge here was among the first to suggest that there is a social dimension to the question of determining whether personal identity obtains, a point Priestley would also use, but to different effect, in defence of his own alternative view.

Samuel Clarke and Anthony Collins

Locke's fission-like examples and his suggestions leaning towards an account of persons as fictions had a remarkable development between 1706 and 1709 in a six-part debate between Clarke and Collins (Clarke 1738: v. 3, 720–913). By all indications this debate was widely known. It was reprinted twice (in 1731 and 1738) and throughout the century is referred to many times. In 1727, a thirty-six page abridgement of the debate was published (Fox 1988: 55, 69).

Clarke, Boyle Lecturer and 'chief lieutenant of Newton', was at the time regarded by many as the most intelligent man of his era. Collins, a disciple of Locke, was at the onset of the debate relatively unknown. His initial challenge to Clarke was in response to Clarke's attempt to establish the immortality of the soul. Their exchange soon developed into a more general consideration of personal identity and of whether matter can think. Clarke defended the traditional view that consciousness could reside only in an immaterial substance, Collins the new view that matter can think.

Surprisingly, perhaps, what we are calling genuine fission examples were introduced into this debate not by Collins, as a way of developing Locke's view, but by Clarke, as a way of objecting to it. Subsequently fission examples were discussed several times in the debate. The basic outline of Clarke's overall argument is simple. He assumed that consciousness is a real property, which, in his sense of 'real property', implied that were consciousness to be a property of a material system every part of the system would have to be conscious (Clarke 1738: 730, 760). Such a result, he maintained, would be absurd. Collins maintained that consciousness can emerge from properties of parts of the system (or be 'superadded' by God to the system) even though the parts themselves are not conscious.

In Clarke's first reply to Collins, he asked Collins to suppose that 'the smallest imaginable Particle of Matter imbued with Consciousness or Thought' has 'by the Power of God' been 'divided into two distinct Parts'. Clarke then asked, 'What will naturally and consequently become of its Power of Thinking?':

> *If* the Power of Thinking will remain only in One of the separated Parts: then either That One Part only, had at first the Power residing in it; and then the same Question will return, upon the Supposition of *Its* being likewise divided; or else it will follow that one and the same Individual Quality may be transferred from one Subject to another; which all Philosophers of all Sects in the World, have always confessed to be impossible. *If*, in the last place, it be said, that upon the Division of the Particle, the Power of Thinking, which was in it, will wholly cease; then it will follow, that That Power was never at all a real Quality inhering or residing in the Substance, (in which mere separation of Parts, makes no Alteration;) but that it was *merely an external Denomination*, such as is *Roundness* in a Globe, which perishes at its being divided: And this, I suppose, will be granted to be sufficiently absurd.
>
> (Ibid.: 761)

In such early passages, Clarke clearly had fission in mind, but he had not yet directed his focus to its implications for personal identity.

In his *Third Defense*, Clarke introduced a fission example to show that Collins' attributing consciousness to material substances leads to a contradiction. The 'contradiction' he had in mind arises from considering consciousness as a real property and yet admitting that it can be separated from the substance in which it inheres. Earlier Clarke had argued on general metaphysical grounds that, even though all material substances transform continuously into other substances by addition or subtraction of particles, it is 'absurd' to suppose that the same numerical property can be 'transferred' from one substance to another. Now he argued that in attributing sameness of consciousness over time to a material substance, Collins must really be attributing it to a 'flux' of substances, which contradicts the assumption of a real property's inseparability from its substance (Ibid.: 787; see also 843).

Instead of denying Clarke's assumption directly, Collins replied by introducing *memory* as the faculty that guarantees the persistence of the same consciousness and, hence, of the person (Ibid.: 809, 819–20). He suggested that the forgetting of past but distant actions can be understood by appeal to a failure of transference in the brain since only if the recollection of past experiences is transferred to new particles of the brain will memory for them be retained. But, then, when such recollections are transferred and consciousness of past actions is maintained, consciousness – and ultimately the person – changes substances. His reply, thus, resulted in shifting the argument to personal identity, and accordingly refocused Clarke's objection.

Clarke initially replied that Collins' account of transference is 'an *impossible* hypothesis':

> That the *Person* may still be the same, by a continual Superaddition of the *like Consciousness*; notwithstanding the whole *Substance* be changed: Then I say, you make *individual Personality* to be a mere *external imaginary Denomination*, and nothing in reality: Just as a *Ship* is called the *same Ship*, after the whole Substance is changed by frequent Repairs; or a *River* is called the *same River*, though the Water of it be every Day new ... But he cannot be *really and truly* the *same Person*, unless the *same individual numerical Consciousness* can be transferred from one Subject to another. For, the continued Addition or Exciting of a *like Consciousness* in the new acquired Parts, after the Manner you suppose; is nothing but a Deception and Delusion, under the Form of Memory; a making the Man to seem himself to be conscious of having done that, which really was not done by him, but by another.
>
> (Ibid.: 844)

In other words, Clarke objected to Collins that if memory were able to guarantee identity of persons, then persons would be fictional.

Clarke, then, introduced the idea of fission to hammer home the point that such a sequence of like consciousnesses is not the same as a series of acts by a single consciousness:

> Such a Consciousness in a Man, whose Substance is wholly changed, can no more make it Just and Equitable for such a Man to be punished for an Action done by another Substance; than the Addition of the like Consciousness (by the Power of God) to two or more new created Men; or to any Number of Men now living, by giving a like Modification to the Motion of the Spirits in the Brain of each of them respectively; could make them All to be one and the same individual Person, at the same time that they remain several and distinct Persons; or make it just and reasonable for all and every

one of them to be punished for one and the same individual Action, done by one only, or perhaps by none of them at all.

(Ibid.: 844–5)

Collins' view is thus shown to be contradictory because it would lead in this imaginary fission-scenario to saying of two or more individuals both that they are and also are not the same person.

Clarke, then, in a variation on his fission example, immediately emphasized the resulting contradiction:

> It is a *Contradiction plain enough*, to say that God's impressing permanently upon a Thousand Mens Minds, after the Manner of the Representation of a Dream, the like Consciousness with that which I find in my own Mind; would make every one of them, to be, not Persons *like* me, but the *same individual Person* with myself.
>
> (Ibid.: 845)

And then again, in the context of considering the resurrection:

> If the *same Person*, after *Annihilation*, could, by restoring of the same *Consciousness*, be created again; he might as possibly be created again, by addition of the same *Consciousness* to new Matter, even before Annihilation of the first: From whence it would follow, that Two, or Two Hundred, several Persons, might All, by a Superaddition of the like *Consciousness*, be *one and the same individual Person*, at the same time that they remain *several and distinct Persons*: It being as easy for God to add *my Consciousness* to the new formed Matter of One or of One Hundred Bodies at this *present Time,* as the Dust of my present Body at the *Time of the* Resurrection. And no Reason can be given, why it would not be as just at any time, to punish for my Faults a new created Man, to whom *my Consciousness* is by the Power of God superadded: … This inexplicable Confusion, wherewith your Doctrine perplexes the Notion of *personal Identity*, upon which Identity the Justice of all Reward and Punishment manifestly depends; makes the *Resurrection*, in your way of arguing, to be inconceivable and impossible.
>
> (Ibid.: 852)

Nothing in what Clarke said suggests that he may have been thinking of the fission-descendants in any of these examples as being co-conscious. Rather, his examples support the charge of contradiction only if the descendants are conceived to be, although replicas, distinct persons.

Collins' reply leaves it unclear whether he understood the force of Clarke's examples:

36

I do allow that each of those Beings would be the *same Person* with Mr. *Clarke*, that is, each of them would have a present Representation of the past Actions of Mr. *Clarke* . . . [Hence,] let there be ever so many thinking Beings that have a present Representation of a past Action, they can all constitute but one and the same Person, because they all agree in, or have a present Representation of the same past Action, wherein *Self* or personal Identity consist.

(Ibid.: 877)

The emphasis in this passage is entirely on the agreement of present mental representations in the replicas' minds. So, it is an open question whether Collins took Clarke's view to be a case of genuine fission or instead one that involves co-consciousness among the replicas.

The possibility that Collins here misinterpreted Clarke is heightened by an analogy Collins drew between the replicas and the parts of a human body:

My consisting of even so great a Bulk of Matter, or even so many distinct Beings, does not constitute different Persons, but constitutes what we call *Self*, by the Sympathy and Concern I have for each part united to me, though I have a distinct Act of Sensation for each part that is at any time affected.

(Ibid.)

Later, however, in responding to problems posed for his view by the doctrine of the resurrection, Collins appealed to the 'Article of Christian Faith, that *the same numerical Particles* that are laid in the Grave, shall be raised at the Resurrection' (Ibid.: 878, emphasis added).

In such passages, Collins took the problem for his view with having several psychological replicas to be that the punishment of twenty distinct beings, all having 'present Representations of the same sinful Actions' would make God's punishment unjust by making it to be 'twenty times as much as the sinful Action deserved' (Ibid.). Strictly speaking, such worries as this one are compatible with the hypothesis that Collins considered the replicas to be co-conscious – the punishment might be twenty times greater because it is inflicted in full measure on each of twenty bodily parts all of which are related to the same consciousness. But such an interpretation is far-fetched. It is more plausible to suppose that what Collins had in mind is that the injustice would result simply from God's bringing about a pain twenty times greater than was merited. This simpler interpretation is also supported by the fact that Collins later explicitly excluded, for moral reasons that again relied on his sense of justice, that God could create '*distinct* thinking Beings, with *each* of them a Consciousness extended to the same past Actions, and attributing them to *themselves*' (Ibid., emphasis added).

In sum, Clarke provided genuine fission examples. Ironically, he also had a view of the self according to which genuine fission is impossible. So, he perceived the *seeming* possibility of genuine fission as an absurdity following from relational accounts of identity. Also ironically, Collins, who had a view of personal identity that allowed him to acknowledge fission as a real possibility, may not have fully followed Clarke's examples. In any case, because this debate was well-known, both fission examples and the idea that they have implications for personal identity theory of a sort Locke had not considered was brought to the attention of eighteenth century theorists.

Henry Grove

From 1706 to 1738, Grove, a dissenting minister, taught at Taunton Academy, one of many schools in England where progressive ideas were seriously and sympathetically considered. Like Watts, who was a good friend and fellow student, Grove was trained in Cartesian metaphysics. But Grove was intrigued by Locke's radical new ideas. Between 1710 and 1720, Grove corresponded with Clarke and also published several essays on the immateriality and immortality of the soul. For present purposes, however, his unpublished lectures are of most interest. In them, he wrote:

> For if consciousness [as Locke claimed] never fails of making Personal Identity, it follows that several men may possibly be one and ye same Person because tis possible they may all agree in an obstinate Fancy that they did a certain action which in truth was done by one of them; And for as much as Personal Identity is ye foundation of Reward and Punishment may consistently with ye strictest Justice be all punish'd for ye Crime of one. Mr. Lock must be interpreted to own this consequence by resolving it into ye goodness of God, as our Security that he will not annex the same consciousness to different Agents and then make them all suffer for but one individual action.
> (Grove 1720: 44)

Since Grove greatly admired Clarke he may, or may not, have gotten this idea from reading the debate between Clarke and Collins. Wherever he got it, his remarks illustrate how easily Locke's critics came to the consideration of fission.

Scriblerus

Independently of such formal philosophical discussions, there are many indications that early in the eighteenth century, fission-like examples were on the minds of thinkers who were interested in the topic of personal identity. Much of this interest, including quite a bit in the popular press, was stimulated by Locke's new account of personal identity (Fox 1988). But, surprisingly, in

Britain it was also nourished by a fascination with the phenomenon of Siamese twins. As early as 1694, Richard Burthogge had reported the phenomenon of '*Child*' who had a double body, that is, 'a double Breast and double Head, and *proper* feelings of all parts' (Burthogge 1694: 264–5). In the summer of 1708, Hungarian Siamese twin sisters toured Europe and captured the imagination of London.

The twins phenomenon inspired a remarkable, humorous commentary of sorts on Locke's theory. Written around 1714, by members of the Scriblerus Club (Alexander Pope, John Arbuthnot, Jonathan Swift, John Gay, Thomas Parnell, Robert Harley, and perhaps others), *The Memoirs of the Extra-ordinary Life, Works, and Discoveries of Martinus Scriblerus* revisits the topic of Siamese twins in the context of a satirical critique of then current debates over the metaphysics of soul, consciousness, and personal identity.[4] Toward the beginning, Scriblerus, the hero of the story, seeks the location of the soul in the body, but cannot find it. In his reflections on his search, the idea that there may be two persons in one body arises. A later chapter rehearses, from Collins' point of view, the debate between Clarke and Collins over thinking matter. Several subsequent chapters deal with Scriblerus' falling in love with and marrying a pair of Siamese twins, who share a single 'organ of generation'. After this marriage, someone else marries just one of the twins, and they all go to court. Scriblerus argues that the twins are one person and share one soul since the organ of generation is obviously the 'seat of the soul'. The other husband argues that in marrying the twins, and then consummating his marriage, Scriblerus committed bigamy, as well as incest. Several judges work out the solution, the result of which is that both marriages are dissolved since 'two persons [the explicit reference is to the husbands, but must also playfully be to the twins] could not have a Right to the entire possession of the same thing, at the same time'. Although not dealing with fission *per se*, the identity problems associated with the case of these Siamese twins expresses in concrete form a sort of puzzlement and amusement that Clarke and Collins discussion of fission must have produced in sophisticated readers of their debate, not the least the members of the Scriblerus Club. There is some evidence that the *Memoirs* were widely read, not only for their humor, but also as philosophy.[5]

Joseph Butler

We know that Butler was familiar with the debate between Clarke and Collins because he twice noted it (Butler 1736: 32, 321). Yet he never directly discussed fission examples. As we shall see, he may have alluded to them. One of the things he did do is to reassert the immaterial substance view of personal identity, often merely repeating Clarke's criticisms of relational views.[6] However, Butler's deft way of doing this suggests that with the possible exception of Clarke, he saw more clearly than anyone else had yet seen what was radical in Locke's view. And Butler's skillful articulation of this radical core in order to reject it may have helped Hazlitt, who greatly admired Butler, to get clearer about which aspects of this radical core he wanted to embrace.

Butler's best known thought on personal identity is his criticism of the memory analysis. Although he has gotten all the credit for seeing how Locke's view might be circular, the criticism itself had surfaced earlier, originally in remarks on Locke's view by John Sergeant, one of Locke's earliest critics, who wrote that 'Consciousness of any Action or any Accident we have now, or have had, is nothing but our Knowledge that it belong'd to us'. He said it follows that 'the Man, or that Thing which is to be the Knower, must have had Individuality or Personality from other Principles, antecedently to this Knowledge call'd Consciousness; and consequently, he will retain his Identity, or continue the same Man, or (which is equivalent) the same Person, as long as he has those Individuating Principles'. Finally, he concluded that 'a Man must be the same, ere he can know or be Conscious that he is the same' (Sergeant 1697: ref. 14, sec. 12). A similar criticism is also clearly implicit in Clarke's insistence, repeated several times in his debate with Collins, that by consciousness Locke must mean: 'That Consciousness by which I *not only Remember* that certain Things were done many Years since but also *am Conscious that they were done by Me, by the very same Individual Conscious Being* who now remembers them' (Clarke 1738: v. 3, 787).[7]

Immediately after making his own famous objection to the memory view, Butler highlighted two other and, in our view, deeper issues for which he is not well known. The issues are, first, that there are important links among identity, responsibility, and self-concern and, second, that on a view such as Locke's it is questionable whether persons (or selves) would be real. Butler introduced these issues by remarking that 'the question' is 'whether the same rational being is the same substance', which, he said, 'needs no answer because Being and Substance, in this place, stand for the same idea. But, he continued, 'the consciousness of our own existence, in youth and in old age, or in any two joint successive moments, is not the *same individual action*, i.e., not the same consciousness, but different successive consciousnesses'. And, yet, 'the person, of whose existence the consciousness is felt now, and was felt an hour or a year ago, is discerned to be, not two persons, but one and the same person; and therefore is one and the same'. From this, he said, 'it must follow' on a view such as Locke's, that:

> it is a fallacy upon ourselves to charge our present selves with any thing we did, or to imagine our present selves interested in any thing which befell us yesterday; or that our present self will be interested in what will befall us tomorrow; since our present self is not, in reality, the same with the self of yesterday, but another like self or person coming in its room, and mistaken for it; to which another self will succeed tomorrow. This, I say, must follow: for if the self or person of

today, and that of tomorrow, are not the same, but only like persons the person of today is really no more interested in what will befall the person of tomorrow than in what will befall any other person.

(Butler 1736: 320–2)

Butler conceded that some may think he is misrepresenting Locke's view since 'those who maintain it allow that a person is the same as far back as his remembrance reaches'. But, he claimed, the Lockeans, that is, Collins, whose replies to Clarke are the basis of Butler's assertions here, 'cannot, consistently with themselves, mean, that the person is really the same . . . but only that he is so in a *fictitious* sense: in such a sense only as they assert, for this they do assert, that *any number of persons whatever may be the same person*' (Ibid.: 322, emphasis added). Yet, Butler insisted, a person or self 'is not an idea, or abstract notion, or quality, but a being only, which is capable of life and action, of happiness and misery', and, hence, definitely not a fiction (Ibid.: 323).

In sum, so far as Butler was concerned, on Locke's account of personal identity, our present selves would have no reason to be especially interested in our past or future selves, and no one would have any reason to hold later selves accountable for what earlier selves had done. Yet, in Butler's view, regardless of our philosophical views we must retain the language of self and person. So, to maintain Locke's view, we would have to consider ourselves to be selves and persons not really but only in a fictitious sense. Butler thought such consequences refute Locke's view. But he thought this not because he thought he could prove Locke's view is false (he admitted he could not), but rather because 'the bare unfolding this notion [that selves are merely fictitious entities] and laying it thus naked and open, seems the best confutation of it' (Ibid.: 322, 325). Others, as we shall see, took a different view. What Butler made explicit to motivate a retreat back from Locke's view, Hazlitt, in particular, would make explicit to recommend an advance beyond it.

David Hume

Hume said nothing on a whole host of issues regarding personal identity that were being hotly debated at the time. In particular, he never discussed whether he thought the relation that bound our present to our past selves was 'sameness of consciousness', as Lockeans maintained, or something else (although, as we shall see, since, among other reasons, we extend our identities beyond the reach of our memories, Hume all but implied that it is not sameness of consciousness). And Hume never discussed examples, such as Locke's prince and cobbler example, that might have shed light on his opinion about what the relation is that binds earlier and later stages of a person. Seemingly he avoided discussing such examples because he thought that all such relations were fictitious and that questions about whether identity is preserved in such cases are 'merely verbal'. Yet, in his less skeptical, more realistic moments, such as in most of Book 2 of the *A Treatise of Human Nature*, Hume seems to have subscribed to a relational view of the self. Needless to say, he never discussed fission directly, and he had little to say, and nothing new, about how personal identity might be analyzed in a way that links it to questions of accountability and interestedness.

However, in the context of pointing out that when distinct objects are related to a common cause, we have a tendency to confuse 'specific' with 'numerical identity', as may happen when we regard as the same continuing noise one 'that is frequently interrupted and renewed' or as the same church one that burns down and then is rebuilt, Hume said, 'Where the objects are in their nature changeable and inconstant'; in the case, say, of rivers changing their water, 'we admit of a more sudden transition, than wou'd otherwise be consistent with that relation'. In other words, we allow that such objects persist, even though we would regard comparable changes in objects that were not in their nature changeable and inconstant as bringing about their cessation. It seems from Hume's subsequent discussion of the church example that he may have been aware of the special problems for judgments of identity that arise in the case of fission. In claiming that, 'without breach of the propriety of language', we might regard the two churches as the same church even if the first was of brick and the second 'of free-stone', he added the caveat, 'but we must observe, that in these cases the first object is in manner annihilated before the second comes into existence; by which means, we are never presented in any one point of time with the idea of difference and multiplicity; and for that reason are less scrupulous in calling them the same' (Hume 1739: 258). This is the closest that Hume comes to discussing fission.

Hume claimed that the self is fictitious. In his view, since all reason or understanding has to work with are diverse perceptions, it is the imagination that provides the links upon which our conception of self is ultimately based, and yet we invariably create the fiction that we are something more than just perceptions imaginatively linked: 'For when we attribute identity, in an improper sense, to variable or interrupted objects, our mistake is not confin'd to the expression but is commonly attended with a fiction, either of something invariable and uninterrupted, or of something mysterious and inexplicable, or at least with a propensity to such fictions' (Ibid.: 255). And further: 'The identity which we ascribe to the mind of man is only a fictitious one, and of a like kind with that which we ascribe to vegetable and animal bodies. It cannot, therefore, have a different origin, but must proceed from a like operation of the imagination upon like objects' (Ibid.: 259). Rather than considering the nature of personal identity *per se*, Hume turned instead, and almost exclusively, to two other questions: first, that of explaining how the fiction of identity arises, not only in the case of persons but in that of anything which seems to persist over time and through changes; and, second, the question of what role the fictional self plays in our emotions and motivations. He thus shifted the emphasis from conceptually analyzing the notion of personal identity to empirically accounting, first, for how it arises and, second, for its functional role.

G. W. Leibniz

Leibniz had a great, though critical, admiration for Locke's new theory of personal identity and tried unsuccessfully to engage Locke in dialogue. Later, Leibniz wrote *New Essays Concerning Human Understanding*. However, Locke died before the book was finished, so, out of respect for Locke, Leibniz decided not to publish it. In 1765, long after Leibniz had died, *New Essays* finally appeared. By then it was too late to have much impact on the debate over Locke's views (although from it Kant got the notion of 'apperception').

In *New Essays*, Leibniz discussed an example that is a curious mixture of fission and fusion. Although this example never found a home in the ensuing debate over personal identity, it found a different one, in our own times, in Putnam's externalist semantics:

> It may be that in another place in the universe or at another time a globe may be found which does not differ sensibly from this earthly globe, in which we live, and that each of the men who inhabit it does not differ sensibly from each of us who corresponds to him. Thus there are at once more than a hundred million pairs of similar persons, i.e., of two persons with the same appearances and consciousnesses; and God might transfer spirits alone or with their bodies from one globe to the other without their perceiving it; but be they transferred or let alone, what will you say of their person or self according to your authors? Are they two persons or the same since the consciousness and the internal and external appearance of the men of these globes cannot make the distinction? It is true that God and the spirits capable of seeing the intervals and external relations of times and places, and even internal constitutions, insensible to the men of the two globes, could distinguish them; but according to your hypotheses consciousness alone discerning the persons without being obliged to trouble itself with the real identity or diversity of the substance, or even of that which would appear to others, how is it prevented from saying that these two persons who are at the same time in these two similar globes, but separated from each other by an inexpressible distance, are only one and the same person; which is however, a manifest absurdity.
>
> (Leibniz 1765: 255–6)

In addition to Leibniz, others (Adam Smith is the premier example) also explored the implications of fission-like examples of a sort that are beyond the confines of the traditional personal identity debate. However, to pursue the interesting uses to which such fission-like examples have been put would take us too far afield.

Abraham Tucker

Currently, Tucker is not well known, but toward the end of the eighteenth century he was a formidable figure. He claimed to be a Lockean but also had original ideas that opposed those of Locke, including views on the unity of consciousness and personal identity. He importantly influenced Paley's theological utilitarianism and he was a hero to Hazlitt, who in 1807 republished an abridged version of Tucker's seven volume, *The Light of Nature Pursued* (1768–77).

Like Clarke, Tucker argued for the simplicity and immateriality of the mind or spirit based on its necessary unity and indivisibility, but in some ways Tucker's arguments are more sophisticated than Clarke's and his overall position closer to Kant's. However, since Tucker held that our experienced unity of consciousness has metaphysical implications for a numerical unity of spirit rather than for a synthetic unity of consciousness, he stands at the end of one tradition rather than at the beginning of another. He discussed personal identity and the unity of mind in two works: *Man in Quest of Himself* (1763) and *The Light of Nature Pursued* (1768–77, III), in both of which he insisted on the fact that the divisibility of matter implies a metaphysical divisibility and that no system of matter could maintain unity of mind and numerical identity of self.

In *Man in Quest of Himself*, Tucker pushed his materialist opponent to the position that there must be a 'fifth element', a single spiritual 'drop' that is the Self and that becomes lodged in the pineal gland where it can make use of the distributed sensory systems of the brain. Then Tucker forced him to admit that the Self-drop can itself be divided, and that were it to divide, mental unity would be dissipated, while the substantial basis of that unity would remain. His hypothetical opponent replied that even though while so divided the person may not be able to have experiences, his substantial base would still be existing and so the person would continue; further, if at a later time the person's Self-drop were brought back together (as it surely could be), then the person would reacquire the ability to experience.

At this point, Tucker introduced a variation on fission and fusion:

> You know the almighty power of Chance, and how in the course of infinite ages she must produce all possible combinations. Now one possible combination is this; that some thousands of years hence half your drop and half mine should join in one pineal gland, and the other halves in some other pineal gland. Will these two compounds be persons having knowledge of their own existence? – I make no

doubt of it. – Will they be distinct and different persons from one another? – Certainly – Which of them will be one of us? – Neither .

(Tucker 1763: 204–5)

The opponent is forced to conclude: 'I can never bring myself to believe that I can become another Person, or part of another Person, or perceive his perceptions, much less by the perceptions of two'. From this position the opponent finally concedes that any such Self-drop may vary in substance even during his life and as a result that his numerical self-identity cannot be based on such a compound material unity.

Tucker's chapter, 'Existence of Mind' in *The Light of Nature Pursued* was greatly admired by Hazlitt as tightly argued metaphysics. And so it is, although today we would no longer accept its arguments, which for the most part are the culmination of eighteenth-century attempts to defend the necessary dependence of unity of mind and individuality of self on immaterial substance. In this work, after arguing that matter is essentially divisible, Tucker turned to our intuitions of our own individuality and uniqueness noting that no matter how skeptical a man becomes none 'ever doubted of his existence, at the instant time when he reflected on it' (Tucker 1768–77: v. 3, 67). He then argued against the notion that the mind or perceptive substance could be a compound, like material substance, on the grounds that 'if composition prevailed in Mind too, every Self must contain a number of little Selves, every Mind many little Minds, and every Sentient principle a multitude of Sentient principles'. Tucker continued: 'But this is a supposal that will not bear the mentioning, for who would not be shocked to hear talk of a half or a quarter of a man's self? Besides, if things sentient were divisible, the parts might be dispersed throughout the four quarters of the world, and a man might have perceptions at the same time in Europe, Asia, Africa, and America' (Ibid.: 69–70). Tucker then rejected the idea that the self could be composed of a compound of non-perceptive components or atoms.

Continuing to pursue another version of this latter possibility, Tucker suggested that his opponent might reply 'that mind is not so much a collection of particular atoms, as a figure or harmony resulting from the order wherein they lie, and therefore may continue the same although some, or all of the atoms be shifted'. Consideration of this possibility then led Tucker to reflect on fission-like replication: 'Besides, where shall we place personality? for there is no difference between similitude and identity in forms . . . therefore two minds composed of atoms, having an exactly similar disposition, must be the same person, and thus there may be a thousand same persons in so many different parts of the globe, as there may be a thousand same forms and harmonies'. Tucker took this consideration as showing that the identity – or rather particularity and uniqueness – of mind cannot be maintained by its form alone. He argued that changes of the form through activities of the mind would imply that we are constantly changing our identities as we perceive and think, as well as when we grow and change character. He thought such a conclusion 'contrary to the apprehensions of all mankind who esteem themselves the same person from cradle to grave, notwithstanding any variations of character and capacity they may have gone through in the interval' (Ibid.: 72–5).

Tucker also argued directly against Locke's view of personal identity, which he interpreted as implying that identity depends on a quality, rather than on a being, and that on any such account 'a man loses his existence or personality every time he loses his consciousness by falling asleep' (Ibid.: 76). Like others, Tucker saw consciousness as providing evidence of our identity rather than as constituting it. He argued that since the same or perfectly similar conscious states can occur in different persons, conscious states per se cannot determine identity but, rather, presuppose the existence of the person whose conscious states they are.

Finally, in arguing against Locke's suggestion that 'the faculty of thinking may be annexed to a system of matter', Tucker entertained problems associated with unity of consciousness and the impossibility that conscious judgments could be distributed spatio-temporally within a system of matter (Ibid.: 77). Using a fission argument similar to that developed earlier when considering 'form', he stated:

> If Self be not a substance but a system of substances ranged in some particular order, there appears no such necessary connection between any one Self and any precise collection of substances or percipient form . . . but that they might have contained any other Self . . . and we must look for some cause yet undiscovered to assign each system its personality. This cause then, before I was existent, might have assigned my personality to any other similar substances disposed in the like order in some distant part of the globe: now why may not this cause do the same at the present instant? . . . therefore there might have been two Myselves some thousands of miles apart. But if such a supposition would shock the ears and understanding of every man it will necessarily follow that every Self must be a substance numerically distinct from all others, of whose identity no other substance nor system of substances can participate. And if a substance, it must be one uncompounded of parts: for I am nothing else besides Myself, nor can contain any thing that is not Me, nor yet can I have parts which are neither me nor any thing else.
>
> (Ibid.: 80–1)

Two hundred years later, we are no longer shocked at the supposition of 'two Myselves'. Only slightly different examples of fission, in which there is a more direct connection between the original and its continuers, such as we shall soon consider in Hazlitt's writings, have revolutionized our conceptions of personal identity and what matters in survival.

Thomas Reid

Reid, who as we shall see in Chapter 5 had read the debate between Clarke and Collins, drew attention to fission examples, albeit briefly, when he said of Locke's view of personal identity that it 'hath some strange consequences, which the author was aware of, Such as, that, if the same consciousness can be transferred from one intelligent being to another, which he thinks we cannot shew to be impossible, than two or twenty intelligent beings may be the same person' (Reid 1785: v. 1, 351). There is every reason to believe that Reid here had in mind what we have called a genuine fission example. In a letter to Lord Kames, which Reid wrote in 1775, he said:

> Dr. Priestley in his last book thinks that the power of perception, as much as the other powers that are termed mental, is the natural result of an organic structure such as that of the human brain. Consequently, the whole man becomes extinct at death; and we have no hope of surviving the grave but what is derived from the Christian revelation. I would be glad to know your lordship's opinion, whether, when my brain has lost its original structure, and when some hundred years after, the same materials are again fabricated so curiously as to become an intelligent being – whether, I say, that being will be *me*; or if two or three such beings should be formed out of my brain, whether they will all be *me*, and consequently be all one and the same intelligent being. This seems to me a great mystery; but Dr. Priestley denies all mysteries.
>
> (Fraser 1898: 97)

So, Reid not only knew about fission examples but, like Clarke, used them to argue against materialism. In general, Reid's view and his criticisms of Locke were similar to Butler's. Like Hume, however, Reid took a greater interest than did Butler in the origins of our empirical understanding of the self.

Fission examples: the legacy

Except for Locke's brief mention of them, fission examples became visible in the debate over personal identity as a potential source of objections to relational theories. Clarke, especially, wielded fission examples like a sword, with which he tried to slay a two-headed dragon, one head of which was relational theories of personal identity and the other the impending natural-ization of the soul. Apparently, in the philosophical culture generally, as the examples of Grove, Butler, and Tucker suggest, Clarke's strategy seemed promising initially and continued to be attractive. But, as we shall see, the sword of fission examples proved to be double-edged. Whereas one side could be used to inflict wounds on relational theories of personal identity, the other side would soon be turned on the concept of personal identity itself; for instance, fission examples seem to have played a role in Hume's ultimate conclusion that 'all the nice and subtle questions concerning personal identity' are merely verbal. In the views of some others, fission examples clearly did become a weapon that was used to attack traditional assumptions about personal identity's importance.

As we have seen, Reid claimed, with disdain, that 'Dr. Priestley denies all mysteries'. Reid was right. Priestley, who was aware of fission examples and the uses to which they had been put in the personal identity debates, seems to have argued independently of fission examples that personal identity is not what matters in survival. Thirty years later, his student, Hazlitt, went further, using fission examples not only to argue that personal identity is not what matters primarily, but to deny altogether the appropriateness of future-oriented self-interest. In Chapter 5, we shall consider the views of Priestley and Hazlitt.

By the time Priestley had finished, the soul was finished, at least as a scientifically useful notion. Although it would linger for quite awhile – indeed throughout the nineteenth century – not only in the scientifically irrelevant and retrogressive backwaters of natural theology, but also on the margins of progressive developments, it had been stripped of its god-like powers. The dogma of reflexive consciousness was also rejected. The way was then open to suggest a developmental view of the acquisition of self-concepts. Hazlitt, as we shall see, was among the first to do this. In the views of many thinkers, the immaterial, immortal, supernatural soul had transformed into the material, mortal, natural mind. Just as in the Christian myth, God, as it were, had become man. But it would not happen without a fierce struggle. On the philosophical battlefield, swords would swing in every direction and not only heads, but also souls, would roll.

3

THE SELF AS SOUL

For decades before the appearance of Locke's *Essay*, philosophers who wrote about self and personal identity were primarily concerned with the details of post-mortem existence – whether the soul would be reunited with a body and, if it would, with what sort of body, and so on. After the appearance of Locke's *Essay*, these questions were largely replaced by two others: whether matter can think; and whether, without recourse to the immaterial soul, personal identity can be explained. Because these naturalistic issues became the focus of interest, discussions of self and personal identity tended inevitably and, as the century wore on, increasingly to gravitate toward this-worldly concerns. But not all of these were empirical concerns.

Toward the beginning of the century, the idea that the soul or mind could be investigated a priori was alive and well. To many thinkers, more seemed to hang in the balance than simply how best to determine our own natures. Materialism and atheism were thought to go hand in hand, as were atheism and debauchery. Stillingfleet (1697), Clarke (1738), and Butler (1726), for instance, were sure that the concession that matter can think would lead all but inevitably to the end of religion and morality. To combat these feared consequences thinkers fought the suggestion that the soul might be material.

Through the first two decades of the eighteenth century, traditional meta-physicians, such as Clarke, could stick to their a priori weapons and only occasionally dirty their hands with empirical analysis of mental phenomena. Eventually, however, even traditionalists who espoused that 'the thinking principle within us' is immaterial and indivisible coupled such commitments with empirical analyses of the soul's activities. In many cases, they did this not grudgingly, but as willing participants in a continually growing collective vision. Berkeley, for example, appended to his thin and somewhat defensive insistence on the immaterial soul, an expansive, empirically based account of vision that made virtually no use of his immaterialist metaphysics. Butler, in his sermons on human nature, did much the same, though not to the same degree. And, toward the end of the century, Reid (1764) was, if anything, more enthused and expansive about the empirical parts of his account than about its metaphysically spiritual underpinnings. In short, even in the theories of traditionally minded thinkers, there was a growing inclination to subordinate rational psychology to empirical investigation. However, only in retrospect has it been clear which way things were going.[1]

Thinking matter

In the *Essay*, the most controversial thing Locke wrote was that matter might think.[2] He put forth this suggestion, in Book IV, almost as an aside. A generation earlier, Hobbes' dogmatically asserted materialism had provoked more unthinking denunciation than genuine discussion. The lesson had not been lost on Locke, who proposed modestly only that it is 'impossible for us, by the contemplation of our own *Ideas*, without revelation, to discover whether Omnipotency has not given to some Systems of Matter fitly disposed, a power to perceive and think'. The reason, Locke claimed, is that 'in respect to our Motions', it is 'not much more remote from our Comprehension to conceive, that GOD can, if he pleases, superadd to Matter a Faculty of Thinking, than that he should superadd to it another Substance [i.e., an immaterial soul] with a Faculty of Thinking; since we know not wherein Thinking consists, nor to what sort of Substances the Almighty has been pleased to give that Power' (Locke 1975: IV.iii.6; 540–1). Thus, unlike Hobbes, Locke did not actually say that matter can think. Rather, he said only that, for all we know, it can think. And either because Locke was genuinely pious, which in fact he was, or because he was clever, which he also was, he tied the *denial* that matter can think to the assertion that God's powers are limited, thus, attempting to disarm his critics.

It did not work. Stillingfleet and others were outraged. For traditionalists the main threat from Locke's seemingly innocent speculation was that if matter can think, then for the purposes of metaphysical and psychological explanation, the immaterial soul might be dispensable. But for those who would develop a science of the mind that was the point. There is no investigating the immaterial soul empirically. Since its nature and essential properties are determined a priori it has no internal structure open to empirical inquiry. For example, it cannot be decided by observation whether the soul is always thinking, or even whether animals have immaterial souls.[3] Although the soul was reputed to be active, perhaps even to be the only thing except for God that is active, it does not develop in any way and, hence, as an object of investigation it is completely static. In sum, once the arguments about whether the immortal soul exists were concluded, one accepted its presence or not. There was nothing much to investigate. By comparison, the phenomena of consciousness were seen to be multifaceted and dynamic. And there was no doubt about their existence. Yet no one had ever tried systematically to account for their behavior. Thus, whether a thinker was for or against Locke's novel suggestion that perhaps matter can think, investigating the mind required empirical inquiry. Early in the century a Clarke might take the high road and resist this descent into merely probable and contingent results. But when it came to the investigation of human nature, the emerging program of empirical psychology was the only game in town. One either played it or took oneself completely out of the action. In resisting its lure, thinkers like Clarke became the last of a dying breed.

Clarke and Collins

Clarke and Collins debated each other for three years. Their point of departure was the question of whether souls are naturally immortal. By *soul*, both of them agreed to mean 'Substance with a Power of Thinking' or 'Individual Consciousness' (Clarke 1738: 750). Clarke defended the traditional idea that souls *are* naturally immortal, since they are immaterial and, hence, indivisible. However, he argued for this view in a novel way, precisely because the newly emerging science of mind forced him to defeat the suggestion that mental properties are emergent. His adversary, Collins, countered that the soul is material. Both agreed that individual atoms are not conscious. The dispute between them turned on the question of whether it is possible that a system of matter can think. Clarke argued that it is not possible, Collins that matter actually does think.

Throughout, Clarke played the part of the traditional metaphysician, albeit one who was extraordinarily well informed scientifically. He thought he knew, largely for a priori reasons, that the soul is indivisible, even though, in his view, the soul is extended! Collins, though not always consistently, played the role of the empirical psychologist. His faltering, but often successful attempts to reformulate traditional metaphysical issues empirically, embodied the birth pangs of a new approach. This new approach was then fully born in subsequent thinkers and grew steadily throughout the century. The debate is, thus, a poignant record of two thinkers' struggle to cope with a rapidly changing intellectual climate, one by hanging onto the old, the other by groping for the new. It is, in microcosm the debate over self and personal identity in the first half of the eighteenth century.

Collins' approach was the progressive side of Locke's, of whom he had been a close personal friend and devoted disciple. Collins even had religious views that were similar to, though perhaps more liberal, than Locke's (Ibid.: 864). Yet Collins was disposed and able to go beyond Locke, particularly in two ways: first, methodologically, if not also ontologically, he was unabashedly materialist; and, second, he replaced Locke's metaphysically awkward *same*-consciousness view of personal identity with a more defensible *connected*-consciousness view. In short, Collins was, as Locke himself seems to have foreseen, what Locke might have become had he lived longer and adapted his views and approach to the newly emerging empirical study of the mind. During the last year of his life, Locke remarked to a third party that he regarded Collins as such a philosophically amiable companion that he numbered his own days by the length of his friendship with Collins. Toward the end of his life, Locke wrote to Collins that he regarded him as one who would extend Locke's own work into the future (Locke 1823: v. 10, 271).

At the beginning of their debate, Clarke and Collins agreed on three basic assumptions: first, that consciousness is a 'real property of the mind'; second, that the individual atoms of which human bodies are ultimately composed are not themselves conscious; and, third, that if consciousness were a property of the body, then since it is not a property of the ultimate constituents out of which the body is composed, it has to be a higher order property of a material system, that is, as we might say, an emergent property.

Clarke was an extreme nominalist. Throughout the debate he denied that any emergent property could be 'real'. While admitting that certain higher level properties, such as the 'Magnitude' and the 'Motion' of a body, could be real, he carefully explained that they enjoyed this status just because they are nothing but the 'sum' of the magnitudes and motions of the ultimate parts out of which the relevant bodies are composed (Clarke 1738: 759). He excluded as real properties of any material system secondary qualities, such as the 'sweetness of a rose', on the grounds that they are effects produced by material systems in some other substance. Finally, he excluded properties such as 'Magnetism' and 'Electrical Attraction' as real properties since they are 'merely abstract Names to express the Effects of some determinate Motion of certain Streams of Matter'. Gravitation, in his view, is a special case. It 'is not a *Quality inhering in* Matter, or that can possibly *result* from any Texture or Composition of it; but only an *Effect* of the continual and regular Operation of some other Being upon it; by which the Parts are all made to tend one towards another' (Ibid.: 759–60).

'Under these *three* Heads', Clarke continued, 'must necessarily be contained all possible Qualities, Modes or Powers whatsoever'. That is, 'they must either be *Qualities really inhering in the Subject to which they are usually ascribed*; or *Modes produced by* it in *some other Subject*; or else *mere Abstract Names, signifying certain Powers or Effects that do not properly reside in any Subject at all*'. Consciousness, he said, since it is a real property, has to be a property of the first sort. But, he argued, were consciousness a property of a system of matter, it would be an emergent property and no emergent property can be a property of the first sort. Hence, in his view, consciousness cannot be a property of a system of matter:

> To suppose any Power or Quality of this kind, arising from, or belonging to any *whole* System of Matter, without belonging to the *several* Parts of which that Whole consists, is a direct and express Contradiction: It is supposing either an *Universal* to exist, without *Particulars*; or an *Effect* to be produced without a *Cause*, or to have more in it than was in the *Cause*; or that a *Quality* is by the Power of God made so to arise out of Nothing, as to be superadded to a

Subject, and to subsist without inhering in that Subject, to which it is at the same time supposed to belong.

(Ibid.)[4]

Throughout the debate, this was the heart of Clarke's argument.

Collins did not challenge Clarke's view that magnetism and electricity are unreal. Instead, he denied that one could know a priori that all emergent properties, and consciousness in particular, are unreal. He claimed that Clarke's attempt to so argue merely begged the question. Whether an emergent property is real, Collins countered, is a matter to be determined case by case, empirically. What, though, do we learn by examining actual cases that is relevant to assessing the ontological status of consciousness? In Collins' view, three things: first, 'by Experience we see that every thing by change of Form becomes every thing. The same Parts of Matter become Parts of *Dung, Earth, Grass, Corn, Sheep, Horses, Men, &c.* and act their Parts under these Mutations'; second, and 'equally matter of fact', in the case of examples such as that of the gestation of a bird, we see 'That the Matter of which an Egg consists, doth intirely constitute the young one, and that the Action of Sensation began under a particular Disposition of the Parts by Motion, without the Addition of an Immaterial and Immortal Soul'; and, third, we learn by experience that there are in some systems of matter 'Power[s] to make or receive a Change, to act or be acted on, that [are] not the Sum or Aggregate of Powers of the same kind' (Ibid.: 758, 767–9)

Consider, for instance, texture. According to Collins:

The Texture, let it be of the Eye, Ear, or any other part of Man is essentially different from the Texture of other Beings, and the Texture of the Parts of the Being itself; and it is from its Texture, as well as from its Magnitude and Motion, that the Matter of which the Eye consists, has a Power to make or receive a Change, to act or be acted on: which Power depends so intirely on the particular Texture, that upon the least Alteration of some Parts of the Eye, it ceases to have a Power of being operated on by external Objects, or of contributing to the Act of Vision.

(Ibid.: 769)

Thus, in Collins' view, experience, not a competing a priori theory, undermines some of Clarke's crucial a priori assumptions.

According to Collins, the basic problem with Clarke's argument is that he was trying to settle by verbal fiat what could be settled only empirically:

Saying *That Consciousness is an Individual Power* (be they ever so many that say so) is but calling Consciousness by another name. It is not giving an account of what Consciousness is, wherein it doth consist, which is requisite to demonstrate from Consciousness, that Consciousness cannot be added to a Being that consists of actually separate and distinct Parts.

(Ibid.)

By 'an account of what consciousness is', Collins meant an analysis of consciousness for which there is empirical evidence. So, what he wanted was not a way of describing consciousness, but a way of analyzing it empirically and then explaining it.

Moreover, in Collins' view, not all items of consciousness are alike. In the case of some, a proper account of what consciousness is would have to be developmental, whereas in the case of others it would have to explain pathology. 'For we know by Experience, that the Soul or Thinking Being undergoes several Changes or Alterations. It has not only different Passions, as Anger, Love, &c. at different times, which are Modifications of the Soul, that begin and have their Period, but has Qualities or Powers, such as Seeing and Hearing, which by the Defect of our Organs plainly cease for a time' (Ibid.: 772–3) In Collins' opinion, the provision of some such account of consciousness was a requirement for any acceptable view, including his own. For 'if one should undertake to demonstrate to me, that Consciousness can only inhere in a System of Matter, and for this Purpose should tell me, that Consciousness is an Organical Operation, I should desire him to tell me wherein Thinking or Consciousness doth consist?' And, Collins continued, 'if he would do that, I should be able to know whether it is an Organical Operation or not: whereas his telling me that it is an Organical Operation, leaves me as ignorant what Thinking is, in what it does consist, as I was before those sounds reached in my ear'.

But Mr. *Clarke* has not said anything to this Question, but barely by calling Consciousness *an Individual Power*. His Argument therefore, stripped of all doubtful Expressions, and resting on the Proofs by which he supports it, is this: *Matter is a Substance consisting always of actually separate and distinct Parts; Consciousness cannot reside in a Being which consists in actually separate and distinct Parts; therefore Matter cannot think, or be conscious.* To support which Connection he has no intermediate Ideas, but by saying, *Consciousness is an Individual Power, and an Individual Power cannot reside in a Being that consists of Parts; therefore Consciousness cannot reside in a Being which consists of Parts*: which carries the Matter not one jot further than merely supposing Consciousness to be a Power which can only reside in Individual Beings.

(Ibid.: 769–70)

Collins, thus, pushed hard.

Clarke, unmoved, gave a four-part response to Collins' requirement that he provide an empirical analysis of consciousness: first, he explained that *'Consciousness*, in the most strict and exact Sense of the Word, signifies neither a *Capacity of Thinking*, nor yet *Actual Thinking*, but the *Reflex Act by which I know that I think, and that my Thoughts and Actions are my own and not Another's'*. Second, he explained that by 'Individual Power' he meant 'such a Power as is *really and truly* in the nature of the Thing itself *One Power*, in opposition to its being such merely in our *abstract Complex Notion'*; by an *individual power*, he continued, 'I mean thereby to express that it is really and truly one undivided Consciousness, and not a Multitude of distinct Consciousnesss added together'. Next, he claimed that 'it would necessarily imply a plain and direct Contradiction, for any power which is really *One* and not *Many* . . . to inhere in or result from a divisible Substance' (Ibid.: 784).[5] So far, then, Clarke stuck to the high road of a priori metaphysics.

In his fourth point, Clarke claimed that if, as Collins asserted, 'the Brain or Spirits be the Subject of Consciousness', and thus the subject of consciousness be 'in perpetual flux and change', then 'That Consciousness, by which I *not only Remember* that certain Things were done many Years since, but also *am Conscious that they were done by Me, by the very same individual Conscious Being* who now remembers them . . . is transferred from one Subject to another; that is to say, that it is real Quality which subsists without inhering in any Subject at all' (Ibid.: 787). Clarke's fourth point, in effect, invited Collins to explain how on his own view, memory could be understood. He, thus, gave Collins an opening to return to the theme that Clarke lacked an empirical analysis of consciousness. In anticipation of Collins' expected reply, Clarke tried to cut him off at the pass, by conceding in advance that his 'affirming Consciousness to be an individual Power, is not giving an Account of what Consciousness is' but then 'neither was it intended to be so'. It is enough, Clarke continued, that:

> Every Man feels and knows by Experience what Consciousness is, better than any Man can explain it: Which is the Case of all simple ideas: And it is not at all necessary to define more particularly what *it is*; but abundantly sufficient that we know and agree what it is *not*, viz., that it is not a Multitude of distinct and separate Consciousnesses; in order to prove that it does not and cannot inhere in a Being, that consists of a Multititude of separate and distinct Parts.
>
> (Ibid.: 790)

It would in the end, then, come down to this: a clash between intuition and science.

As we know from the continuation of this debate into our own times, this particular conflict may be unresolvable. What would become clear, however, on the way to this end – and this seems to be a lesson that was not lost on subsequent thinkers, including those who embraced Clarke's traditional immaterialist account of the soul – is that while intuition might be a sufficient basis to resist the reduction of the mental to the material, it was impotent as a source of explanations of mental phenomena.

Collins returned to this latter theme again and again, as in the following remarks:

> Thinking or Human Consciousness begins, continues and ends, or has Generation, Succession and Corruption, like all other Modes of Matter; as like them it is divided and determined, simple or compounded, and so on. But if the Soul or Principle of Thinking be undivided, how can it think successively, divide, abstract, combine or ampliate, retain or revive Impressions in the memory? And how can it be capable, partly or wholly, to forget any thing? All which *Phaenomena* are naturally conceived, and may be commodiously explained by the Springs and Movements, and Receptacles; by the Vigor, Perfection, Disorder or Decay of a bodily Organ, but not by any thing indivisible.

Collins even illustrated how, on his view, explanations for some of these phenomena could be forthcoming:

> It is so far from being absurd to annex human Consciousness to so flux a Substance as the Brain, that it will rather be absurd to annex it to any other Substance but so flux a one as the Brain: For if we utterly forget, or cease to be conscious of having done many things in the former Parts of our Lives which we certainly did, as much as any of those things which we are conscious that we have done; and if in fact we do by degrees forget every thing which we do not revive by frequent Recollection, and by again and again imprinting our decaying Ideas; and if there be in a determinate Time a partial or total flux of Particles in our Brains: What can better Account for our total Forgetfulness of some things, our partial Forgetfulness of others, than to suppose the Substance of the Brain in a constant Flux? And what can better show that Consciousness is not transferred from one Subject to another, than our forgetting totally or partially, according to the Brain's being more or less in a Flux?

Collins then continued by explaining how he would account for remembrance:

> I can know 'I' did something in the past despite this flux which may involve no residual particles that were part of the original system at the time of an event: Consciousness of having done [an] Action is an

Idea imprinted on the Brain, by recollecting or bringing into View our Ideas before they are worn out; which continues in me, not only the Memory of the Action itself, but that I did it. And if there is now and then a Recollection of a past Action, Mr. Clarke may, by what I have said, conceive a Man may be conscious of things done by him, though he has not one Particle of Matter the same that he had at the doing of those things, without *Consciousness's being transferred from one Subject to another* in any absurd Sense of those words.

(Ibid.: 807–9)

This illustrates what Collins meant by *an account of consciousness*.

Clearly Collins thought that in the cases of memory and forgetting he could not only give an account of consciousness, but give one that would explain how consciousness, over time, could be transferred from a material system of the brain initially composed of certain particles to one composed of another, without changing the individual subject of consciousness whose brain is involved. By our contemporary standards, his explanation – that it is by repeatedly recollecting that we keep our memories from decaying beyond recall – may seem crude (Ibid.: 809, 870). But crude or not, it was a genuine scientific explanation, and Clarke had nothing comparable to offer in its stead.

Rather, Clarke accused Collins of 'begging the Question by, assuming the impossible Hypothesis' that the subject in Collins' example who originally had the experience that subsequently would be remembered and any subject who subsequently remembered it would be the same:

Supposing it were *possible*, that the *Memory* in general of such or such an Action's having been done, might be preserved in the Manner you suppose; yet it is a manifest Contradiction, that the *Consciousness* of its being done by *me*, by *my own individual self* in particular, should continue in me after my whole Substance is changed; unless *Consciousness* could be transferred from one Subject to another, in the absurdest Sense of those Words. For to suppose that one Substance should be *Conscious* of an Action's having been done by itself, which really was not done by it, but by another Substance, is plainly supposing an individual Quality to be transferred from one Subject to another, in the most absurd Sense; as is plain that *Consciousness* is a *real, individual Quality*, and different from bare *general Memory*.

Clarke then declared that on Collins' account, consciousness, rather than being a real individual quality, is a '*fleeting transferrable Mode or Power*':

That the *Person* may still be the same, by a continual Superaddition of the *like Consciousness*; notwithstanding the whole *Substance* be changed: then I say, you make *individual Personality* to be a mere *external imaginary Denomination*, and nothing in reality: just as a *Ship* is called the *same Ship*, after the whole substance is changed by frequent Repairs; or a *River* is called the *same River*, though the Water of it be every Day new.

And so, on Collins' view, the self, in effect, would be a *fiction*:

> But he cannot be *really and truly* the *same Person*, unless the *same numerical Consciousness* can be transferred from one Subject to another. For, the continued Addition or Exciting of a *like Consciousness* in the new acquired Parts, after the Manner you suppose; is nothing but a Deception and Delusion, under the Form of Memory; a making the Man to seem himself to be conscious of having done that, which was not done by him, but by another.
>
> (Ibid.: 844–5)

Thus, Collins' attempt to characterize how consciousness could be understood on the hypothesis of the brain as its material substrate had forced Clarke, and as we shall see, Collins also, to recognize what was thought to be a decisive implication of Collins' hypothesis. The implication is that the apparent unity of self-consciousness actually involves a series of numerically different acts of consciousness, whose subject cannot be one simple individual being. In Clarke's mind, it was a conclusive refutation of Collins' view that this consequence followed from it.

For his part, Collins embraced the consequence. He eventually distinguished between the immediate subject of an action or state of consciousness, and the organized being, or brain, which is the substantial base for the sequence of states of consciousness. In response to Clarke's concerns about transference of consciousness from one subject to another, Collins admitted that 'The Quality of a Subject can only be the Quality of that Subject wherein it exists, and not of another Subject. The Motion of a System of Matter can only be the Motion of that System'. Thus:

> The Consciousness of any Being can only be the Consciousness of that particular Being. And I further observe, that the Motion of a System of Matter one Day can never be the Motion of the same numerical System the next Day, nor the Consciousness of Yesterday be the same numerical Consciousness that I have to Day, let the Being that is conscious in me be divisible or indivisible.

So, the mode of a substance, once the mode ceases, can never be the same as another mode of the same kind, whether it is a mode of the same or a different substance. It follows, Collins continued, that:

It is thus as intelligible to me that the Memory of Things should be preserved by a Being in a Flux, as by a Being that is not so. For the individual Consciousness To-Day, can neither in an indivisible or divisible Being be the individual Consciousness To-morrow; that Consciousness is a perfectly distinct Action in both Beings from the preceding Consciousness the Day before. And whenever Mr. Clarke accounts for an indivisible Being's remembrance of an Action or Thought, I promise to account for Memory in a divisible Being.

(Ibid.: 819–20)

In response to Clarke's attempted proof of the impossibility that consciousness could reside in the substance of the brain, Collins replied that it 'is plain, that all Mr. Clarke's Propositions are founded on his considering Consciousness to be something else than that I contend it is'. Thus, the exchange, which began over the issue of the immateriality of the soul and the possibility of matter thinking, expanded to include a discussion of alternative theoretical interpretations of consciousness and its relations to the substance and activities of the brain.

Ultimately, Collins appealed to an analogy between consciousness and the property of roundness to blunt the force of Clarke's claim that emergent properties cannot be 'real'. Collins pointed out that individually the arches out of which a circle is composed are not round, but collectively, when properly arranged, they are round. Yet roundness, as even Clarke admitted, is a real property. In this final part of the debate between them, the question turned on whether this analogy is a good one. Clarke, of course, claimed that it is a bad analogy. In the end, he claimed that what made roundness a real property of the circle is that although the arches are not individually round, they have a 'tendency' toward roundness. He denied that the same could be said of the material atoms out of which Collins was claiming conscious systems might ultimately be composed. Collins, on the other hand, claimed that the atoms did indeed have a tendency toward consciousness (Ibid.: 860, 890, 894).

Since neither Clarke nor Collins had a principled way of setting the limits to such 'tendencies', there was no way to resolve this impasse. So, Clarke simply reiterated the nominalist thesis with which he began:

You intend to make *Thinking* not a real *Quality*, but a *mere empty Name* or *external Denomination*, such as I at first ranked under the *Third Head*. For the most complex Modes of Motion possible, whatever *Name* we give them, is nothing but a *mere external Denomination*. *Thinking* therefore, according to you, being only a *very complex Mode of Motion* [or *of any other Quality of Matter*] is likewise nothing but a *mere external Name or Denomination* of that Mode. Which Notion of yours concerning Thinking, is certainly a mere *Chimera*; and a very absurd one.

(Ibid.: 899)

Clarke then returned to his point that what consciousness is can be known intuitively.

This may seem a disappointing outcome. But it is consequential. For, in the end, eighteenth century readers of this debate were left with a choice among three options. First, as Clarke had done, they could stay with the a priori, immaterialist view of the soul and give the back of their hands to the emerging scientific study of the mind. Second, they could somehow combine their commitment to the a priori, immaterialist view of the soul with the emerging scientific study of the mind. Or, finally, as Collins had done, they could throw off the traditional metaphysical view of self and cast their lot entirely with the emerging scientific study of the mind. Early in the century, when Clarke and Collins had their debate, it seemed to many that the real choices were between the first and the third of these options. But as the century progressed, it increasingly became apparent to virtually everyone that the real choices were between the second and the third options. By mid-century no serious thinker eschewed the scientific study of the mind. The worm had turned.

Shaftesbury

The movement toward empiricism in the study of mind was matched by a movement toward empiricism in the study of morals and prudence. The issues of self and personal identity linked these domains. Collins had been one of the first of Locke's students to embrace materialism as a research strategy for the study of mind. Shaftesbury was one of the first of his students to embrace materialism as a research strategy in ethical theory. But whereas Collins thought that he got his impetus toward materialism from Locke, Shaftesbury thought that he got his by opposing Locke.

Born in 1671, Anthony Ashley Cooper, the third Earl of Shaftesbury, was educated under Locke's personal direction. Yet, by the time Shaftesbury reached maturity, there were important differences in their respective philosophies. For instance, Shaftesbury dismissed Locke's laborious objections against innate ideas as 'one of the childishest disputes that ever was' (Rand 1900: 345–7). And whereas Locke thought that morality, like geometry, could be derived from a priori principles, Shaftesbury thought that all we need to know about morality emanates from human nature. Ironically, since Shaftesbury was the first to champion 'moral sense', in ethical theory he was more empirical than the father of empiricism. One could almost say that what Locke was to the Cartesians on the issue of innate ideas, Shaftesbury was to Locke on the issue of moral principles.

In one respect, Shaftesbury and Locke were similar. Both tried to avoid constructive metaphysics. But whereas Locke argued at length against metaphysical views he rejected, Shaftesbury tried to jettison metaphysics altogether, claiming that metaphysical questions were unanswerable and metaphysical answers both paradoxical and too far removed from what one needs to know to live a good and happy life to be worth pursuing. When it came to constructive metaphysics, Locke, for the most part, retreated to a theological pragmatism, Shaftesbury to a purely secular pragmatism.

Yet, Shaftesbury too became embroiled in metaphysics, particularly in opposing the mind–body dualism of his day, to which he thought Locke had made too many concessions. Shaftesbury advanced in its stead a neutral monism that shaded into materialism. A friend and admirer of Bayle, he attacked dualism with skepticism:

> As for what is said of 'A material unthinking substance being never able to have produced an immaterial thinking one', I readily grant it, but on the condition of this great maxim of nothing being ever made from nothing may hold as well on my side as my adversary's. And then, I suppose, that whilst the world endures, he will be at a loss how to assign a beginning to matter, or how to suggest a possibility of annihilating it . . . The poor dregs of sorry matter can no more be made out of the simple pure substance of immaterial thought, than the high spirits of thought or reason can be extracted from the gross substance of heavy matter. So let the dogmatists make of this argument what they can.
> (Shaftesbury 1711: v. 2, 69–70)

In Shaftesbury's view, Nature, a single great unity, with both mental and material attributes, is capable of varying degrees of purpose and mentality.

Shaftesbury agreed with Hobbes and Locke that it is life that unifies animate matter, and that life should be understood mechanistically: it is in virtue of the 'sympathising of parts' that we find in a tree that it 'is a real tree, lives, flourishes, and is still one and the same even when by vegetation and change of substance not one particle in it remains the same' (Ibid.: 99–100). However, he suggested that trees form a natural kind, whereas, as we have seen, Locke's nominalism about essences can be taken to imply that for him there are only nominal kinds.

Shaftesbury rejected the idea, prevalent at the time, that unless one's theory of personal identity supports the idea of survival and is compatible with divine rewards and punishments, people will lose their incentive to be moral. He believed, instead, in a religion of nature, in acting morally now for its own sake, and professed no concern whatsoever for the afterlife, writing in disgust that 'philosophy seems at present to be the study of making virtue burdensome and death uneasy'. He recommended that people 'make the most of life and least of death', by doing 'the most good, and that the most freely and generously, throwing aside selfishness, mercenariness, and such servile thoughts as unfit us even for this world, and much more for a better':

> This is my best advice; and I leave with you, as that which I have lived and shall die by. Let every one answer for their own experience, and

speak of happiness and good as they find it. Thank heaven I can do good and find heaven in it, I know nothing else that is heavenly. And if this disposition fits me not for heaven, I desire never to be fitted for it, nor come into the place.

(Rand 1900: 345–7)

Shaftesbury concluded: 'I ask no reward from heaven for that which is reward itself. Let my being be continued or discontinued, as in the main best. The author of it best knows, and I trust Him with it. To me it is indifferent, and always shall be so.'

In regard to personal identity, Shaftesbury stressed that, as 'the meanest anatomist can tell us, the "stuff" out of which we are composed is constantly changing, with complete replacement every "twice seven years".' Beyond that, he claimed that peoples' characters also are constantly changing: ' 'Tis good fortune if a man be one and the same only for a day or two. A year makes more revolutions than can be numbered.' Still, Shaftesbury conceded, 'when he comes to suffer or to be punished for . . . vices, he finds himself . . . still one and the same'. He concluded, 'You see, therefore, there is a strange simplicity in this you and me, that in reality they should be still one and the same, when neither one atom of body, one passion, nor one thought remains the same' (Shaftesbury 1711: v. 2, 101).

What accounts for this strange simplicity in 'our real and proper self'? It is not clear how Shaftesbury answered this question, but through the voice of a participant in a dialogue, he seems to have reached a conclusion surprisingly like Locke's own: 'As accidental as my life may be, or as random that humour which governs it, I know nothing, after all, so real and substantial as myself. Therefore if there be that thing you call substance, I take for granted I am one. But for anything further relating to this question . . . I am determined neither way' (Ibid.).

Even so, Shaftesbury seems reluctantly to have rejected Locke's account of personal identity, but not to embrace another. The problems he saw with Locke's view were due to pathologies of memory. So, for instance, in *Miscellaneous Reflections* (Ibid.), which may have been influenced by the Clarke–Collins debate, he stated, 'That there is something undoubtedly which thinks, our very doubt itself and scrupulous thought evinces.'

But in what subject that thought resides, and how that subject is continued one and the same, so as to answer constantly to the supposed train of thoughts or reflections which seem to run so harmoniously through a long course of life, with the same relation still to one single and self-same person, that is not a matter so easily or hastily decided by those who are nice self-examiners and searchers after truth and certainty.

He continued:

> But the question is, 'What constitutes the We or I?' and 'Whether the
> I of this instant be the same with that of any instant preceding or to
> come?' For we have nothing but memory to warrant us, and memory
> may be false.

Shaftesbury had no answer to this problem, confessing in the end that 'I take
my being upon trust'. Then it was moral pragmatism to the rescue:

> Let others philosophise as they are able: I shall admire their strength
> when, on this topic, they have refuted what able metaphysicians
> object, and Pyrrhonists plead in their own behalf. Meanwhile there is
> no impediment, hindrance, or suspension of action on account of
> these wonderfully refined speculations. Argument and debate go
> on still. Conduct is settled. Rules and measures are given out and
> received. Nor do we scruple to act as resolutely upon the mere suppo-
> sition that we are, as if we effectually proved it a thousand times, to
> the full satisfaction of our metaphysical or Pyrrhonian antagonist.
> This to me appears sufficient ground for a moralist.
>
> (Ibid.: 275–6)

In all of this, there is a curious similarity to Locke. The main difference is that
whereas Locke slid over the question of faulty memory, Shaftesbury admitted
that it could not be solved. Both appeal in the end to a kind of pragmatism,
but whereas Locke's was theological and both other- and this-worldly,
Shaftesbury's was secular and completely this-worldly.[6]

Shaftesbury, like Locke, also took as central the question of our 'concernment' for our earlier and later selves:

> Now to be assured that we can never be concerned in anything here-
> after, we must understand what it is which concerns or engages us in
> anything present. We must truly know ourselves, and in what this self
> of ours consists. We must determine against pre-existence, and give a
> better reason for our having never been concerned in aught before
> our birth than merely 'because we remember not, nor are conscious'.
> For in many things we have been concerned to purpose, of which we
> have now no memory or consciousness remaining. And thus we may
> happen to be again and again to perpetuity, for any reason we can
> show to the contrary. All is revolution in us. We are no more the self-
> same matter or system or matter from one day to another. What
> succession there may be hereafter we know not, since even now we
> live by succession, and only perish and are renewed.
>
> (Ibid.: 34–5)

Shaftesbury took the conclusion to these speculations to be a kind of skepticism regarding self-concern: ''Tis in vain we flatter ourselves with the assurance of our interests ending with a certain shape or form. What interested us at first in it we know not, any more than how we have since held on, and continued still concerned in such an assemblage of fleeting particles. Where besides or in what else we may have to do, perchance, in time to come, we know as little, nor can tell how chance or providence hereafter may dispose of us.'

Shaftesbury's journal, entitled *Philosophical Regimen* was not published until the beginning of the twentieth century (Rand 1900). Written as a dialogue between the author and himself, in it Shaftesbury leans heavily on the meditations of Marcus Aurelius and the discourses of Epictetus. Although the emphasis is on moral issues and on the social or 'artificial' self, entries on the 'natural self' enter into those on personal identity, covering some of the same ground as found in his published works, including further reflections on self-concern:

> The metaphysicians and notable reasoners about the nice matters of identity, affirm that if memory be taken away, the self is lost. And what matter for memory? What have I to do with that part? If, whilst I am, I am but as I should be, what do I care more? and thus let me lose self every hour, and be twenty successive selfs, or new selfs, 'tis all one to me: so I lose not my opinion. If I carry that with me 'tis I; all is well. If that go, memory must go too: for how one without the other? If thou preservest this true opinion of self (as not body) even whilst in a body, it will not be surely less confirmed to thee when thou shalt find thyself (if such be the case) even out of a body. If the now do not belie thee, the hereafter cannot. If the present state allow it, the future must demonstrate it: and the better surely for thee, that thou hast thus thought and begun thus with thyself whilst here. – But why these ifs? Why the conditioning? Wouldst thou bargain as others do? – What views? what fancies? – The now; the now. Mind this: in this is all.
>
> (Ibid.: 136–7)

Sounding rather Buddha-like, Shaftesbury was a thinker who, in many ways, was ahead of his time. Had he argued more fully, he might have been profoundly influential. As it is, his influence on the subsequent personal identity debate was probably mostly by way of suggestion. And in spite of his tendencies toward skepticism and mysticism, his main influence was to encourage the empirical study of morality in human nature. He, thus, had an important impact on several eighteenth century figures who attempted to naturalize human nature, including philosophers such as Hutcheson, Butler and Hume, rhetoricians and aestheticians such as George Campbell and Lord Kames, and others in France and Germany.

George Berkeley

Before Berkeley closed his *Philosophical Commentaries* (1948) to write his *An Essay Towards a New Theory of Vision* (1709/1837) and *A Treatise Concerning the Principles of Human Knowledge* (1710/1965) he noted to himself his final retreat from any investigation of personal identity: 'The Concrete of the Will & understanding I must call the Mind not person, lest offense be given . . . Mem: Carefully to omit Defining of Person, or making much mention of it' (Berkeley 1948: 87; item 713).[7] Apparently Berkeley felt that his thoughts about personal identity had led him to ideas that were religiously dangerous. And so they had. He had begun with something like a Lockean conception of personal identity but, then, as a consequence of his attempt to eliminate all abstract ideas, including not only those of material but also of spiritual substance, he found himself forced to a skeptical position, more like that of Hume than Locke, from which he felt he had to retreat. Finally he came to assume – almost dogmatically and in the tradition of Descartes and Clarke – an underlying simplicity and unity to our minds that can be known immediately through our actions.

In Berkeley's earliest notes in his *Commentaries*, composed before he had reached this final destination, he wrote: 'Time train of ideas succeeding each other' (4), 'Duration not distinguish'd from existence' (5), and 'Time a sensation, therefore onely in mind' (13). This is followed by the note: 'Eternity is onely a train of innumerable ideas. hence the immortality of ye Soul easily conceived. or rather the immortality of the person, yt of ye soul not being necessary for ought we know' (14). And later: 'Nothing properly but persons i.e. conscious things do exist, all other things are not so much existences as manners of ye existence of persons' (24). From this beginning Berkeley finds a unity of person in the sequence or train of ideas, the 'percepi' for which the person is the 'percipere'. Later he was to summarize his position as: 'Existence is percepi or percipere'. (429).

However, problems arose for Berkeley when he focused on what would maintain identity within his system: 'No identity other than perfect likeness in any individuals besides persons' (192); and 'On account of my doctrine the identity of finite substances must consist in something else than continued existence, or relation to determin'd time and place of beginning to exist, the existence of our thoughts (wch being combin'd make all substances) being frequently interrupted, & they having divers beginnings, & endings' (194). From these thoughts he raised the question: 'wherin consists identity of Person? not in actual consciousness, for then I'm not the same person I was this day twelvemonth, but while I think of wt I then did. Not in potential for then all persons may be the same for ought we know' (200) (to which he added the clarificatory note, 'two sorts of Potential consciousnesses Natural & praeternatural [here] I mean the latter' (202)). Much later, he was to use the first objection in his dialogue, *Alciphron: Or, the Minute Philosopher*

(1732/1837), in which the minute philosopher is modelled on 'free thinkers' like Collins, and perhaps even written with the Clarke–Collins debate specifically in mind. In that dialogue, Berkeley proposed that the same *man* might be several *persons* if there is a complete break in consciousness between the man's earlier and later phases. His main objection against the 'same consciousness' view, which probably was the source of a similar, but better known objection in Reid, divides a man into three phases, A, B, and C, and shows that defining a person in terms of consciousness leads to a contradiction when the C-person has remembrances of B but not of A, and the B-person has remembrances of A.

In Berkeley's *Commentaries* these difficulties about identity first led him to the conclusion that 'It seems improper & liable to difficulties to make the Word Person stand for an Idea, or to make our selves Ideas or thinking things ideas' (523). Still trying to avoid what seems to follow from his general position, he claimed: 'I am the farthest from Scepticism of any man. I know with an intuitive knowledge the existence of other things as well as my own soul, this is wt Locke nor scarce any other Thinking Philosopher will pretend to' (563). But, then, in an amazing series of notes shortly thereafter, he seems forced to a Humean interpretation of his own views: 'We think we know not the Soul because we have no imaginable or sensible Idea annex'd to that sound. This the Effect of prejudice' (576). 'Certainly we do not know it. this will be plain if we examine wt we mean by the word knowledge. Neither doth this argue any defect in our knowledge no more than our not knowing a contradiction' (576a). 'The very existence of Ideas constitutes the soul' (577). 'Consciousness, perception, existence of Ideas seem to be all one' (578). 'Consult, ransack yr Understanding wt find you there besides several perceptions or thoughts. Wt mean you by the word mind you must mean something that you perceive or yt you do not perceive. a thing not perceived is a contradiction. to mean (also) a thing you do not perceive is a contradiction. We are in all this matter strangely abused by words' (579). 'Mind is a congeries of Perceptions. Take away perceptions & you take away the Mind put the Perceptions & you put the mind' (580). 'Say you the Mind is not the Perceptions. but that thing whch perceives. I answer you are abus'd by the words that & thing these are vague empty words wthout a meaning' (581). Consistent with this view he again addressed, but this time more positively, the problem of discontinuity: 'No broken Intervals of Death or Annihilation. Those Intervals are nothing. Each Person's time being measured to him by his own Ideas' (590).

We see some residues of this position in Berkeley's treatment of Time in the *Principles*, as well as in his discussion there of the resurrection (Berkeley 1965: 69–70). In both discussions, continuity of self seems restricted to continuity of trains of ideas. Like Hume, the early Berkeley did not deny that there is an underlying connecting link between conscious states but instead denied only that we can know its nature other than as a 'congeries of Perceptions'. But a strictly empirical approach to self-knowledge was not one that Berkeley could maintain. He soon wrote: 'Say you there must be a thinking substance. Something unknown whch perceives & supports & ties together the Ideas. Say I, make it appear there is any need of it & you shall have it for me. I care not to take away any thing I can see the reason to think should exist' (637)

Berkeley's initial approach to unity was through the Will and Under-standing:'Doctrine of Identity best explain'd by Takeing the Will for Volitions, the Understanding for Ideas. The difficulty of Consciousness of wt are never acted etc. solv'd thereby' (681). But, then, realizing that 'activity' is the important element here (673; 683), and that 'The will & the Understanding may very well be thought two distinct beings' (709) he concluded: 'The Spirit the Active thing that wch is Soul & God is the Will alone The Ideas are effects impotent things' (712). At this point he decided to drop all talk of person and to focus on Mind (713, cited above). However, he was still worried about what makes for unity: 'You ask do these volitions make one Will. wt you ask is meerly about a Word. Unite being no more' (714). Not satisfied with this answer, he continued: 'Qu[estion]: wt mean you by My perceptions, my Volitions? Res[ponse], all the perceptions I perceive or conceive etc are mine, all the Volitions I am Conscious to are mine' (744) and 'We see no variety or difference betwixt the Volitions, only between their effects. Tis One Will one Act distinguish'd by the effects. This will, this Act is the Spirit, operative, Principle, Soul etc' (788). Becoming more confident that he has found the key in a unified will he concluded: 'While I exist or have any Idea I am eternally, constantly willing, my acquiescing in the present State is willing' (791).

It is not long after these earlier notes that Berkeley's position solidified into the substantial view of Spirit also to be found in his published works: 'The Substance of a Spirit is that it acts, causes, wills, operates, or if you please (to avoid the quibble yt may be made on ye word it) to act, cause, will, operate its' substance is not knowable not being an Idea' (829) and 'But the Grand Mistake is that we know not wt we mean by we or selves or mind. etc. tis most sure & certain that our Ideas are distinct from the Mind i.e. the Will, the Spirit' (847). Having convinced himself of the substantial self, independent of ideas, he concluded: 'I must not give the Soul or Mind the Scholastic Name pure act, but rather pure Spirit or active Being' (870). And reminding himself of his earlier theory: 'Dangerous to make Idea & thing terms Convertible, that were the way to prove spirits are Nothing' (872). Hume, relishing just this danger, would adopt the theory that Berkeley disowned.

Did Berkeley ever return to these dark thoughts? Originally the *Principles* was intended to be in three parts: the first, on matter; the second, on mind; the third, on God. The *Principles*, as we now have them, is just the first of this projected three-part work. Berkeley never wrote the third part, on God. However, he did write the second part, on mind, apparently before he published, in 1713, the first edition of *Three Dialogues between Hylas and Philonous* (Berkeley 1965: 103–211). By his own account, he 'lost' the one and only copy of his all but completed manuscript of Book II of the *Principles*.[8]

He never returned to the project. No one knows what Berkeley actually wrote, or what, had he returned to the project, he would have written.

In his published writings, Berkeley, in *Alciphron* (1732/1837), considered Locke's view that personal identity consists in sameness of consciousness. But Berkeley's closest approach to the issues about self that so frightened him in his youth seems to be in the third part of the *Three Dialogues*. There, in the course of discussing the contradictory nature of material objects, Hylas (Berkeley's materialist antagonist) objects to Philonous (Berkeley's spokesperson): 'But the same idea which is in my mind cannot be in yours or in any other mind. Does it not, therefore, follow from your principles that no two can see the same thing? And is not this highly absurd?' (Ibid.: 193).

Philonous responds to this by taking the view that at least in its application to material objects that are composite and persist over time, how we should understand *identity* or *sameness* is a merely verbal matter, to be decided on pragmatic grounds. He says that 'If the term "same" be taken in the vulgar acceptation, it is certain' that 'different persons may perceive the same thing, or the same thing or idea exist in different minds'. He then notes that 'words are of arbitrary imposition', and adds:

> But if the term 'same' be used in the acceptation of philosophers who pretend to an abstracted notion of identity, then, according to their sundry definitions of this notion (for it is not yet agreed wherein that philosophical identity consists), it may or may not be possible for divers persons to perceive the same thing. But whether philosophers shall think fit to call a thing the 'same' or no is, I conceive, of small importance.
>
> (Ibid.: 194)

Philonous, then, imagines two philosophers who use the word 'same' differently. He says:

> But who sees not that all the dispute is about a word, to wit, whether what is perceived by different persons may yet have the term 'same' applied to it? Or suppose a house whose walls or outward shell remaining unaltered, the chambers are all pulled down, and new ones built in their place, and that you should call this the 'same', and I should say it was not the 'same' house – would we not for all this perfectly agree in our thoughts of the house considered in itself?
>
> (Ibid.)

Hylas says that materialists 'suppose an external archetype to which referring their several ideas they may truly be said to perceive the same thing'. Philonous, then, replies that on his view too, one can suppose there is an external archetype, so long as 'external' means to one's own mind and not to 'that mind which comprehends all things'. Philonous concludes, 'But then, this serves all the ends of *identity*, as well as if it existed out of a mind' (Ibid.: 195).

Particularly in light of Berkeley's having 'lost' Part II of the *Principles*, what is fascinating about these exchanges is his willingness, when it comes to the identity of material objects to take the view that whether an object is identical with its earlier phases is largely a verbal matter, to be determined pragmatically in light of the uses to which the notion of identity is put. This, of course, is very similar to the view that Hume took about disputes over identity in general, including the identity of persons.

Did Berkeley, in the manuscript for Part II of the *Principles* or in writing the *Three Dialogues,* ever consciously connect such thoughts about the identity of material objects to the issue of the identity of selves? Although there is no direct evidence, it seems likely that he did. In the third edition of *Three Dialogues*, which was published in 1734, a few pages before the exchange between Hylas and Philonous just discussed, Berkeley inserted four new paragraphs about the soul, which included Hylas' objecting:

> Notwithstanding all you have said, to me it seems that, according to your own way of thinking, and in consequence of your own principles, it should follow that you are only a system of floating ideas without any substance to support them. Words are not to be used without a meaning. And as there is no more meaning in *spiritual* substance than in *material* substance, the one is to be exploded as well as the other.
>
> (Ibid.: 178)

This, of course, is close to Hume's objection in the *Treatise*, published just five years later. To the objection, Philonous replies indignantly:

> How often must I repeat that I know or am conscious of my own being, and that I *myself* am not my ideas, but somewhat else, a thinking, active principle that perceives, knows, wills, and operates about ideas. I know that I, *one and the same self*, perceive both colors and sounds.
>
> (Ibid.; emphasis added).

So, Berkeley introduced the notions of *identity (sameness)*, just a few pages before Philonous takes the view that in its application to material objects we can afford to be relativists about *identity*. Barring the discovery of new manuscripts or additional information about Berkeley's unpublished thoughts, whether at this point in his life he saw the general application of his relativistic thoughts to the identity of selves must remain a matter of speculation. However, as we have shown, it is not a matter of speculation that Berkeley, at least early in his career, was deeply conflicted about the nature of the soul.

Whatever Berkeley's true views, he chose to keep secret his early fascination with the sort of account of self which Hume would later make famous. It seems to us that in his youth, Berkeley rushed ahead with what turned out to be a dangerous empirical approach, later to retreat to the safe ground of more comfortable a priori notions. He had gone to the edge of an abyss, peered over, and drew back in horror. Hume would go to the same edge, peer over, lose his footing, and stumble in. The subsequent free fall frightened even Hume, who in the Appendix to the *Treatise*, tried desperately on his way down to grasp at something.[9]

Both Berkeley and Hume consoled themselves with empirical studies. Berkeley, in his *An Essay toward a New Theory of Vision* (1709/1837) and *Theory of Vision Vindicated and Explained* (1733/1837), developed accounts of mentality that were thoroughly empirical and made little use of his official immaterialistic theory of the soul. Not only was he apparently quite conflicted about his own official account of the soul, he was capable of leaving it behind to study the mind in a way that even Collins might have admired. In contrast, although Clarke and Berkeley subscribed to similar views of the soul, their approaches to the empirical study of mind could hardly have been more different.

Henry Grove

During the eighteenth century, as the soul became naturalized, what was once philosophy of soul became philosophy of mind. During the early part of the century, in major texts the word 'soul' occurs about equally often with the word 'mind'. By the end of the century, the word 'soul' has been almost entirely replaced by 'mind'. For instance, in Berkeley's *Principles* (1710), the word 'soul' occurs nearly as often as the word 'mind'. In his scientific work on vision, published at about the same time, he used only the word, 'mind'. And in the 1730s, the skeptic, Hume, in the *Treatise*, used both *soul* and *mind* equally in contexts where in a previous era the word 'soul' would have been used. By contrast, after mid-century, Reid, the ordained minister, whose major source for philosophical ideas was Hume, used only the word 'mind' in those same contexts. Thus, throughout the century, in empirically oriented works, as 'the thinking principle in man' increasingly became the object of naturalistic investigation, the term 'mind' gradually replaced 'soul', even among thinkers, such as Reid, who maintained a traditional belief in the immaterial soul.

'Pneumatology' was a term of major significance throughout most of the eighteenth century. Originally a scholastic term, at the beginning of the century it meant the philosophy of spirits, a discipline which included philosophy of the human spirit (psychology), philosophy of pure spirits other than God (angelology), and philosophy of God (theology). Throughout the seventeenth century, pneumatology maintained this threefold structure. However, during the eighteenth century, and increasingly as the century wore on, pneu-matology became more and more associated with the philosophy of the human spirit (psychology) and less with that of other spirits. After mid-century, pneumatology became the science of the human mind, and through analogy, the science of brute minds. By the end of the century, the term all but disappeared and was replaced by 'philosophy of mind' or 'mental philosophy', from which, toward the mid-nineteenth century, 'psychology' emerges. Thus, pneumatology, the philosophy of spirits, ultimately gives birth to psychology, the science of mind. Meanwhile, in the early nineteenth century, what continued to be called pneumatology devolved into a speculative discipline dealing with apparitions and ghosts.[10]

From the perspective of our own times, Henry Grove, is almost invisible. He is known, if at all, mainly for his contributions to *The Spectator*, for which he was greatly admired by Samuel Johnson. Nevertheless, Grove is worth remembering, for he was a keen and original thinker. For instance, in an essay on benevolence in *The Spectator*, in which he argued against Hobbes' idea that self-love is the root of sympathy and benevolence, Grove was an early advo-cate of the idea that we have a natural disposition to compassion. He may even have introduced the term 'disinterested benevolence' into the eighteenth-century discussion of altruism.[11] As indicated in the last chapter, Grove discussed fission examples. And, as we shall see below, he was an acute critic of Locke on personal identity, and even expressed a famous objection to Locke that is used later by Berkeley and Reid, and for which Berkeley generally gets the credit.

Beyond these accomplishments, Grove is useful, for present purposes, as an example of a teacher who, in the early part of the century, was grappling with the changes that were then just beginning to occur in pneumatology. As such, he contrasts usefully with Reid, another teacher of pneumatology, who we shall consider in Chapter 5. Posthumously, Groves' writings on ethics were published, but not his lectures on pneumatology. However, his lectures were recorded by a student, probably in the early- to mid-1720s.[12] From these lecture notes we can glimpse how pneumatology was taught during the early eighteenth century.

Grove began by noting the transition of most interest to us, the shift in pneumatology from an a priori to an empirical discipline. He said, 'Pneu-matology, by some styled the special part of metaphysics, by Mr. Locke a branch of Physics or natural philosophy', signifies 'a discourse of spirits, which shall also serve for the definition of the thing itself'. Grove continued by noting that 'the common notion of a Spirit is [of] an immaterial cogitative Being' and that 'the main foundation of this Definition is the usual Belief that a power of thinking belongs only to immaterial Substance'. Others, he says, have been persuaded 'that matter may think, nay probable that this is real Fact & yt ye Soul, which is conscious to itself of its thinking, is a system or compo-sition of matter'. The issue, Grove thinks, turns on how Spirit is defined, the materialists having left 'out the consideration of its Essence; viz a Spirit is a Being possessed of a Power of Thinking'. But which definition is better, Grove thinks, cannot simply be intuited or laid down by fiat, but has to be determined by inquiry (Grove 1720: 1).

Grove then rehearsed the traditional taxonomy of pneumatology: 'Human Soul or that thinking Principle *whatever it be* which every man is sure he has within him'; 'Angelical Mind united to none or to a thin etherial Body'; 'The great and everblessed God' (Ibid.: 2; emphasis added). As is clear from his use of the placeholder, 'whatever it be', Grove attempted to introduce his topic without taking sides. He mentioned Locke's new view of pneumatology as a natural philosophy, while also characterizing the traditional metaphysical view.[13] And against the backdrop of the dominant Cartesian notion of the soul as an immaterial thinking substance, Grove presented the hypothesis that matter can think. He, then, proposed different definitions of spirit or soul, without deciding among them. Yet since his course is clearly one intended to be about spirits, he proposed to consider all three traditional levels of mind or spirit. As it turned out, the human mind is the dominant topic.[14]

Grove eventually defended his own partly a priori, partly empirical thesis that the soul is an immaterial substance that acts independently of the body, with which it is in union. In doing so, he considered arguments from Cartesians, Cambridge Platonists, Locke, Clarke, and others. For instance, he argued against the Cartesian view that the soul is *essentially* a thinking thing (he thought it is only *accidentally* a thinking thing), but he sided with the Cartesians against Locke, in holding that the soul is, in fact, always thinking. In defending this latter position, Grove argued against Locke's view that thinking does not occur during sleep, yet he rejected the Cartesian view that the soul, in sleep, thinks independently of the body. Grove's position is that during sleep, imagination or irrational thinking occurs, as the body dominates over the soul. He held that we forget this thinking because it is so irrational.

Grove criticized Locke's account of personal identity, on the grounds that since each act of consciousness is separate 'there would not be one immaterial Substance: but a train of them equal to ye number of ye several acts of thinking'. He paraphrased Locke as replying that 'ye same Consciousness is common to all and they will be but one Person, one rational intelligent Being'. To which, Grove countered, aptly enough, that 'Mr. Lock's Chapter of Identity and Diversity' is so 'plentifully stor'd with absurdities, that tis great Pity it should have a Place in a Book of so good sense and solid coherent Thinking' (Grove 1720: 39).

One of Grove's original and interesting arguments against Locke's theory appears later in Berkeley and Reid:

> A person any time to Day can recollect a certain act he did yesterday and therefore is throughout this Day ye same Person he was then, before a month perhaps is past he forgets yesterday's action and tho

72

assured by others that he did it can himself remember no such thing. When therefore he shall have forgotten what he did yesterday he will not be ye same Self he was then, but tho he forgets what he did yesterday, he may be perfectly conscious of some thing he does to Day and will therefore be ye same Individual Person he is to Day, but he is throughout ye whole of this Day ye same Person he was yesterday, and if a Month hence he will be ye same Person he was to Day and to Day he is ye same Person he was yesterday, then a month hence he will be the same person he was yesterday and yet he will not neither, because he will not then be conscious of what he did yesterday.

(Ibid.: 43)

In sum, the problem, in Grove's view, is that 'If Consciousness be the ground of Personal Identity, and where the same consciousness is wanting there no longer remains ye same Person, a man may be and may not be one and ye same Person at the same time' (Ibid.: 42–3).[15]

Joseph Butler

Born in 1692, Butler was sent to the dissenting academy at Tewkesbury where, as a 21-year-old student, he boldly criticized Samuel Clarke's a priori proofs of God's existence. Clarke was so impressed with Butler's criticisms that he included and replied to them in his collected works. Subsequently he became Butler's long-term friend and advisor. Butler then left the academy to pursue a career in divinity at Oxford, after which, in 1718, he obtained the position of preacher at Rolls Chapel. Later he obtained a parsonage at Haughton, and then, in 1725, at Stanhope, where he became even more isolated from his friends in London. During his last year at Stanhope, his father died. There is reason to believe that these were not happy years for Butler.[16] In 1733, Butler returned to London, where he became a member of the intellectual society that was maintained around Queen Caroline. Berkeley also was a member.

From the point of view of the story that concerns us, it is almost as if there were two Butlers. Early-Butler wrote *Sermons on Human Nature* (1726), late-Butler *The Analogy of Religion* (1736). Early-Butler was a natural historian of human nature, optimistic about the prospects for empirical discoveries. Late-Butler was distrustful of empirical investigation into human nature and sceptical about its value. In sum, early-Butler befriended empirical inquiry, late-Butler tried to defang it.

At the beginning of the preface to his *Sermons*, published three years after the original edition of the *Sermons*, Butler expressed the spirit of the work as a whole by distinguishing two paths to knowledge of morality, which he said, 'exceedingly strengthen and enforce each other'. One, he said, takes its origin from inquiring into 'the abstract relations of things', the other by examining 'a matter of fact, namely, what the particular nature of man is, its several parts, their economy or constitution'. The point of the second approach, he said, is 'to determine what course of life it is, which is correspondent to this whole [human] nature'. Both approaches, he wrote, would yield the same results: 'our obligations to the practice of virtue'. However, in the first, a priori approach, 'the conclusion is expressed thus, that vice is contrary to the nature and reason of things', whereas in the second, empirical approach, 'that it [vice] is a violation or breaking in upon our own nature'. Butler said that while the first is a 'direct formal proof, and in some respects the least liable to cavil and dispute: the latter is in a peculiar manner adapted to satisfy a fair mind; and is more easily applicable to the several particular relations and circumstances in life'. Butler said that in the *Sermons* he would chiefly follow the second, empirical method (Butler 1726: 181).

In the *Sermons*, Butler also follows a third approach, what today we would call *conceptual analysis*. For instance, from the fact that 'the very idea of an interested pursuit necessarily presupposes particular passions or appetites; since the very idea of interest or happiness consists in this, that an appetite or affection enjoys its object', he concluded that 'it is not because we love ourselves that we find delight in such and such objects, but because we have particular affections toward them' (Ibid.: 192). Thus, unlike in Butler's own characterization of his second, empirical method, it actually combines empirical *and* a generous dose of conceptual analysis to show how human nature is in accord with moral ideals, many of which are simply taken as obvious.

How did Butler link human nature to this obvious morality? He supposed that by examining humans empirically, we can discern their purpose, that is, how nature (and ultimately God) intended that humans should function. 'Every work both of nature and of art', he said, 'is a system' in which parts are related to a whole. 'And as every particular thing, both natural and artificial, is for some use or purpose out of and beyond itself, one may add, to what has already been brought into an idea of a system, its conduciveness to this one or several ends' (Ibid.: 201). Butler followed this observation by comparing human nature to a watch. He took 'appetites, passions, affections, and the principle of reflection' to be analogous to the parts of the watch. The question for him, then, concerned how these parts must work together to function properly. One can determine empirically, he said, that some parts are meant to be subservient to others and, in particular, that 'reflection or conscience' is meant to lead:

> There is a principle of reflection in men, by which they distinguish between, approve and disapprove their own actions. We are plainly constituted such sort of creatures as to reflect upon our own nature. The mind can take a view of what passes within itself, its propensions, aversions, passions, affections, as respecting such objects, and in such degrees; and of the several actions consequent thereupon. In this survey it approves of one, disapproves of another, and towards a third

74

is affected in neither of these ways, but is quite indifferent. This principle in man, by which he approves or disapproves his heart, temper, and actions, is conscience; for this is the strict sense of the word, though sometimes it is used so as to take in more. And that this faculty tends to restrain men from doing mischief to each other, and leads them to do good, is too manifest to need being insisted upon.

(Ibid.: 201)

Butler never questioned his assumption that in human affairs we already know when things go as they should and when they run amok. On the basis of this assumption, he argued that we can determine empirically that when conscience does lead, humans function properly, that is, promote good and avoid 'mischief'.

There are disanalogies between artifacts and humans. Chief among these is that 'a machine is inanimate and passive: but we are agents'. 'Our constitution', Butler said, 'is put in our own power. We are charged with it; and therefore accountable for any disorder or violation of it' (Ibid.: 184). Once again, there is an easy transition in Butler's thought between what he took to be a simple observable fact – that we are agents and, hence, can control our behavior – to a normative conclusion, put forth as obvious – that we are, therefore, accountable for violations of our 'nature'. Such, in the *Sermons*, are the optimistic uses for moral ends to which the new empirical philosophy of human nature is put.

In the *Analogy*, published ten years later, Butler's tone is changed. Now the project is mainly to show that on empirical grounds one can prove very little. Butler began by trying to shift the burden of proof from that of showing that we survive our bodily deaths to that of showing that bodily death is the end. We are entitled, he says, to suppose that everything continues, unless we discover some *positive* reason to think that it stops. 'This', he said, 'is that kind of presumption or probability from analogy, expressed in the very word continuance, which seems our only natural reason for believing the course of the world will continue to-morrow'. He then inferred, rather implausibly, that this 'shows the high probability that our living powers will continue after death, unless there be some ground to think that death is their destruction' (Butler 1736: 82).

Don't we know 'from the reason of the thing' that when death comes, our bodies decay? Butler conceded the point. But, what, he asked, does that have to do with *our* fate? Such 'effects [disintegration of the body] do in no wise appear to imply the destruction of a living agent'. The key word, for Butler, in this implausible observation, is *imply*. For, he said, just 'as we are *greatly in the dark*, upon what the exercise of our living powers depends, so we are *wholly ignorant* what the powers themselves depend upon'. We know, from 'sleep' or 'swoon' that we can retain our mental powers, even though we have lost the capacity to exercise them. 'Since then we *know not at all* upon what the existence of our living powers depends, this shows further, there can no probability be collected from the reason of the thing, that death will be their destruction: because their existence *may* depend upon somewhat in no degree affected by death; upon somewhat quite out of the reach of this king of terrors'. Nor 'can we find any thing throughout the whole *analogy of nature*, to afford us even *the slightest presumption*, that animals ever lose their living powers; much less, if it were possible, that they lose them by death: for we have no faculties wherewith to trace any beyond or through it, so as to see what becomes of them. This event removes them from our view. It destroys the *sensible* proof' (Ibid.: 83–4). On the other hand, what we do know from observing nature is that animals and insects, as well as humans, can survive great changes other than death. This, Butler claimed, makes it more plausible to suppose that we can also survive the great change that comes with bodily death. It is not just that we lack evidence, drawn from *experience*, for the *negative* conclusion that when our bodies decay we cease. It is also, he said, that we have evidence, drawn from *reason*, for the *positive* conclusion that we survive.

In contrast to the method he followed in the *Sermons*, Butler here appealed for his supporting evidence not to empirical observation but to the Platonic argument that destruction is decomposition and that 'since consciousness is a single and indivisible power . . . the subject in which it resides must be so too'. Thus, supposing that the 'living agent each man calls himself' is 'a single being, which there is at least no more difficulty in conceiving than in conceiving it to be a compound, and of which there is the proof now mentioned; it follows that our organized bodies are no more ourselves or part of ourselves, than any other matter around us'. To his credit, Butler conceded that 'the simplicity and absolute oneness of a living agent cannot indeed, from the nature of the thing, be properly proved by experimental observations.' 'But', he said, 'as these *fall in* with the supposition of its unity, so they plainly lead us to *conclude* certainly, that our gross organized bodies, with which we perceive the objects of sense, and with which we act, are no part of ourselves' (Ibid.: 86–7).

Butler, more than any other eighteenth century critic of Locke, took Locke's observations about the role of appropriation in self-constitution seriously, which Butler then tried to use for his own ends. It is 'easy to conceive', he said, 'how matter, which is no part of ourselves, may be appropriated to us in the manner which our present bodies are' (Ibid.: 86). But, he continued, where there is appropriation, there must be an appropriator. Locke had an appropriator in 'man', which he distinguished from 'person' and allowed might be merely a material organism. Butler believed that he had already shown that the appropriator must be something simple and indivisible, and, hence, could not possibly be a material organism. This simple and indivisible appropriator, he assumed, is who we truly are. What this being appropriates, he went on to conclude, is not thereby part of itself, something it *is*, but, rather, merely something it *owns*.

Butler astutely conceded that this appropriator might be a simple *material* entity. But, he said, since 'we have *no way of determining by experience* what is the certain bulk of the living being each man calls himself, and yet, till it be determined that it is larger in bulk than the solid elementary particles of matter, which there is no ground to think any natural power can dissolve, there is no sort of reason to think death to be the dissolution of it, of the living being, even though it should not be absolutely indiscerpible'. And since each of us has already 'passed undestroyed through those many and great revolutions of matter, so peculiarly appropriated to us ourselves; why should we imagine death will be so fatal to us?' (Ibid.: 87–8). Thus, Butler, although drawing on Plato, has learned from Locke that, for all we know, the thinking principle within us is material. Butler, in effect, adapted Plato's argument for immortality to the purposes of an age in which materialism was on the rise. For Butler, it is our simplicity, not our immateriality, that ensures our survival. The a priori had been recast in an empirical mold.

The heart of Butler's view is his claim that our bodies are not us, but things we own, our instruments. We are agents that use these instruments. It is as if our bodies were artifacts – as if, in relation to them, we are pilots in a ship: 'We see with our eyes only in the same manner as we do with glasses'. 'Upon the whole, then, our organs of sense and our limbs are certainly instruments, which the living persons, ourselves, make use of to perceive and move with: there is not any probability, that they are any more; nor consequently, that we have any other kind of relation to them, than what we may have to any other foreign matter formed into instruments of perception and motion, suppose into a microscope of a staff' (Ibid.: 89–90).

When Butler turned to the topic of personal identity per se, the story is much the same. Here, particularly in the uses he made not only of the notion of appropriation but also of that of concernment, he showed that he had learned his lessons from Locke: 'For, personal identity has been explained so by some, as to render the inquiry concerning a future life of no consequence at all to us the persons who are making it' (Ibid.: 328). Butler, in response to what he clearly saw as the dangers of empirical analysis, proposed that we take as primitive the idea of *personal identity*. Like the notion of *equality*, he said, it defies analysis. Just as by observing two triangles, he said, we can determine intuitively that they are equal, so also by observing ourselves in the present and remembering ourselves in the past, we can determine intuitively that we have persisted, and not just in 'a loose and popular sense' of *same*, such as we might employ in saying of a mature oak that it is the same tree as stood in its spot fifty years previously, even though it and that former tree have not one atom in common. Rather, we can determine that identity of persons obtains in 'the strict and philosophical sense', which requires sameness of substance: 'In a loose and popular sense, then, the life, and the organization, and the plant are justly said to be the same, not withstanding the perpetual change of the parts. But in a strict and philosophical manner of speech, no man, no being, no mode of being, no anything can be the same with that, with which it hath indeed nothing the same' (Ibid.: 330).

In Butler's view, even though we can determine intuitively through memory that we are the same as some person who lived earlier, our current consciousness of that fact is not the same as our consciousness in the past. Each episode of consciousness is a mode of the being who is conscious. The modes come and go. The being persists. Thus, even if it were possible to provide a conceptual or empirical analysis of *personal identity*, it would not be possible to do so by appealing to sameness of consciousness, which is one more reason, he thought, if one were needed, why Locke's account of the matter will not do. On the other hand, if, *per impossible*, our being did just consist in successive acts of consciousness, then 'it must follow, that it is a fallacy upon ourselves, to charge our present selves with anything we did, or to imagine our present selves interested in anything which befell us yesterday; or that our present self will be interested in what will befall us to-morrow; since our present self is not, in reality, the same with the self of yesterday, but another like self or person coming in its room, and mistaken for it: to which another self will succeed to-morrow' (Ibid.: 331–2).

In other words, in Butler's view, if selfhood were as Locke has portrayed it, we would have no reason to be *concerned* either with past or future stages of ourselves, for these would be ourselves only in a *fictitious* sense. In an apparent allusion to fission, Butler insisted that *calling* people to whom we are only so related ourselves would not make them ourselves (see p. 41). But can Butler *show* that the unwelcome conclusion that persons are fictions is actually false? Not really, and he knows it. True to his method, though, he did not feel that he had to show it. Why show what is obvious? 'The bare unfolding this notion, and laying it thus naked and open, seems the best confutation of it' (Ibid.: 332).

In comparing Butler's approach with those of other great philosophers of his times, certain contrasts stand out. Unlike Locke, for instance, he was not particularly interested in tracking down the sources of our ideas and principles in experience. Nor was Butler interested in explaining empirically the mechanics of self-constitution; if anything, he had a negative interest in that sort of empirical inquiry. Otherwise, however, Butler was interested in explaining how humans function, particularly in so far as their minds contribute to the ways they function. However, his concern with mental functioning was not, like Hume's, in articulating laws of association or explaining the role, say, that belief in our own identities plays in the formation of our attitudes and emotions. Butler showed no interest in such questions. His passion was not to follow the argument wherever it might lead, his objective not knowledge for knowledge's sake.

Butler had ulterior motives. He came to the empirical study of the mind already armed with a traditional array of moral and metaphysical conclusions. In this respect he was like Clarke. Yet whereas both Butler and Clarke were intent on showing that nothing we can learn empirically will upset truths derived from metaphysics and revelation, Clarke's way of showing this, so far as human mentality is concerned, was to refuse to get involved, except to refute the views of others. By contrast, Butler, in the *Sermons* at least, entered enthusiastically into the empirical investigative process. Only later, and perhaps disillusioned, did he retreat to what may have seemed to be the relative safety of rational psychology. However, he had such a clear-headed understanding of the arguments of those he opposed, he *may* have realized that he sought refuge in a house that was on fire. Subsequently, he retired from writing philosophy.

Several years after Butler had published the *Analogy*, Hume wanted to meet him, and tried to present him with a copy of his recently published *Treatise*. It seems that Hume even deleted from the *Treatise* a chapter on miracles because he intended to give a copy of it to Butler and thought the chapter might upset him. Butler was absent when Hume came to call. There is no record of Butler's reaction to Hume's book. Later, Hume said in a letter, that he heard that Butler was recommending that people read his *Moral and Political Essays*. Curiously, Butler was well acquainted with David Hartley, who was a neighbour for several years. Indeed, in 1752 Hartley was one of the physicians who was called to treat the failing Bishop on his deathbed. As noted, Butler was also friends with Clarke and Berkeley, from the previous era. By the time Butler died, any attempts to justify traditional beliefs in the immaterial soul, as he had done by 'analogy to nature', and as Clarke and Berkeley had done by means of a priori arguments, no longer convinced the growing group of more empirically oriented philosophers of human nature, which prominently included Hume and Hartley. With Butler's death came the end of an era in which religion had dominated the philosophy of human nature. Henceforth, in the eighteenth century empirical philosophy would dominate it. Later still, but gradually and in stages, psychology would become an experimental science.

4

HUMAN NATURE

Throughout the eighteenth century Newton's *Principia* was held as an arche-type of good science. In the emerging empirical philosophy of human nature, everyone wanted to accomplish what Newton had accomplished in natural philosophy. Almost everyone thought it could be done. There were two inhibiting factors. The more obvious of the two, even to most thinkers of the time, was the continuing influence of religious beliefs. The more subtle was a problem that is not fully resolved even in our own times: the unhelpful mixing of what we now take to be philosophy and psychology.

Hume, the greatest of the mid-century philosophers of mind, had freed himself from the shackles of religious belief. But he was also one of the most indiscriminate mixers of philosophy and psychology. And he did not even stumble into his own preferred style of mixing. He consciously adopted it. He began by criticizing his contemporaries' approach to the study of human nature and then proposing a radical alternative, which was what today we would call *foundationalism*. But Hume recommended foundationalism, not only as an epistemological and metaphysical view, but also as a scientific research program.

The best way to understand what it meant to adopt Hume's approach as a scientific research program is to compare it with that of other mid-century philosophers of human nature, such as Adam Smith and Edmund Law. To read Adam Smith on human sympathy, a topic to which Hume tried to apply his new methods, you would hardly even know that there was such a thing as religion or that there was anything to philosophy but ethical theory. The uses to which Smith put his empirical inquiries into sympathy often got in the way of his ethical theory. But unlike in the case of Hume's foundationalism, the complications hardly ever go the other way round. As we shall see, it is difficult-to-impossible to separate Hume's philosophy from his science. But one can easily excise Smith's ethical theory from his empirical inquiry into sympathy without detracting from the empirical inquiry. We shall do so below.

Edmund Law provides another interesting contrast with Hume. Although Law was a clergyman, when it came to plumbing the depths of self and personal identity, he deftly marginalized both religion and all but the most pragmatic of philosophical concerns. He was, of course, at one with Hume in marginalizing religion. But there could hardly be a more striking contrast than the ways in which Hume and Law incorporate philosophy into what they hoped were properly scientific perspectives. Hume, in applying his foundationalism to the consideration of personal identity, was led into deep and profound complications that even he could not resolve. Law, on the other hand, adopted a purely pragmatic, legal approach to the same topic. So far as questions of self and personal identity are concerned, his only foray into metaphysics is his doctrine of 'the sleep of the soul'. But unlike Hume's theories, Law's doctrine is intended not to provide new foundations for the study of mind, but rather to clear away metaphysical debris that blocks the way to more promising empirical approaches. Law aimed to protect religion by freeing it from a competition that it cannot win, and to free science by avoiding a confrontation that can only distract it from its more promising empirical projects.

David Hume

When Locke published the *Essay*, he dreamt of the emergence of a science of human nature. But in developing his account of self and personal identity, he was under the grip of several a priori assumptions that inhibited the development of that science. Chief among these was the Cartesian notion that all consciousness is reflexive. In addition, Locke had ulterior motives. Nothing is more central to his account of personal identity than his distinction between person and man (= human), but that distinction was an important one for him largely because it allowed him to suggest that matter might think while at the same time accommodating the Christian dogma of the resurrection.

When Hume published the *A Treatise of Human Nature* (1739), he talked as if a science of human nature had already emerged. In developing his account of self and personal identity, he had gotten beyond both the a priori assumption that all consciousness is reflexive and the dogma of the resurrection. Nevertheless, he too had a dream about the new empirical philosophy of human nature. His dream was not of its emerging but of its assuming its rightful position among the sciences. In Hume's view, that position was at the *foundation* of a mighty edifice of human knowledge. Whereas today we tend to think of physics as the most fundamental science, Hume thought of the 'science of man' as the most fundamental. And the reason Hume thought this is that only this new science would build an account based on experience (rather than things), which for him was our ultimate source both of evidence and meaning. Hence, in Hume's view, only this new science could include what today we would call the foundations of *epistemology* and *metaphysics*.[1] 'There is no question of importance', Hume said, 'whose decision is not comprised in the science of man; and there is none, which can be decided with any certainty, before we become acquainted with that science'. In explaining 'the principles of human nature', he continued, 'we in effect propose a complete system of the sciences, built on a foundation almost entirely new, and the only one upon which they can stand with any security'.

After making this point about the need for secure foundations, Hume lamented the then current status of the new science of human nature. Progress has been slow, he pointed out, and disputes abound. The remedy, he thought, was 'to leave the tedious lingering method', which he thought was superficial and piecemeal, 'and, instead of taking now and then a castle or village on the frontier, to march up directly to the capital or centre of these sciences, to human nature itself'. When once we conquer this central position, Hume waxed enthusiastically, 'we may every where else hope for an easy victory'. And thereby we may 'extend our conquests over all those sciences, which more intimately concern human life'.

How, then, to proceed to the prize: to human nature itself? The first step, Hume thought, was to reveal the basis on which any genuine science of human nature must be built. That, he said, is 'experience and observation'. From our current point of view, it may seem that Hume could not have begun more innocently. Yet this seemingly innocent first step masked what, in retrospect, we can see to be an important confusion. Simply put, Hume failed to distinguish between what *we* would call *philosophy* and what we would call *science* – more specifically, what we would call, on the one hand, *metaphysics* and *epistemology* and, on the other, empirical *psychology*. Hume included them all, often in an unhappy mixture, in his newly restructured science of human nature. And it was this sort of indiscriminate mixing, as much as anything, that retarded the growth of his new science.

Moreover, Hume's confusion on this issue was not a peripheral mistake, but was central to his perspective. It was *because* he thought that the science of human nature – what today we would call *psychology* – includes philosophy that he also thought the science of human nature was not just another science, but the foundation of all the sciences. This new science, in his view, would not only *itself* be founded on experience and observation, but – and this is how it would be the foundation of all the sciences – would *explain* how *all* knowledge, including whatever is discovered in any of the other sciences, also is founded on experience and observation.

As it happened, however, for psychology to find its feet as a science it had to abandon such epistemological and metaphysical pretensions. Its practitioners had to realize that it was not their job, *qua* psychologists, to get to the absolute bottom of things. Happily, that task could be left to philosophers. Rather, it was their job, as psychologists, to explain human behavior. To do that, they had to take certain things for granted that in a more philosophical frame of mind could be seen to be deeply questionable. Since Hume stood near the beginnings of the new science of human nature he was understandably confused about the need for a division of labor. Fortunately, he did not stick consistently to his idea that the science of human nature would be the foundation of all the sciences. Sometimes, he seemed to see, if only through a glass darkly, that the new science would have a different mission.[2]

The contrast between what we are calling, somewhat anachronistically, the *philosophical* and the *scientific* approaches is especially poignant in Hume's account of self and personal identity. In Book I of the *Treatise*, at the heart of his account is his argument that belief in the substantial self is an illusion. More generally, he is intent on showing that belief in the persistence of anything is an illusion. This is what today we would call philosophy, rather than psychology. And it is Hume, the skeptical metaphysician, at his destructive best. In the remainder of Book I, Hume addressed the task of explaining why people are so susceptible to the illusion of self. And in Book II he explained how those dynamic mentalistic systems in which we represent ourselves to ourselves, as well as to others, actually work. In these more psychological projects, Hume took for granted many things that in Book I he had subjected to withering skeptical criticism. This is Hume the psychologist at his constructive best.

For the *science* of human nature – eventually psychology – to leave philosophy behind, it was not, as is often suggested, just, or even primarily, a question of psychologists learning, toward the end of the nineteenth century, how to become experimental. Experimental design and data collection, important as they have become, were not in the eighteenth century the main lesson that the emerging science of human nature had to learn. The main lesson then was how to take the right things for granted. These were things that metaphysicians and epistemologists, especially in Hume's day, but even today, are loath to take for granted. Ironically, contrary to Hume's suggestion in his preface to the *Treatise*, what was required for the new science of human nature to surge forward was not that it become more fundamental, but that it become less so.

Hume saw it differently. In his view, it was necessary to get down to what is fundamental, which for him were 'impressions', the ultimate source of all knowledge. Locke had already argued that the ingredients of human knowledge – that is, the ideas in terms of which people formulate meaningful beliefs – come from experience. However, Locke thought that in addition to experience, rational intuition and a priori metaphysics were in certain crucial respects sources of knowledge about the world. Hume, by contrast, thought that *only* experience was a source of knowledge about the world.[3] In the *Treatise* he even suggested that geometry is a posteriori.

In a way, Hume was right that before the new science could surge forward, philosophers had to get to the bottom of things. His austere phenomenalistic metaphysics and epistemology cleared the construction site of the obstructing boulders of religion and traditional metaphysics. But Hume's metaphysics and epistemology should never have been regarded as an essential part of the new structure. He had forged a potent weapon of destruction that once it had done its work, was not only almost useless for the constructive task which lay ahead, but actually became an obstacle in its own right.

Hume's radical empiricism, whatever we may think of it, was the source of some of his most philosophically influential thoughts about self and personal identity, especially of his idea that neither the notion of substance, in general, nor that of substantial self, in particular, has a basis in experience. In Hume's view, there are no (simple) *impressions* corresponding to these ideas: 'For my part, when I enter most intimately into what I call *myself* I always stumble on some particular perception or other' and 'never can catch *myself* at any time without a perception, and never can observe any thing but the perception' (Hume 1739: 252). Hence, the 'ideas' of substance and of substantial self are not really even *ideas* but, rather, empty words, which some misguided metaphysicians have used to formulate mistaken (in Hume's view, literally unintelligible) beliefs.

Since all ideas come from impressions and there is no impression of a 'simple and continu'd' self, there is no idea of such a self. This critique of traditional views led Hume to formulate his alternative 'bundle' conception of the self and also to compare the mind to a kind of theatre. None of the actors – the 'perceptions [that] successively make their appearance; pass, re-pass, glide away and mingle in an infinite variety of postures and situations' – is the traditional self. None, strictly speaking, is either 'simple' at a time or identical over time. Beyond that, Hume claimed, humans do not even have minds, except as fictional constructions. Thus, although the mind may be a kind of theatre, there is one crucial respect in which it differs from real theatres. There is, Hume says, no site for the mental performance, at least none of which we can have knowledge; that is, so far as we know, the mind does not even exist! Rather, there 'are the successive perceptions only, that constitute the mind; nor have we the most distant notion of the place, where these scenes are represented, or of the materials, of which it is compos'd' (Ibid.: 253).

With these philosophical preliminaries out of the way, Hume turned to the psychological task of explaining how objects that are constantly changing, including the materials out of which we ourselves are constructed, nevertheless seem to persist. He asked, 'What then gives us so great a propension to ascribe an identity to these successive perceptions, and to suppose ourselves possest of an invariable and uninterrupted existence thro' the whole course of our lives?' Before answering this question, he distinguished 'betwixt personal identity, as it regards our thought or imagination, and as it regards our passions or the concern we take in ourselves'. He added that the first of these issues – personal identity, as it regards our thought or imagination – 'is our present subject' and that 'to explain it perfectly we must take the matter pretty deep'. Among other things, that meant to him that we must account for the identity that we attribute to plants and animals, 'there being a great analogy betwixt it, and the identity of a self or person' (Ibid.).

What, though, is the difference that Hume had in mind in distinguishing between his two ways of regarding personal identity? It is between, on the one hand, explaining why we regard anything that changes, including ourselves, as persisting over time (this is personal identity as it regards our thought or imagination); and, on the other, explaining the role that belief in ourselves as things that persist plays in the ways we represent ourselves to ourselves and to others (this is personal identity as it regards our passions or the concern we take in ourselves). The first of these questions occupies Hume in most of the remainder of Book I. The second occupies him in most of Book II.

In explaining personal identity as it regards our thought or imagination, the crucial psychological question for Hume was that of figuring out what causes us to forge a succession of perceptions into a persisting object. His answer is one word: resemblance. That, Hume said, 'is the cause of the confusion and mistake, and makes us substitute the notion of identity, instead of that of related objects'. When successive perceptions resemble each other, he said, it is easy to imagine that the first simply persists. In fact, 'our propensity to this mistake' is so ubiquitous and strong 'that we fall into it before we are aware'. And even when we become aware of our error 'we cannot long sustain our philosophy, or take off this biass from the imagination'. So, we suppose that objects that change persist. In and of itself, Hume suggested, that is not so bad. But 'in order to justify to ourselves this absurdity', we make up a story, often one in which the principle character is the notion of substance; that is, we invent the fictions of '*soul*, and *self*, and *substance* to disguise the variation' in our perceptions. When, as in the case of 'plants and vegetables', we cannot fool ourselves into believing that the persistence of an underlying substance accounts for the persistence of the organism, we invent an equally 'unknown and mysterious' surrogate – presumably, Hume here means 'life', as in the views of Hobbes and Locke – to connect the successive and different perceptions (Ibid.: 254–5).

Later Hume would claim – probably at least with Locke's prince and cobbler example in mind – that 'all the nice and subtile questions concerning personal identity' are merely verbal. In the present context, though, he insisted that 'the controversy concerning identity is not merely a dispute of words'. Usually, he continued, when people attribute identity 'to variable or interrupted objects' their 'mistake' is 'attended with a fiction' (Ibid.: 255). They believe that the identity, which they have claimed obtains, is not just their (perhaps pragmatically motivated) decision to regard distinct but similar, objects as the same. Rather, they believe that those objects really are the same, perhaps even that what makes them the same is the existence of some unifying substance, such as soul, or some unifying mode, such as life or consciousness. Thus, in Hume's view, normally it is not just that someone, in full knowledge of the facts, innocently chooses to *call* distinct objects which resemble each other the same object, but rather that the person who chooses to do this is immersed in a cloud of metaphysical confusion.

Hume then committed himself to the view, which he may well have gotten from Locke, that 'any mass of matter, of which the parts are contiguous and connected', remains the same just if no part of it is subtracted or foreign part added (even if the particles are rearranged). Yet if the alteration in the mass of matter is 'trivial', Hume said, 'we scruple not' to pronounce it the same since the passage of our thought from the earlier to the later object is 'so smooth and easy' (Ibid.: 255–6).

What affects whether the passage of our thought is smooth and easy? Resemblance, of course, but subject to these additional considerations: first, the size of the change relative to the size of the whole (rather than merely the absolute size of the change); second, whether the change is gradual and insensible (rather than sudden and obvious); third, whether the various parts of the objects under consideration have a 'reference' to each other, as they would have if they contributed 'to some *common end* or purpose'; and, fourth, whether there is 'a *sympathy* of parts to their *common end*', that is, whether there is a 'reciprocal relation of cause and effect in all their actions and operations', such as obtains, say, in the case of plants and animals (Ibid.: 257).

In addition, Hume pointed out that when distinct objects are related to a common cause, we have a tendency to confuse 'specific' with 'numerical identity', as may happen when we regard as the same a continuing noise 'that is frequently interrupted and renewed' or as the same a church that burns down and then is rebuilt. Finally, 'where the objects are in their nature changeable and inconstant' – in the case, say, of rivers changing their water – 'we admit of a more sudden transition, than wou'd otherwise be consistent with that relation'. That is, we allow that such objects persist, even though we would regard comparable changes in more stable objects as bringing about their cessation (Ibid.: 258).

As we saw in Chapter 2, it seems from Hume's discussion of the church example that he may have been aware of the special problems for judgments of identity that arise in the case of fission. Hume clearly did take the view that we can explain personal identity on the same principles as we would explain the identities of all other 'compounded and changeable' things and that personal identity is equally illusory: 'the identity which we ascribe to the mind of man is only a fictitious one' (Ibid.: 259). Whether fission examples eased Hume's way to this conclusion is unknown.[4] However, he was sensitive to the objection that in showing that personal identity is relational, rather than substantial, he had not *thereby* shown that it is fictitious. Hume continued by noting that 'a question naturally arises concerning this relation of identity; whether it be something that really binds our several perceptions together or only associates their ideas in the imagination'; that is, 'whether in pronouncing concerning the identity of a person, we observe some real bond among his perceptions, or only feel one among the ideas we form of them'? The issue, Hume claimed, 'we might easily decide'. It is enough if we remember that 'the understanding never observes any real connexion among objects'. 'Even the union of cause and effect', he added, 'when strictly examin'd, resolves itself into a customary association of ideas' (Ibid.: 259–60).

Here, Hume seems to draw conclusions from philosophy for empirical psychology. For instance, in his view, since we know from epistemology that causation cannot be anything more than constant conjunction, the only remaining task is to explain why we tend mistakenly to attribute more than that to causal relationships, not only in general but in specific cases. For such explanations Hume retreats to his thesis that the only relations between objects that we can observe are resemblance and contiguity. So, he assumes, the explanation must lie there. Resemblance and contiguity are all there *is* to causation since they are all that there *can be* to it. This is Hume the philosopher.

However, In Book II of the *Treatise*, Hume proposed specific causal theses: for instance, ones having to do with interactions between pride or sympathy and systems of self-representation. In justifying these more specific causal theses, it does not do to retreat to talk of resemblance and contiguity, as he sometimes attempts to do, any more than in this more realistic context it would do to think of minds merely as fleeting systems of sensory impressions which come and then go 'with an inconceivable rapidity'. The world of psychological science, like the world of everyday life, is a world of relatively stable objects and relationships. Confirmation in psychology is carried out within, not beneath, this realistic context.

From the fact that we never observe any real bond among our perceptions, 'it evidently follows', Hume continued, 'that identity is nothing really belonging to these different perceptions, and uniting them together; but is merely a quality, which we attribute to them, because of the union of their ideas in the imagination, when we reflect upon them'. Resemblance, contiguity, and causation 'are the uniting principles in the ideal world, and without them every distinct object is separable by the mind, and may be separately consider'd, and appears not to have any more connexion with any other object, than if disjoin'd by the greatest difference and remoteness'. It is, then, Hume concluded, on one or more of these three relations 'that identity depends; and as the very essence of these relations consists in their producing an easy transition of ideas; it follows, that our notions of personal identity, proceed entirely from the smooth and uninterrupted progress of the thought along a train of connected ideas, according to the principles above explain'd' (Ibid.: 260).

So, which of these three relations comes into play when we consider the 'successive existence of mind or thinking person'? Not contiguity, Hume said. That leaves only resemblance and cause and effect. With regard to resemblance, he considered the case of someone who retains the same memories, which, of course, resemble each other over time. That is, if you remembered yesterday an event that happened a year ago and then remembered today, in the same way, that same event, the two memories, considered just as mental phenomena in the present, would resemble each other. In such a case, Hume said, 'the memory not only discovers the identity, but also contributes to its production, by producing the relations of resemblance among the perceptions' (Ibid.: 261). In other words, whereas for Locke memory produced personal identity by ensuring *sameness* of consciousness, for Hume it promotes the fiction of personal identity by producing *resemblances* among successive conscious states.

So far, so good. But when Hume turned next to causality, his language became more realistic. He said that 'we may observe that the true idea of the human mind, is to consider it as a system of different perceptions or different existences, which are linked together by the relation of cause and effect, and mutually produce, destroy, influence, and modify each other'. Impressions give rise to ideas which, in turn, give rise to still further impressions. 'One thought chases another, and draws after it a third, by which it is expelled in its turn'. Hume then famously mused:

> I cannot compare the soul more properly to any thing than to a republic or commonwealth, in which the several members are united by the reciprocal ties of government and subordination, and give rise to other persons who propagate the same republic in the incessant changes of its parts. And as the same individual republic may not only change its members, but also its laws and constitutions; in like manner the same person may vary his character and disposition, as well as his impressions and ideas, without losing his identity. Whatever changes he endures, his several parts are still connected by the relation of causation.
>
> (Ibid.: 261)

Here, it sounds as if Hume's project were to recommend a relational theory of personal identity, rather than to explode its pretensions. However, it is unclear whether he intended such apparently realistic causal talk to be interpreted in the light of his earlier skeptical pronouncements or whether he is here revealing, perhaps without even recognizing that he is doing so, that in accounting for the unity of the mind, he is not himself of one mind.

In Locke's view, memory played a crucial role in constituting personal identity. In Hume's view, it does so also, but for different reasons:

> As memory alone acquaints us with the continuance and extent of this succession of perceptions, it is to be considered, upon that account chiefly, as the source of personal identity. Had we no memory, we never should have any notion of causation, nor consequently of that chain of causes and effects, which constitute our self or person. But having once acquired this notion of causation from the memory, we can extend the same chain of causes, and consequently the identity of our persons beyond our memory, and can comprehend times, and circumstances, and actions, which we have entirely forgot, but suppose in general to have existed.
>
> (Ibid.: 261–2)

So, in Hume's view, memory contributes to producing personal identity not only by creating resemblances among successive perceptions but also by revealing to us that our perceptions are causally linked. However, once we see that our perceptions are causally linked, we then use this new information as a basis for extending our identities to periods of our lives that we do not remember.

Hume then brought up the topic of forgetfulness: 'Who can tell me, for instance, what were his thoughts and actions on the 1st of January 1715, the 11th of March 1719 and the 3rd of August 1733? Or will he affirm, because he has entirely forgot the incidents of these days, that the present self is not the same person with the self of that time; and by that means overturn all the most established notions of personal identity?' Hume said that, in his view, which presumably he intended to contrast with the views of Locke and perhaps also Collins, 'memory does not so much produce as discover personal identity, by shewing us the relation of cause and effect among our different perceptions' and that 'it will be incumbent on those who affirm that memory produces entirely our personal identity, to give a reason why we can thus extend our identity beyond our memory' (Ibid.: 262).

Hume extended his critique by questioning the seriousness of trying to make fine-grained distinctions, perhaps especially in the case of specially contrived, hypothetical examples, such as Locke's prince and cobbler example, about whether personal identity obtains. He said, 'Identity depends on the relations of ideas; and these relations produce identity, by means of that easy transition they occasion. But as the relations, and the easiness of the transition may diminish by insensible degrees, we have no just standard by which we can decide any dispute concerning the time when they acquire or lose a title to the name of identity'. It follows, Hume said, that 'all the disputes concerning the identity of connected objects are merely verbal, except so far as the relation of parts gives rise to some fiction or imaginary principle of union' (Ibid.).

In sum, Hume's view seems to be that disputes about identity are merely verbal, if they are about which relations, were they to obtain, would constitute identity. But the disputes are based on substantive mistakes, if the disputants suppose that what is merely successive is *really* the same. In any case, the disputes are about fictitious imaginary constructs. That is all there is to identity over time and through changes.

Thus, Hume may have thought that a crucial difference between Locke and himself on the question of personal identity is that whereas Locke thought that there is a fact of the matter about whether a person persists, Hume did not, but rather thought that there is a fact of the matter only about the circumstances under which the illusion of persistence is nourished. In his capacity as a psychologist, Hume tried to explain what those circumstances were. But he did not stop there. As soon as he moved on to the largely psychological concerns that dominate Book II of the *Treatise*, he became deeply involved in what today we would call social psychology of the self. In doing so, he abandoned, but probably without realizing that he had done so, the project of marching up directly to 'the capital or centre of the sciences, to human nature itself'. In his capacity as social psychologist of the self, Hume returned to 'the frontier'.

The transition, in Hume's thought, from skeptical philosophy to the most general sorts of associational issues, and then to specific psychological hypotheses about how self-representations function in our mental economy can be nicely illustrated in terms of one of Hume's less complicated, but from our point of view, more interesting discussions in Book II, his short chapter, 'Of the Love of Fame' (Ibid.: 316–24). Here, Hume said that besides the more basic causes of pride and humility, which previously in Book II he had already discussed, there is in the opinions of others a 'secondary' cause of pride, 'which has an equal influence on the affections'. 'Our reputation, our character, our name', Hume continued, 'are considerations of vast weight and importance; and even the other causes of pride, virtue, beauty, and riches, have little influence, when not seconded by the opinions and sentiments of others'. However, he added, to explain why the love of fame is so important, it will be necessary to 'first explain the nature of *sympathy*' (Ibid.: 316).

For our purposes, three things about Hume's conception of sympathy are especially interesting. The first is that in the case of some of Hume's examples, it seems that what he means by *sympathy* is what today we would call *emotional contagion*. That is, it seems that we catch another's emotions more or less as we might catch their colds, by intimate contact: 'A good-natured man finds himself in an instant of the same humour with his company'. 'A chearful countenance infuses a sensible complacency and serenity into my mind; as an angry or sorrowful one throws a sudden damp upon me. Hatred, resentment, esteem, love, courage, mirth, and melancholy; all these passions I feel more from communication, than from my own natural temper and disposition' (Ibid.: 317). In other words, in the case of many mental states, one person's being in that state and in proximity to another greatly increases the likelihood that the other will also be in that state. However, in explaining how this process works, Hume goes considerably beyond a merely external descriptive account.

How, then, does sympathy happen? Hume said that we infer (implicitly and unconsciously?) the mental states of others from observing their bodies and behavior: 'any affection' that 'is infused by sympathy' is 'at first known only by its effects, and by those external signs in the countenance and conversation, which convey an idea of it'. Then, the idea of whatever mental state we take others to be in is 'converted into an impression, and acquires such a degree of force and vivacity, as to become the very passion itself, and produce an equal emotion as any original affection' (Ibid.).

But how are such ideas converted into impressions? In perhaps his most curious remark in the *Treatise*, Hume said, 'It is evident that the idea, or rather impression of ourselves is always intimately present with us, and that our consciousness gives us so lively a conception of our own person, that it is not possible to imagine that any thing can in this particular go beyond it' (Ibid.). What is so curious about this remark is that, in Book I, Hume had made quite a show of revealing that we have no impression of self, at least none corresponding to what some philosophers had understood by *self*. Now, rather surprisingly, Hume reveals that we do after all have an impression of self, and not just any old impression, but one that is quite extraordinary. We have an impression of self that is *always* with us and that is as *lively* as any impression *could possibly be*. Yet, Hume offered not a word of explanation about what this impression is like, or how it compares to the impression of self which he earlier claimed we do not have, or why our having the impression of self which he now says we have could (or could not) have misled us into thinking that we also have the supposed impression of self which he earlier argued we do not have.

The rest of Hume's explanation is almost as puzzling, but primarily for its ambiguity and seeming inconsistency. Hume said:

> Whatever object, therefore, is related to ourselves, must be conceived with a like vivacity of conception, according to the foregoing principles; and though this relation should not be so strong as that of causation, it must still have a considerable influence. Resemblance and contiguity are relations not to be neglected; especially when, by an inference from cause and effect, and by the observation of external signs, we are informed of the real existence of the object, which is resembling or contiguous.
>
> (Ibid.: 317–8)

In these remarks, when Hume said, 'whatever object', which object did he have in mind? It may seem that he was here referring to a mental state that one person has 'caught' from another. But what he then said in the next paragraph suggests that the object that he had in mind is the other person himself. Whatever 'object' Hume had in mind, in his view, it 'must be conceived with a like vivacity of conception, according to the foregoing principles'. But which principles are those – the ones he has just explained, having to do with emotional contagion, or ones he had earlier explained, having to do with pride and humility? Either way, and regardless of which object Hume had in mind, it is difficult to make sense of the quoted remarks. And when he added, 'Though this relation should not be so strong as that of causation, it must still have a considerable influence' we are left completely in the dark. Non-causal *influence*! What will Hume think of next?

Hume continued by remarking that just as different peoples' bodies are basically alike, so also are their minds, 'and this resemblance must very much contribute to make us enter into the sentiments of others, and embrace them with facility and pleasure'. In addition to such general similarities among people, there may, in particular cases, be some 'peculiar similarity in our manners, or character, or country, or language' and, if there is, then this too 'facilitates the sympathy'. So, 'the stronger the relation is betwixt ourselves and any object, the more easily does the imagination make the transition, and convey to the related idea the vivacity of conception, with which we always form the idea of our own person' (Ibid.: 318).

In sum, Hume's explanation, in this part of the *Treatise*, of how sympathy works is that it involves two steps. First, we infer what another's mental state is from observing his external appearance and behavior, and thereby introduce into our own minds the idea of his state. Second, we bring that idea of the other's state into 'proximity' with our own vivacious and ongoing impression of ourselves, and thereby upgrade the idea of the other's state into an impression, in the process converting it into one of our own mental states, say, our own cheerfulness, rather than merely our idea of another's cheerfulness. Ironically, in so far as the mechanism for sympathy that Hume postulates involves what today we would call *emotional contagion*, Hume suggested that the real emotional contagion is not between ourselves and another, but wholly internal to ourselves. We acquire our idea of the other's mental state by means of inference, not emotional contagion. The contagion, to the extent that it is involved in the mechanism of sympathy, is not inter-personal but intra-personal, that is, it occurs internally to one individual, when that individual upgrades an idea into an impression. And an idea is thus upgraded by its 'catching' the vivacity of our ongoing impressions of ourselves.

But unlike in the simplest cases of emotional contagion – for instance, when one baby cries because it is put down next to another crying baby – Hume obviously thought that sympathy involved one's *imagining* an actual or possible internal state of the other.[5] This becomes particularly clear, later in the *Treatise*, in Hume's section, 'Of the mixture of benevolence and anger with compassion and malice', where he introduced a variation on the first step of his two-step account of how sympathy works. Instead of saying that the initial occasion of sympathy is an inference we make to another's mental state based on observing him, Hume allows that 'we often feel by communication the pains and pleasures of others, which are not in being, and which we only anticipate by the force of imagination'. To illustrate what he has in mind, Hume says, 'supposing I saw a person perfectly unknown to me, who, while asleep in the fields, was in danger of being trod under foot by horses, I shou'd immediately run to his assistance; and in this I shou'd be actuated by the same principle of sympathy, which makes me concern'd for the present sorrows of a stranger' (Ibid.; 385). In a case like the one in this example, one does not merely infer what the other is feeling, but must *imagine* what the other *would* be feeling under certain unrealized conditions, or perhaps what the other *ought* to be feeling under certain unrealized conditions, which are obviously imaginative activities. But so also is imagination involved in the standard case in which one infers what another person is currently feeling. Both sorts of cases contrast sharply with the simplest examples of emotional contagion (e.g., the crying babies), in which another's external behavior simply causes one to behave similarly.

Returning now to Hume's account in his section on 'the love of fame', he said that other relations besides mental resemblance between ourselves and others can add 'new force' to sympathy: 'The sentiments of others have little influence when far removed from us, and require the relation of contiguity to make them communicate themselves entirely'. Returning, next, to more realistic causal talk, he noted that biological relations also matter: 'The relations of blood, being a species of causation, may sometimes contribute to the same effect; as also acquaintance'. Such relations, when combined, 'convey the impression or consciousness of our own person to the idea of the sentiments or passions of others, and makes us conceive them in the strongest and most lively manner' (Ibid.: 318).

Hume said that since there is no difference between impressions and ideas except for 'different degrees of their force and vivacity' and since 'this difference may be removed, in some measure, by a relation betwixt the impressions and ideas, it is no wonder an idea of a sentiment or passion may by this means be so enlivened as to become the very sentiment or passion':

> The lively idea of any object always approaches its impression; and it is certain we may feel sickness and pain from the mere force of imagination, and make a malady real by often thinking of it. But this is most remarkable in the opinions and affections; and it is there principally that a lively idea is converted into an impression. Our affections depend more upon ourselves, and the internal operations of the mind, than any other impressions; for which reason they arise more naturally from the imagination, and from every lively idea we form of them.
>
> (Ibid.)

Hume concluded that 'this is the nature and cause of sympathy; and it is after this manner we enter so deep into the opinions and affections of others, whenever we discover them'. Continuing in his role as social psychologist, Hume then went on to elaborate his account of the ways in which attendant circumstances affect our mechanisms of sympathy; for instance, he pointed out that 'though fame in general be agreeable, yet we receive a much greater satisfaction from the approbation of those whom we ourselves esteem and approve of, than of those whom we hate and despise'. But there is little in all of this that affects his account of how sympathy works, as an internal mechanism.

What, for present purposes, is chiefly interesting about Hume's account of sympathy is the way in which he tried to formulate a dynamic model of mental operations in which the conception of self plays a role. The fact that he did this at all, and some of the details of the way that he did it, suggest that he had a sophisticated understanding of self-conceptions in general, and of sympathy in particular. And, as we have seen, often he did. But sometimes he did not. For instance, in his section, 'of the pride and humility of animals', he remarked that 'almost in every species of creatures, but especially of the nobler kind, there are many evident marks of pride and humility'. For instance:

> The very port and gait of a swan, or turkey, or peacock show the high idea he has entertain'd of himself, and his contempt of all others. This is the more remarkable, that in the last species of animals, the pride always attends the beauty, and is discover'd in the male only. The vanity and emulation of nightingales in singing have been commonly remark'd.

> (Ibid.: 326)

What passages such as these show is that Hume, for all his sophistication about self-conceptions, was still a long way from considering, let alone understanding, the true mechanisms of how ideas of self arise developmentally. In sum, when it came to understanding self-conceptions – what they are, how they arise, what roles they play in our mental lives, and so on – Hume, though often amazingly perceptive, could also be quite naive.

Adam Smith

Smith, who was a good friend and confidant of Hume, took over the post at the University of Glasgow of his former teacher, Hutcheson, when the latter retired. Ultimately Smith would make his mark as an economist. But, his first love was moral psychology. His lectures at Glasgow led to a book, *The Theory of Moral Sentiments* (1859), in which he put forth such a perceptive and rich account of sympathy that, had his book been more influential, it might have been to sympathy what Locke's account of personal identity was to that topic.

In its being sensitive both to the internal complexity of sympathy and to the great variety of guises in which it appears, Smith's account was light-years ahead of that of Hutcheson and even a clear advance on that of Hume. And, unlike Hume, Smith managed to investigate the phenomenon of sympathy scientifically, in a way that did not require a statement of his epistemological and metaphysical views. Nevertheless, Smith did have what today we would regard as philosophical concerns, having to do with ethical theory, and even to a large extent constructed his account in the service of these concerns. But these normative philosophical concerns, at least in Smith's hands, were much less intrusive than metaphysics and epistemology had been in Hume's.

Nevertheless, commentators on Smith, from Reid to the present day, often miss the empirical richness of Smith's account of sympathy by being overly concerned with the ways in which its unclarities complicate the uses to which he tried to put it for purposes of ethical theory.[6] In our view, if one leaves ethical theory to one side and focuses just on Smith's account of sympathy as a psychological phenomenon, one of the great virtues of his account – arguably its greatest virtue – is his extraordinary sensitivity to that phenomenon.

Smith was the first to draw attention to the ways in which differences of degree in the extent to which people sympathize with others complicate how we should account for sympathy. Although the issue is implicit throughout his discussion, in the context of making the point that sympathy is not 'a selfish principle' he raised it explicitly. 'When I sympathize with your sorrow or your indignation', he said, 'it may be pretended indeed, that my emotion is founded in self-love, because it arises from bringing your case home to myself, from putting myself in your situation, and thence conceiving what I should feel in the like circumstances'. 'But', he continued, 'though sympathy is very properly said to arise from an imaginary change of situation with the person principally concerned, yet this imaginary change is not supposed to happen to me in my own person and character, but in that of the person with whom I sympathize'. For instance, 'when I condole with you for the loss of your only son, in order to enter into your grief I do not consider what I, a person of such a character and profession, should suffer, if I had a son, and if that son was unfortunately to die: but I consider what I should suffer if I was really you, and I not only change circumstance with you, but I change persons and characters' (Smith 1759: 317).

What is most perceptive about these remarks is Smith's recognition that in imagining yourself in another's situation, you can do so to different degrees. In some cases, you just imagine yourself in the other's situation by altering circumstances external to your person – say, having to do with familial relations and the fates of people you care about. In other cases, you imagine yourself in the other's situation by altering your own 'person and character'. When Smith talks of his becoming 'really you' and 'changing persons', sometimes he seems to mean merely that in imagination he would cross the boundary between mere external circumstances and internal ones; that is, he would alter not only circumstances external to his person but also his own person and character. Other times, Smith talks as if, in imagination, he would 'really [become] you', retaining no vestige of himself. On balance, Smith usually seems to mean just the former. But he is ambiguous enough that there is no way to be absolutely sure. What we can be sure of is that Smith was alive to the issue.

We shall not here attempt to give a complete summary of Smith's account of sympathy. We want merely to illustrate some of the ways in which, like Hume in Book II of the *Treatise*, Smith entered wholeheartedly into the project of constructing a dynamic model of some of those mental systems in which the line between self and other is an issue. In discussing Hume, we viewed him, in part, through the lens of a contemporary distinction between the philosophy and psychology of personal identity that is current in our own times. We pointed out that Hume had a foot in both camps. Leaving aside Smith's ethical theory, if we view through the same lens his account of sympathy as a mental and behavioral phenomenon, his account falls squarely on the psychological side of the ledger. Smith exhibited little interest in the sorts of foundational issues with regard to personal identity (or, any other epistemological or metaphysical topic) that preoccupied Locke and Hume. Smith's focus was on characterizing how our minds actually work.

Smith had two central preoccupations that permeated his entire account. One, which we will not stress, has to do with selfishness. He was intent on showing that, so far as our natural propensities are concerned, we are not completely selfish. 'How selfish soever man may be supposed', he began his book, 'there are evidently some principles in his nature, which interest him in the fortune of others, and render their happiness necessary to him, though he derives nothing from it except the pleasure of seeing it'. Smith said, 'Of this kind is pity or compassion, the emotion which we feel for the misery of others, when we either see it, or are made to conceive it in a very lively manner'. Smith's target, in this part of what he has to say, was pretty obviously Hobbes (and perhaps also Locke and Mandeville), his heroes pretty obviously Hutcheson and Hume, though Smith is not explicit on the point. For the most part, he discussed issues and examples, not persons or theories. He rarely named names.

Smith's other central preoccupation was with accounting for the mechanics of sympathy, which he did mainly by commenting on examples. He said that since 'we have no immediate experience of what other men feel, we can form no idea of the manner in which they are affected, but by conceiving what we ourselves should feel in the like situation'. If 'our brother is upon the rack', he said, we discover what he suffers not by our senses, which cannot 'carry us beyond our own person', but by our imaginations, which help us to form an idea of what another experiences 'by representing to us what would be our own [experience], if we were in his case'. 'By means of imagination, 'we place ourselves in his situation, we conceive ourselves enduring all the same torments, we enter as it were into his body, and become *in some measure* the same person with him'. Thereby, we 'form some idea of his sensations, and even feel something which, though weaker in degree, is not altogether unlike them' (Ibid.: 9, emphasis added). Thus, in an important respect, Smith is squarely in the tradition of Hume. In imagination we replicate the impressions of the person with whom we are sympathetic, to which we have no direct access, by means of our own past or present impressions. And we determine which of our own impressions to bring into play by imagining ourselves in the other's external circumstances and perhaps also in adopting some of his internal characteristics. Smith concluded that once we have done this, the other's 'agonies, when they are thus brought home to ourselves . . . begin at last to affect us, and we then tremble and shudder at the thought of what he feels' (Ibid.).

Smith is aware that sometimes sympathy is simply emotional contagion. He said that sympathy 'may be seen to arise merely from the view of a certain emotion in another person'. In such cases, passions 'may seem to be trans-fused from one man to another, instantaneously and antecedent to any knowledge of what excited them in the person principally concerned'. For instance, when grief or joy is 'strongly expressed in the look and gestures of any one', they 'at once affect the spectator with some degree of a like painful or agreeable emotion. A smiling face is, to every body that sees it, a cheerful object; as a sorrowful countenance, on the other hand, is a melancholy one' (Ibid.: 11). Yet Smith was much more interested in the forms of sympathy which are not instantaneous and depend on the sympathizer's precon-ceptions.

Smith distinguished a variety of examples, among them the case in which we simply *react* to imagining ourselves in the other's *situation*, but with our own current awareness of what is happening to him or is about to happen to him. In some cases, our and the other person's awareness of the situation might be alike in relevant respects: 'the mob, when they are gazing at a dancer on the slack rope, naturally writhe and twist and balance their own bodies, as they see him do, and as they feel that they themselves must do if in his situation'. In other cases, our awareness might be superior to that of the person with whom we sympathize: when we see an object about to fall on another's leg, then, whether or not he also sees it, 'we shrink and draw back our own leg' and when the object 'does fall, we feel it in some measure, and are hurt by it as well as the sufferer'. In his discussion of such examples, Smith showed that he is aware of sympathy as a *bodily* phenomenon. 'Persons of delicate fibres and a weak constitution of body complain, that in looking on the sores and ulcers which are exposed by beggars in the streets, they are apt to feel an itching or uneasy sensation in the correspondent part of their own bodies'. And Smith showed that he is aware of what we might call the counter-factual character of sympathy: 'horror arises from conceiving what they themselves *would* suffer, if they really were the wretches whom they are looking upon, and if that particular part in themselves was actually affected in the same miserable manner' (Ibid.:10).

It is not just pain or negative mental states that call forth 'our fellow-feeling' and it is not even just information about real others that calls it forth. Positive emotions, such as joy, even 'our joy for the deliverance of those heroes of tragedy or romance who interest us', is, Smith said, 'as sincere as our grief for their distress'. He added that, 'in every passion of which the mind of man is susceptible, the emotions of the by-stander always correspond to that, by bringing the case home to himself, he imagines should be the sentiments of the sufferer'. And, yet, Smith pointed out, some passions more easily provoke sympathy than others. 'The furious behaviour of an angry man is more likely to exasperate us against himself than against his enemies' since 'we are un-acquainted with his provocation'. But since 'we plainly see what is the situation of those with whom he is angry, and to what violence they may be exposed from so enraged an adversary' we readily 'sympathize with their fear or resentment'. Thus, our knowing what provokes a passion can affect whether we sympathize. In situations in which we may have to choose with whom we should be sympathetic, our being able to see the source of another's passion makes it easier to sympathize with him. But in the case of such examples, it is not just knowledge of causes, Smith thought, that determines with whom we sympathize but also the kind of passion involved. 'The very appearances of grief and joy', for instance, 'inspire us with some degree of the like emotions' because 'they suggest to us the general idea of some good or bad fortune that has befallen the person in whom we observe them' (Ibid.:10–11).

Yet even in the case of emotions with which we are disposed to be sympathetic, Smith thought, background information – for example, with respect to what causes the emotion – plays a key role in determining whether we actually are sympathetic: 'Even our sympathy with the grief or joy of another, before we are informed of the cause of either, is always extremely imperfect'. And 'general lamentations, which express nothing but the anguish of the sufferer, create rather a curiosity to inquire into his situation, along with some disposition to sympathize with him, than any actual sympathy'. In Smith's opinion, sympathy 'does not arise so much from the view of the passion, as from that of the situation which excites it', where what he means by 'the view' is our general understanding of the situation (Ibid.:11–12).

In some cases of sympathetic reaction, our knowledge of the situation might be superior to that of the person with whom we sympathize not, as in the example of the object about to strike someone's leg, because we, but not the person, know what is about to happen, but because we know what the person with whom we sympathize *ought* to feel: 'We blush for the impudence and rudeness of another, though he himself appears to have no sense of the impropriety of his own behaviour; because we cannot help feeling with what confusion we ourselves should be covered, had we behaved in so absurd a manner' (Ibid.:12). Clearly, Smith saw in sympathy an extremely complicated mental operation. It is not even, he thought, that, in sympathy, rather than feeling what we imagine others are actually feeling, we feel instead what *we* would be feeling if we were in their situations. Rather, in some cases at least, we feel what we would be feeling, if we were in the other's situation, subject to the qualification that we are simultaneously able to view ourselves from our present perspective. Smith, thus, built into his model of how sympathy works a related and quite sophisticated model of mental dissociation.

Smith illustrated this dissociative aspect of sympathy in terms of three additional examples, the first of which has to do with insanity: 'Of all the calamities to which the condition of mortality exposes mankind, the loss of reason appears, to those who have the least spark of humanity, by far the most dreadful'. But 'the poor wretch, who is in it, laughs and sings perhaps, and is altogether insensible of his own misery'. Smith concluded that 'the anguish which humanity feels, therefore, at the sight of such an object, cannot be the reflection of any sentiment of the sufferer'. Rather, 'the compassion of the spectator must arise altogether from the consideration of what he himself would feel if he was reduced to the same unhappy situation, and, what perhaps is impossible, *was at the same time able to regard it with his present reason and judgment*' (Ibid.: 12, emphasis added). Smith next considered sympathy with infants, in which the same sort of considerations arise.

Finally, Smith considered the interesting case of sympathizing with the dead:

> And overlooking what is of real importance in their situation, that awful futurity which awaits them, we are chiefly affected by those circumstances which strike our senses, but can have no influence upon their happiness. It is miserable, we think, to be deprived of the light of the sun; to be shut out from life and conversation; to be laid in the cold grave, a prey to corruption and the reptiles of the earth; to be no more thought of in this world, but to be obliterated, in a little time, from the affections, and almost from the memory, of their dearest friends and relations. Surely, we imagine, we can never feel too much for those who have suffered so dreadful a calamity. The tribute of our fellow-feeling seems doubly due to them now, when they are in danger of being forgot by every body; and, by the vain honours which we pay to their memory, we endeavour, for our own misery, artificially to keep alive our melancholy remembrance of their misfortune. That our sympathy can afford them no consolation seems to be an addition to their calamity; and to think that all we can do is unavailing, and that, what alleviates all other distress, the regret, the love, and the lamentations of their friends, can yield no comfort to them, serves only to exasperate our sense of their misery.
>
> (Ibid.: 12–13)

Yet, Smith insisted, the happiness of the dead is unaffected by such circumstances

Smith said that in the case of the dead, the sympathizer's feelings arise not only, as in other cases of sympathy, from our putting ourselves in the other's situation but, rather, from 'our lodging, if I may be allowed to say so, our own living souls in their inanimated bodies, and thence conceiving what would be our emotions' (Ibid.:13). In other words, our feelings arise not from imagining what the dead actually feel or even what we would feel if we were in their situation but, rather, what we would feel if we were buried alive, paralysed but fully conscious, thought to be dead by all of our friends and acquaintances, with no hope whatsoever of escape. Thus, we despair but not so much for the dead, or even for their condition, as for ourselves. In sympathizing with the dead, to paraphrase Dylan Thomas, we rage, as it were, at the dying of the light.

Clearly, Smith had come a long way from merely viewing sympathy as emotional contagion, and he was as concerned with how sympathy affects us as he was with how it works. In particular, he was concerned with what he called, 'the pleasure of mutual sympathy', the fact that 'nothing pleases us more than to observe in other men a fellow-feeling with all the emotions of our own breast' nor 'shocks' us more than the observation of its absence. Smith saw in this phenomenon an expression of our deepest values, which, he thought, give the lie to egoism. According to the thinkers Smith hoped to refute, especially Hobbes and Mandeville, because 'man' is 'conscious of his own weakness, and of the need which he has for the assistance of others', he 'rejoices whenever he observes that they adopt his own passions', for he is then assured of their assistance; and he 'grieves whenever he observes the contrary, because he is then assured of their opposition' (Ibid.:13–14).

In contrast to the idea that, in such cases, it is power (augmented control over one's own circumstances) that is primarily the issue, Smith thought that on many occasions when we rejoice in mutual sympathy, and despair in its absence, 'both the pleasure and the pain' are 'felt so instantaneously and on such frivolous occasions' that 'neither of them can be derived from any such self-interested consideration'. Smith conceded that in some cases, and to some extent, we may by sympathizing enliven our own pleasurable emotional reactions, as 'when we have read a book or poem so often that we can no longer find any amusement in reading it by ourselves, we can still take pleasure in reading it to a companion'. But, he said, even this cannot be the whole story: 'The sympathy, which my friends express with my joy, might, indeed, give me pleasure by enlivening that joy: but that which they express with my grief could give me none, if it served only to enliven that grief' (Ibid.:14).

So, it is not just that our emotional states are enlivened by those of others. It is also that the mere correspondence between their states and ours can move us, and sometimes move us profoundly, by relieving our otherwise terrible sense of emotional isolation, of being trapped in our own interior drama in a way that excludes others:

> Sympathy, however, enlivens joy and alleviates grief. It enlivens joy by presenting another source of satisfaction; and it alleviates grief by insinuating into the heart almost the only agreeable sensation which it is at that time capable of receiving. It is to be observed accordingly, that we are still more anxious to communicate to our friends our disagreeable than our agreeable passions, that we derive still more satisfaction from their sympathy with the former than from that with the latter, and that we are still more shocked by the want of it.
> (Ibid.: 14–15)

When we are already connected, we do not need to be reconnected or to have our connection augmented through sympathy: 'The agreeable passions of love and joy can satisfy and support the heart without any auxiliary pleasure'. But 'the bitter and painful emotions of grief and resentment more strongly require the healing consolation of sympathy' (Ibid.: 15).

It is a question, it seems, of overcoming self-enclosure, and connecting to others. In Smith's view, such connecting is sufficiently valuable and pleasurable to us that we will sympathize with another's distress, and hence to some extent experience their distress ourselves, in order to connect:

> As the person who is principally interested in any event is pleased with our sympathy, and hurt by the want of it, so we, too, seem to be pleased when we are able to sympathize with him, and to be hurt when we are unable to do so. We run not only to congratulate the successful, but to condole with the afflicted; and the pleasure which we find in the conversation of one whom in all the passions of his heart we can entirely sympathize with, seems to do more than compensate the painfulness of that sorrow with which the view of his situation affects us.
>
> (Ibid.: 15–16)

Thus, 'it is always disagreeable to feel that we cannot sympathize with him, and instead of being pleased with this exemption from sympathetic pain, it hurts us to find that we cannot share his uneasiness' (Ibid.: 16). Thereby, Smith explained what, from Hume's view, emerged as a puzzle. If Hume's account had been the whole truth, we would have had a powerful motive not to sympathize with the negative emotions of others, since in doing so we set in motion a process that converts their distress into our distress. Smith, in contrast, recognized the value of negative emotions and offered an explanation of their function.

Smith also was concerned to relate the sympathizer's internal life with their external behavior. For instance, our response to our inability to sympathize even with another's unpleasant emotion may encourage us to abuse them: 'If we hear a person loudly lamenting his misfortunes, which, however, upon bringing the case home to ourselves, we feel, can produce no such violent effect upon us, we are shocked at his grief; and, because we cannot enter into it, call it pusillanimity and weakness. It gives us the spleen, on the other hand, to see another too happy or too much elevated, as we call it, with any little piece of good fortune' (Ibid.). In other words, we want not so much to be 'in synch' with others, as for them to be in 'synch with us'. And we want this, not so much to increase our power or even to heighten the emotion which we may have in common with those with whom we sympathize, but simply because it feels good.

All such thoughts both concern personal identity in a larger sense and also illustrate how Smith, the psychologist, confined himself to what Hume had earlier characterized as 'the frontiers' of human nature. In Smith's moral psychology, there is no 'march up directly to the capital or centre' of human nature, at least not to the place where Hume located that center. Even when it came to personal identity *per se*, indeed even when Smith teetered on the brink of discussing fission examples, he avoided talk of substance (and of what links successive stages of a person) in favor of discussing the phenomenon of dissociation, the first since Locke to consider it seriously.

Smith's interest in dissociation, which seemingly was quite independent of Locke's interest in it, was in its relation to conscience. In that context, Smith, like Locke, addressed fission-like examples. Smith said, 'When I endeavour to examine my own conduct, when I endeavour to pass sentence upon it, and either to approve or condemn it, it is evident that, in all such cases, I divide myself, as it were, into two persons; and that I, the examiner and judge, represent a different character from that other I, the person whose conduct is examined into and judged of' (Ibid.: 113).[7] We know there are two personas, or persons, Smith continued, because they have different roles: 'The first is the judge; the second the person judged of. But that the judge should, in every respect, be the same with the person judged of, is as impossible, as that the cause should, in every respect, be the same with the effect (Ibid.: 135).

Smith had different names for this judge, which he repeated often and interchangeably, always talking of the judge as if he were a stern father: 'the man within the breast', 'the great inmate', 'the awful and respectable judge', 'the impartial spectator'. In Smith's view, people are virtuous to whatever degree they identify with this disinterested persona. Thus, he says that 'the man of real constancy and firmness, the wise and just man who has been thoroughly bred in the great school of self-command' does 'not merely affect the sentiments of the impartial spectator. He really adopts them. He almost identifies himself with, he almost becomes himself that impartial spectator, and scarce even feels but as that great arbiter of his conduct directs him to feel' (Ibid.: 146–7). One gets the impression that it was not easy to be Adam Smith.

That is as far as Smith took his discussion of dissociation. In Locke's thought about dissociated personalities, amnesiac barriers mark the boundaries among personas (which, for Locke, are separate persons). Smith never discussed the issue of amnesiac barriers. In fact, he rarely even mentioned memory, one of the most telling signs that the sorts of worries about personal identity that animated Locke and his critics did not interest Smith. Rather, Smith lets identifications with interested and disinterested points of view mark the salient boundaries among personas, which, for him, probably were not literally separate persons. And in thinking about such issues, as we saw earlier in the case of Leibniz, Smith hit upon an aspect of fission-like examples which, while not salient to eighteenth-century theorists, would resonate later, in the nineteenth century, with thinkers whose interests in dissociation transcended the limited confines of the traditional personal identity debate. And it would resonate later still, in our own times, with thinkers investigating the child's acquisition of a theory of mind.[8]

Edmund Law

As we have seen, Locke's views on personal identity were immediately attacked by philosophers and theologians, especially by those who wished to defend the immortality of the soul. Clarke, Berkeley, Watts and Butler were among his leading critics. But there were others, such as Collins, Hume, and Priestley, who would try to develop something like a Lockean account into a new naturalism of self and identity. There were also a few who intended merely to defend what they took to be Locke's view, without putting forth a new view of their own. Among these were Catharine Trotter (Cockburn), Vincent Peronnet, and Edmund Law. Of these, Law was the most original.

The situations that these defenders of Locke had to face were quite different. Trotter's early defense of Locke, in 1702, was in opposition to Thomas Burnet's determined attempt to ignore, first, that Locke distinguished man from person and, second, that Locke did not deny the existence of an immaterial soul so much as he tried to provide an account of personal identity that was independent of it. Trotter perceptively defended Locke on both of these points. She also argued – again in her later publication of 1726 – that Locke's account of personal identity successfully resolved difficulties about the resurrection.

Vincent Perronet wrote two defenses of Locke's account of personal identity. In the second, which was published in 1738, he replied to the criticisms of Butler and Watts (Perronet 1738). Perronet there insisted that the question of personal identity hinges on the proper forensic definition of *person* and reiterated what he took to be the importance of Locke's distinction between human and person: 'I think it must appear sufficiently plain, that by *Person*, Mr. *Locke* does not mean either a *Man*, or any other *living Agent*, in general; but only such a Rational Being, as is *actually* conscious of its own Behaviour; *capable* of a Law, and *answerable* for its Actions. So that One in a Phrensy, not withstanding him being a *Man* or *living Agent*, would not however, according to Mr. *Locke*, be esteem'd a *Person*'. Perronet then asked:

> Is the *Mad* Man *justly* punishable for what the *Sober* Man did? If he be not, then we must allow that something more is necessary to constitute the *same* Person, in Mr. *Locke's* Sense, than bearly being the *same Man*. He that has lost his Understanding, and the Remembrance of his Crimes, is yet the *same living Agent*, and may, I presume, be call'd the *same Guilty Man*: But if he be not the *same Conscious Being*, or the *same proper Object of Punishment*, he is not in Mr. *Locke's* phrase, the *same Person*. And indeed his Opinion, that God Almighty will punish no Man hereafter for any Crime, but what is first brought home to his Mind and Conscience, seems to have plain Reason, if not plain Revelation, on its Side.
>
> (Ibid.: 7–10)

But Perronet did not deal with two issues: whether Locke's notion of *person* picked out a substance; and whether Locke's account could avoid the kind of contradiction based on memory that Berkeley, in *Alchiphron* (1732), had recently proposed (see pp. 65–6).

Law was the next defender of Locke. In 1731, he had translated William King's, *An Essay on the Origin of Evil*, to which he added voluminous notes, often presenting Locke's views on various matters. He also added John Gay's, 'A Preliminary Dissertation Concerning the Fundamental Principle of Virtue or Morality', which was the first attempt to explicate the source of morality not on any supposed innate 'moral sense' but on 'observation and imitation of others' and on laws of association. Gay's essay was to have a great influence on Hartley's association psychology (King 1731: xxxiii). In 1769, Law published, *A defence of Mr. Locke's opinions concerning Personal Identity*. Although Law's piece was sparked by an anonymous essay on personal identity published that year, he said little about the objectionable essay and turned quickly to defending his version of Locke's view.

It is a mark of how much the philosophical climate, in 1769, had changed since Perronet, thirty years earlier, had published his defense of Locke that Law could defend Locke as he did and not pay a heavy personal price. Just a year after Perronet's defense, Book I of Hume's *Treatise* had been published. Although Hume's early impact was mostly indirect, by midcentury there were far fewer defenders of the notion that personal identity was based on a simple, immaterial, immortal soul. Law, himself, in a work on religion in which he had discussed the idea of the 'sleep of the soul', had argued that Scripture did not support the notion that between death and resurrection the soul separates from the body (Law 1759). If Law had published either his defense of this idea or his defense of Locke much earlier in the century, he would have been viciously attacked. By mid-century, he could make such assertions and not even lose his position at Cambridge. Indeed, not long afterwards, despite much debate over his views, Law was appointed Bishop of Carlisle, a major position in the Church. Times had changed.[9]

The changes were no doubt due in part to continuing philosophical debate, such as had occurred between Clarke and Collins, over whether human thinking must have an immaterial substantial base. Locke had proposed the possibility of 'thinking matter', which at first had sounded the alarms of heresy. By mid-century the simple immaterial substance view was much less certain, and alternatives to it much more palatable. As a result, Law could supplement his review of Christian sources by remarking 'that all *philosophical* arguments drawn from our notions of *matter*, and urged against the possibility of life, thought, and agency being so connected with some portions of it as to constitute a *compound Being* . . . or person, are merely grounded on our ignorance'. Law conceded that there were difficulties about the relations of mind and body, but argued that the word *substance* would not help to solve any of them. 'He that carefully attends to the workings of nature',

Law said, 'and sees how oft the several classes of beings run into each other, will not find very much weight in arguments grounded upon ontological distinctions only'. And were such arguments to establish an 'essential difference' between mind and body, they could show at most that mind 'might possibly be conceived to subsist apart from' body, that is, to 'be sustained in a new manner, and with new perfections by the Deity; but whether he will actually so sustain it, can, I apprehend, be known only from his *word*; which represents the thing, we see, in quite another light: nor indeed ever seems to countenance this nice speculation, by treating *man* in any such intricate, abstracted way' (Law 1759: 414–16).

In his 1769 defense of Locke on personal identity, Law responded to the worry that *person*, on Locke's account, might not pick out a substance, but only a mode, by agreeing that *person* picked out only a mode. Then, relying heavily on Locke's remarks on the use of substance terms in ethics, Law argued, in effect, that the word *person* also picked out what deserved to be regarded as a virtual substance:

> Now the word person, as is well observed by Mr. Locke . . . is properly a forensic term, and here to be used in the strict forensic sense, denoting some such quality or modification in man as denominates him a moral agent, or an accountable creature; renders him the proper subject of laws, and a true object of rewards and punishments. When we apply it to any man, we do not treat him absolutely, and in gross; but under a particular relation or precision: we do not comprehend or concern ourselves about the several inherent properties which accompany him in real existence, which go to the making up the whole complex notion of an active and intelligent being; but arbitrarily abstract one single quality or mode from the rest.
>
> (Law 1769: 145–6)

Thus, in Law's interpretation of Locke, a person is human, but denuded of all human properties except those that are relevant to forensic issues.

In agreement with Locke's view that general moral truths, like the truths of geometry, are eternal and hypothetical, Law claimed that the particulars of which they are true are not concrete but 'abstract'. Geometry is about particular, concrete objects, he said, but about them only in so far as they have certain characteristics and not others. For instance, it is about particular spherical objects, but only so far as they are spherical. This restriction of focus licenses talk of a merely geometrical sphere, which functions as a kind of surrogate – if you like, virtual – substance. In Law's view (and also in his interpretation of Locke's view), it is this sort of restriction of focus that makes the subject matter of geometry abstract. It is also what makes persons abstract.

The forensic issues that interested Law had to do mainly with accountability. Forensics, in his view, is about persons, but only in so far as they have certain characteristics and not others. For Law, the characteristic that mattered most about humans is consciousness. Thus, persons are humans, but only in so far as they are conscious. As a consequence, he reasoned, persons, in reality, are modes of humans, but modes which it is convenient to talk about as if they were substances. So much for persons. What about their identities?

In Law's version of Locke's view, one person is identical with another just if he is accountable for the other's behavior. What makes a person accountable is 'nothing more, than his becoming sensible at different times of what he had thought or done before: and being as fully convinced that he then thought or did it, as he now is of his present thoughts, acts, and existence' (Ibid.: 147). Law argued that personal identity, in this sense, is a social distinction, 'a creature of Society, an abstract consideration of man, necessary for the mutual benefit of him and his fellows', that is, 'a mere forensic term'. Law said that to inquire after 'the criterion or constituent' of personal identity is to inquire in what circumstances societies 'have in fact agreed to inflict evil upon individuals, in order to prevent evils to the whole body from any irregular member' (Ibid.: 180).

Law earlier gave an example of just how far, in his view, the moral and forensic distinction between man and person reaches, or should reach, in criminal justice, and how it depends on consciousness:

> And whence then does this difference in any one's moral capacity arise, but from that plain diversity in his natural one? from his absolute irretrievable want of consciousness in one case, and not in the other? Suppose now that one in the former state kills a man; that he, or some part of what we call him, was ever so notoriously the instrument, or occasion of that death; yet if he was either then insensible of the fact, or afterwards became so, and so continued: *Would he be any more guilty of murder, than if that death had been occasioned by another person? since at that time he was truly such, or at least is so now*, notwithstanding that most people might be apt to judge him still the same, from a sameness in outward circumstances . . . from his shape, mien, or appearance.
>
> (Ibid.: 151, emphasis added)

Thus, according to Law's account of Locke's theory, in order for someone now to be the same person as someone who performed an act previously, the person now must either actually recollect or be capable of being induced to recollect having performed that act, with the same consciousness he had at the time. Such a capacity can come and go. Hence, Law viewed personal identity as an abstract mode of a substance rather than as a substance itself.

Nevertheless, it is not just human societies that rely on consciousness as the criterion of personhood and accountability:

> This distinct consciousness of our past actions, from whence arise all the ideas of merit and demerit, will most undoubtedly be regarded with due weight in foro divino; and indeed has its due weight in foro humano, whenever it can be with certainty determined: wherever this appears wanting, all judicial proceedings are at an end. How so plain soever any criminal act were, the man would now-a-days be acquitted from guilt in the commission of it, and discharged from the penalties annexed to such fact, could it at the same time be as plainly made out, that he was incapable of knowing what he did, or is now under a like incapacity of recollecting it.
>
> (Ibid.: 147)

God and Locke have the same view of personhood.

Law recognized that this account stresses certain features of Locke's view at the expense of others. He said that Locke defined *person* in a 'popular sense' when he defined it as 'a thinking intelligent being, that has reason and reflection, and can consider itself as itself, the same thinking being, in different times and places'. But, Law continued, 'when the term is used more accurately and philosophically, it stands for one especial property of that thing or being, separated from all the rest that do or may attend it in real existence'. The crucial property is 'rationality', not all of it, but 'so far only, as it makes a human 'capable of knowing what he does and suffers, and on what account, and therefore renders him amenable to justice for his behaviour' (Ibid.: 155–6). In the Appendix to his essay, Law suggested that Locke had 'incautiously defined the word' *person* and that 'the expression would have been more just, had he said that the word stands for an attribute, or quality, or character of a thinking intelligent being' (Ibid.: 166–7).

Law further suggested that *person* is better defined in the Ciceronian sense of mode or mask, and that when a person is so defined:

> as an intelligent being subject to government and laws, and accountable for his actions . . . all difficulties that relate to a man's forgetting some actions, &ct. now vanish . . . and it amounts to no more than saying that a man puts on a mask – continuing to wear it for some time – puts off one mask and takes another, i.e. appears to have consciousness – to recollect past consciousnesses – does not recollect, &ct.
>
> (Ibid.: 167)

By taking this virtual-substance approach to personal identity, Law believed that such paradoxes of memory as the one proposed by Berkeley (which he briefly mentioned) can be ignored. For Law, such paradoxes have no practical import. 'To dwell upon those surprising consequences that might attend the transfering the same consciousness to different beings [a reference to fission?], or giving the same being very different ones, is merely puzzling and perplexing the point, by introducing such conclusions as never really existed, and would not alter the true state of the question if they did' (Ibid.: 197). By thus pushing forensic concerns to their limit, Law was able to make a move not available to Locke himself. He was able to displace the traditional concept of the self or person as a pure, simple immaterial substance, or as a vital union of an immaterial soul with a material body, with a view of persons as abstract modes or attributes of a substance. In doing so he was able to make Locke's view more consistent with itself, but only by forfeiting the notion that a person is some kind of substance.

That Law, the Bishop of Carlisle, could exhibit a confidence in this conclusion, which is Lockean in spirit, but which Locke, himself, would hardly have dared to utter, is indicated in the following concluding passage:

> Well then, having examined a little into the nature, and enumerated some few properties of an abstract idea in general, and shown that this particular one before us can be nothing more, we may find perhaps that however fluctuating and changeful this account may be judged to render personality; how much soever it may fall short of some sublime systems about purely immaterial substances, and perfectly independent principles of thought; yet there is no help for these changes in the seat of personality; since, in the last place, we know of nothing more stable and permanent in our constitution that has the least pretence to settle and support it. All parts of the body are to a certain degree in perpetual flux, nor is any one of them, that we are acquainted with, concerned in the present case more than another. As to the mind, both its cogitative and active powers are suspended (whether they be so or not is a matter of fact, in which experience only, and not subtile argumentations drawn from the nature of an unknown, perhaps imaginary, essence ought to decide) during sound sleep: Nay, every drowsy nod (as Mr. Locke expresses it) must shake their doctrine, who maintain that these powers are incessantly employed.

Law continued:

> To the difficulties so often objected, of this being a 'new creation', and making the same thing have 'two beginnings of existence'; — We may observe, that it would indeed be an absurdity to suppose two beginnings of existence, if the identity of a substance, being, or man

108

were inquired into; but when the inquiry is made into the artificial abstract idea of personality, invented for a particular end, to answer which consciousness only is required, beginning and end of existence are quite out of the question, being foreign to any consideration of the subject.

(Ibid.: 159–62)

Law's views on the 'sleep of the soul' would importantly affect Priestley. But Law's radical view of persons as abstract particulars would not be further developed during the eighteenth century.

5

THE SELF AS MIND

Toward the beginning of the eighteenth century, soul theorists were still eager to defend the immaterial substantiality of the soul against those who would account for self and personal identity along relational lines. They had not yet felt the winds of history blowing against them. As the century wore on, the winds eventually became a gale. Soul theorists could not help but notice. One effect of their noticing had to do with their willingness to defend the view that the soul is immaterial. Clarke's bravado contrasts nicely with the defensiveness of Berkeley and Butler, and, with the subsequent reluctance of soul theorists, after Hume, even to do battle on the issue. Another effect is that for soul theorists, toward the beginning of the century, it was enough simply to defend the immateriality of the soul and related a priori doctrines, such as the reflexivity of consciousness, without also contributing to the emerging science of human nature. Again, Clarke is the premier example. Later in the century, many soul theorists bracketed their commitment to the immateriality of the soul in order to conduct meaningful empirical research.

Berkeley is a case in point. While the immateriality of soul is crucial to his metaphysics, it is almost irrelevant to his inquires into vision. Similarly, in Butler's case, while the immateriality of the soul is central to his defense, in the *Analogy*, of immortality, it is almost irrelevant to his more empirically motivated concerns in the *Sermons*. Later still, while many important theorists, such as Hartley, Tucker, and Reid remained committed to the existence of an immaterial soul, there was little swagger in their attempt to defend this commitment, if, indeed, they attempted to defend it at all. In their contributing to the newly emerging science of mind, they managed for the most part to put their commitment to the soul outside of the focus of their inquiries and also safely out of the line of fire. In sum, soul theorists, at least the ones that we now think mattered, tended to change their approach from the beginning to the middle of the eighteenth century. Not only did they begin to embrace the empirical study of human nature, but they found ways in their empirical theorizing to marginalize their view that the soul is immaterial.

A symptom of these changes is that in the last half of the century there emerged a pattern of theoretical allegiances of a kind that would have been unimaginable in the first half. Increasingly, in debates between theorists, it did not matter what one's view was of the immaterial soul. Thus, Hartley, the dualist, was an ally of Priestley, the materialist, while Reid, the dualist, attacked both. And while the main influences on Tucker, the dualist, were Locke, Clarke, and Hartley, it was not Locke and Hartley's dualism that mattered to Tucker, but their more scientific pursuits. It is only a slight exaggeration to suggest that Priestley could have put forth the very same views he did, even if, like Hartley, he had been a dualist; and Reid could have put forth most of his views, even if he had been a materialist. The philosophy of human nature had largely disengaged from both religion and philosophy. In the process, it had become the science of mind.

As a consequence of this disengagement, a new sort of methodological dispute arose that had to do more with technique than with metaphysics. Earlier in the century, Hume had criticized those of his contemporaries who were following 'the tedious lingering method'. But his recommended alternative was to append a foundational epistemology and metaphysics to the fledgling science of human nature. In the last third of the century, as we shall see, methodological disputes began to arise that were more internal to the new science. At issue in these new disputes was not whether to enlarge the domain of the new science by incorporating metaphysics, but of how best to generate and test empirical hypotheses. As we have just seen, by the latter third of the century most of those who were at the center of the new research programs had already figured out how to marginalize their background religious and metaphysical commitments. With the field of battle thus cleared of intruders, the way was open to fine tune more internal aspects of strategy and tactics.

David Hartley

Hartley, the son of a minister and himself trained to be a minister, could not accept the notion of eternal punishment and, so, decided instead to become a physician. Perhaps as a result of this mixed training, his thought is both exact and speculative, and his speculations both naturalistic and theological.[1] His main work, *Observations on Man, His Frame, His Duty and His Expectations* (1749) is part physiology (vibrations in the brain), part psychology (association of ideas), and part Christian theology. It combines a necessitarian metaphysics, mechanistic associationist psychology, and a vision of moral and religious development which has as its end 'perfect Self-annihilation and the pure Love of God' (Hartley 1749: v. 2, 282).

Although Priestley greatly admired Hartley, in his 1775 edition of Hartley's work, he decided that only the part dealing with laws of association merited republication because the theory of vibrations was mere speculation and the religious ideas irrelevant. Yet Hartley's thoughts on physiology theoretically grounded his associational psychology, and he often illustrated his psychology with examples that led directly to his theology. In addition, although the particular form of his physiological hypothesis quickly became outdated, his suggestion that there is an intimate and dependent relationship between mental and physical events in the brain and his speculations about what that relationship is greatly advanced materialist trends in psychology, including Priestley's own materialism.

However, Hartley was a methodological materialist, not also a substantive (metaphysical) one. In this respect, he differed from Collins before him and Priestley after. Hartley believed that 'man consists of two parts, body and mind', where the mind 'is that substance, agent, principle, &c. to which we refer the sensation, ideas, pleasures, pains, and voluntary motions'. However, he accepted Locke's concession that it is *possible*, for all we know, that matter thinks:

> Matter, if it could be endued with the most simple Kinds of Sensation, might also arrive at all that Intelligence of which the human Mind is possessed: Whence this Theory must be allowed to overturn all the Arguments which are usually brought for the Immateriality of the Soul from the Subtlety of the internal Senses, and of the rational Faculty. But I no-ways presume to determine whether Matter can be endued with Sensation or no.
>
> (Ibid.: v. 1, 511–12)

Hartley doubted that either problems with materialism or prescientific intuitions we may have about unity of consciousness could be used to prove that the soul is immaterial. He said that 'it is difficult to know [even] what is meant by the Unity of Consciousness', adding that the main problem with materialism is 'that Matter and Motion, however subtly divided, or reasoned upon, yield nothing more than Matter and Motion still'. But it was, he said, 'foreign to [his] Purpose' to pursue the issue.

Hartley's humility about ontological questions extended to issues involving the afterlife. It is worth noting, he said, 'that the Immateriality of the Soul has little or no Connexion with its Immortality; and that we ought to depend upon Him who first breathed into Man the Breath of the present Life, for our Resurrection to a better' (Ibid.: 512). Thus, although Hartley had metaphysical and theological views, which he expressed side by side with his more scientific ones, he never used the former to determine the content of the latter. He was a physico-theologian, as Bacon, Boyle, Locke, and Newton had been before him, but in his scientific work it was the physico side that prevailed. In his case, like Locke's, his epistemological views engendered a deep humility, mixed with true religious piety, about the extent to which, through reason, humans can know metaphysical and religious truths.

In stark contrast to his metaphysical and theological humility, Hartley's associationist psychology is boldly speculative. There he claimed that all human nature is built out of associations of sensations and consequent ideas, whose origins are in physical impressions in the organism. Previously, in 1700, in the fourth edition of the *Essay*, Locke had introduced the notion of associ- ation of ideas, but had presented associations as obstacles to rational thought. He did not see the power that the concept of association might have as a fundamental and extremely general productive principle of the mind. Hume did see this, and, independently of Hume, so did Hartley. However, Hartley differed from Hume in using the principle in conjunction with his physio- logical hypothesis to provide a general account of human nature, beginning with sensations, and including not only memory and imagination, but reason- ing, the emergence out of pleasure and pain of the various passions (e.g., ambition, self-interest, and sympathy), and the development of involuntary and voluntary action. For Hume, association was a principle in the service of philosophy; for Hartley, it was a principle in the service of the first truly general account of human and animal psychology, which, as it happened, laid an important part of the groundwork for the more scientific, association psychology that developed in the nineteenth and early twentieth centuries.

Hartley thought that his association theory was empirically testable. He used it as a springboard for what he took to be experientially grounded speculations about the way mental systems work and complex behaviors develop. For instance, in the case of compassion ('affections by which we grieve for the misery of others') in children, he said:

> When their Parents, Attendants, &c. are sick or afflicted, it is usual to raise in their Minds the nascent Ideas of Pains and Miseries, by such Words and Signs as are suited to their Capacities; they also find themselves laid under many Restraints on this Account. – And these and such-like Circumstances have raised the Desires and Endeavours to remove the Causes of these their own internal uneasy Feelings, or, which is the same thing, of these Miseries of others (in all which they are much influenced, as in other like Cases, by the great Disposition to imitate, before spoken of); and a Variety of internal Feelings and Desires of this Kind are so blended and associated together, as that no Part can be distinguished separately from the rest; the Child may properly be said to have Compassion.
>
> (Ibid.: 475)

Thus, in Hartley's view, it is primarily a child's own discomfort and its association with the discomfort of others that leads to the child's compassion; for in relieving the pain of others, a child's own 'associated' pain would also be relieved.

Hartley proposed that associations operate on bodily activities even when the mind is only partly involved. For instance, he proposed that 'voluntary and semi-voluntary Motions are deducible from Association':

> After the actions, which are most perfectly voluntary, have been rendered so by one set of associations, they may, by another, be made to depend upon the most diminutive sensations, ideas, and motions, such as the mind scarce regards, or is conscious of; and which therefore it can scarce recollect the moment after the action is over. Hence it follows, that association not only converts automatic actions into voluntary, but voluntary ones into automatic.
>
> (Ibid.: 104)

Through such remarks, Hartley laid the foundation for a mechanistic physiological psychology which, in the long run, presupposed that an overly strict distinction between the powers of mind and body could only inhibit fruitful theoretical development.

Hartley's holism about the mind and its physiological underpinning included an extended discussion of maladies of the mind and their effects on reasoning. The maladies are understood as vibrations gone awry, in a reciprocal causal relationship with one's sense of self: 'The same Increase of Vibrations makes all the principal Ideas appear to affect *Self*, with the peculiar interesting Concern supposed to flow from personal Identity; so that these Vibrations exert a reflected Influence upon themselves by this means' (Ibid.: 398–9). In discussing madness, Hartley says that if someone 'whose nervous System is disordered' were 'to turn his Thoughts accidentally to some barely possible Good or Evil', the 'nervous Disorder' might increase 'the Vibrations belonging to its Idea so much, as to give it a Reality, a Connexion with *Self*' (Ibid.: 401).[2]

In discussing how the idea of God emerges in children, Hartley suggested that 'children in their first Attempts to decypher the Word God, will suppose it to stand for a Man, whom they have never seen, and of whom consequently they form a compound fictitious Idea, consisting of Parts before generated by Men, whom they have seen'. Then, when children later 'hear that God cannot be seen, having no visible Shape, no Parts: but that he is a spiritual infinite Being; this adds much to their Perplexity and Astonishment, and by degrees destroys the Association of the fictitious visible Idea before mentioned with the Word God'. Combining these and other observations and hypotheses, he concluded that 'amongst *Jews* and *Christians*, Children begin probably with a definite visible Idea of God; but that by degrees this is quite obliterated, without any thing of a stable and precise Nature succeeding in its room; and that, by farther Degrees, a great Variety of strong secondary Ideas, *i.e.* mental Affections (attended indeed by visible Ideas, to which proper Words are affixed, as of Angels, the general Judgment, &c.), recur in their Turns, when they think upon God' (Ibid.: 486–8).

Turning next to the 'Love of God', Hartley speculated that in the first instance it is 'evidently deduced' either directly or indirectly 'from [self-]interested Motives', such as 'the Hopes of a future Reward' but that subsequently, 'after all the several Sources of the Love of God have coalesced together, this Affection becomes as disinterested as any other; as the Pleasure we take in any natural or artificial Beauty, in the Esteem of others, or even in sensual Gratifications' (Ibid.: 490). In Hartley's view, all interest has its foundation in sensation. In some, disinterested love eventually takes over and culminates in the dominating disinterested love of God. In his view, by means of a mechanical process, which is properly studied in empirical psychology, it can be determined that the human mind undergoes a developmental sequence from sensual self-interest to a felicitous love of God, and to the anticipation of an afterlife, in which this felicity continues.

Abraham Tucker

Tucker is now known primarily for his contributions to associationist psychology and to ethical theory. As an early utilitarian, he influenced Hazlitt and William Paley, the latter of whom said in his preface to his *Principles of Moral and Political Philosophy* (1785), that he had found in Tucker 'more original thinking and observation upon the several subjects that he has taken in hand than in any other, not to say than in all others put together' (Brown 1970: 95). Since Paley's book for many years was widely used as a text at Cambridge and elsewhere, Tucker's reputation remained alive into the next generation.

Tucker's main scientific contributions were in the fields of action-theory and associationistic psychology. He gave a more refined analysis of what is involved in human action than had previous thinkers and, while agreeing with Locke that compatibilism is the proper account of free will, he criticized Locke's view that desire is always prompted by uneasiness. So far as mental mechanics is concerned, Tucker argued that the fusion of elementary ideas into complex ones could not be understood on the basis of the association of ideas.

For present purposes, Tucker is chiefly interesting as a fascinating example of a thinker who was torn between two traditions. Because he could not accept the crude attempts of Hartley and other materialists of his day to account for the phenomena of consciousness, he was driven to embrace the views of Clarke, whom he revered. One could almost say that what Collins had been to Locke's views, Tucker was to Clarke's. But Tucker was too committed to an empirical methodology to accept Clarke's theories for a priori reasons. And in his attempt to justify Clarke's views empirically, he emptied them of virtually all of their metaphysical content.

In his contributions to action theory, Tucker occasionally touched on questions about self and personal identity similar to some of the questions that we have been tracking. For instance, in response to the question of when it is appropriate to say of an action that it is *one's own*, he proposed that the answer has to do with the action's having being caused by one's own motives without the intervention of anyone else's voluntary activity; and as Harry

Frankfurt and others have been in our own times, Tucker was convinced of the relevance of second-order desires to the question of free will (Ibid.:105, 135).[3] However, it is not Tucker's action theory but some of his more fanciful speculations, derived from his reflections on unity of consciousness, that best illustrate the facet of his thought that is of most interest to us.

Early in 1763, Tucker published, *Free-Will, Foreknowledge, and Fate* (1763a). It was criticized in a periodical for being 'greatly deficient in physiological knowledge' of the basis of human individuality, and for assuming an unwarranted immaterialism. Later in the same year, he published *Man in Quest of Himself: Or a Defence of the Individuality of the Human Mind, or Self* (1763b), in which he responded to this criticism by trying to explain why there can be no satisfactory materialist account of personal unity. His main argument for this, which drew heavily on Clarke's arguments (he even cited Clarke on the title page), was based on the simplicity of self or mind and the divisibility of matter. Yet Tucker did not, as Clarke had done in his debate with Collins, dismiss materialism from an external perspective as 'an impossible hypothesis'. Instead, in the foregoing two books and his later *The Light of Nature Pursued* (1768–77), he developed a four-stage strategy for dealing with materialism. First, he assumed that morality is justified. Then, he argued for a theologically based utilitarianism, according to which morality would not be justified if there were no afterlife with divine rewards and punishments. Then, he argued that there could be no afterlife unless the soul is immaterial and, hence, naturally immortal. Finally, he tried to show that on the basis of materialism one cannot account for unity of consciousness. It is the latter two arguments only that concern us.

Tucker's main arguments for the immateriality and natural immortality of the soul appeared in a footnote in *Free-will* (1763a) and were subsequently repeated at greater length in *Man in Quest of Himself* (1763b) and *The Light of Nature Pursued* (1768–77). In the footnote, he claimed that 'Perception cannot be made up of no perceptions; nor received by a number of atoms jointly, unless received by each of them singly' no more than 'whispers heard by a thousand men' can 'make together a [resounding] audible voice'. He also argued – on the basis of Clarke's nominalistic thesis that 'existence belongs only to individuals' since compound things are merely collections of substances and, as such, have no existence apart from that of their parts – that just as 'if the King were to incorporate six hundred men into a regiment, there would not be six hundred and one Beings therefore, one for the regiment, and one for each of the men', so 'neither when a multiple of atoms run together to form a human body, is there a Being more than there was before: nor would there be a Being lost out of nature upon its dissolution' (Tucker 1763a:190–1). While an atomist might conclude from this that ontologically a human being or person must be merely fictional, like the regiment, Tucker, instead, argued that people are exceptions since 'no man can doubt of his own existence, or that he has a personality belonging to him distinct from all other Beings'. He reasoned that since 'I can never cease to be myself, nor become another person' I must exist as something over and above the parts out of which I am composed: 'There is one being the more in nature for my existence; and were I annihilated there would be a Being the less'.

Using the simplicity argument of his predecessors, Tucker then argued for 'the individuality of mind, or spirit of man, and consequently its perpetual duration: for nature can only destroy compounds by dissolving their parts, but individuals cannot be destroyed without a miracle, that is, an immediate exertion of Omnipotence' (Ibid.: 191). In sum, since all natural bodies are composed of atoms, then all of them – except humans – are analogous to the King's regiment in that they are merely compositions of atoms, not new substances or beings in addition to the atoms of which they are composed. But we are certain of our own existence as real individuals, with our own unique personalities. So, we cannot be merely composed of atoms.

There is no indication in any of Tucker's works that he had read Hume's *Treatise*. So, he may not have been exposed to Hume's argument that we have no introspective access to ourselves as simple beings, nor to Hume's contention that we are as 'artificial' in our mental or personal unity as our bodies are in their material unity. Understandably, the reviewer of Tucker's book on free will suggested that if a Regiment is an artificial Being, then so is a human Being. Tucker, thus, was forced to argue further for his presumed unity and individuality of the self. He began to do this in *Man in Quest of Himself* (1763b) by suggesting that we have 'the strongest idea of substance' from our own Being. He then argued that 'what is properly You and your Existence' cannot depend on the individual material atoms of which your body is composed since these may be lost even though you persist. Nor can it depend on the continued existence of your perceptual organs or the nerves of the brain since (he assumed) you also persist whether or not these are available for use. Finally, he argued that if materialism were true, the self would have to be composed of a 'fifth element', to be placed at a location in the brain where it can 'receive notices' from the organs of perception and then control the organism's activities.

As we saw in Chapter 2, Tucker used examples of both fission and fusion to argue that this 'fifth element' could be divided and reappear in other brains at other times. He said, for instance, that two persons could contribute to form one new person, who would never experience himself as either of these contributing persons. Quite apart from such exotic possibilities, Tucker claimed that it is likely that in the normal course of events the particles of which any such fifth element is composed would change constantly throughout an individual's life, compatibly with the individual person's persisting. He concluded:

> Then if *You* are a real Being and substance, and are not barely a form
> or mode of existence in something else, and if your Existence and

Personality remains the same throughout all the stages of life, from infancy to extreme old age, notwithstanding all the changes of particles in your drop; may we not argue, as we did before, concerning the nerves and the organs, that they are no parts of *You*, but channels to convey perception to something else, which is numerically and substantially *Yourself*?

(Tucker 1763b: 206)

Tucker assumed that the materialist has no answer to this question. He, thus, concluded that the individual is a simple indivisible, immaterial substance.

Tucker then asserted that 'into whatever composition this Individual enters, we esteem it *Ourselves* for the time, notwithstanding fluctuation of its parts; provided they fall into the same connection, and serve the same uses their predecessors did before' (Ibid.). The conclusion that Tucker reached is, in many respects, hardly different from that of Descartes, that the mind is an indivisible, immaterial substance, attached to a body and controlling it from a central location in the brain. However, Tucker went on to argue that while an individual spiritual substance is necessary for perception and action, it is not sufficient. In his view, without a body of some sort, an immaterial spirit can neither perceive nor act, nor know itself as a self, nor think. Tucker's naturalistic sympathies ran deep.

Beginning with a view of self as immaterial soul which might have placed him in the seventeenth century, Tucker could not accept that the soul thinks independently of the body and then through its mental activity affects the body. Instead of this, he claimed that 'a pure creative spirit [would be] no more a thinking than a walking or speaking substance'. He said that the faculty of thinking, or reasoning', rather than 'a primary property of the mind', is a product of its 'composition with a certain system of matter', namely, a fine corporeal substance, which he called 'mental organization' (Tucker 1763a: 76).

Tucker claimed that the same spirit could attach itself to different human bodies. In this, he departed even further from Descartes, Clarke, and Butler. Tucker claimed that the spirit could not carry any residue of its previous bodily existences with it. In attaching itself to different bodies it would become different persons. Thus, it follows, on his view, that identity of spirit has little to do with personal identity. And he had another reason, connected with his recognition of the importance of self-concern, for denying that identity of spirit has much to do with personal identity. He said that 'our concern lies only with the future and it behoves us to shape our behaviour in such a manner as may make our condition happy hereafter', and that 'If we could demonstrate our Pre-existence ever so clearly, we could not expect to know what passed with us in that state, nor gather from thence a fund of experience whereon to build observations for regulating our future conduct' (Ibid.: 171). So, our pre-existence does not matter to us.

But, then, why should our post-existence (in the afterlife) matter? Wouldn't our future self be in the same position of ignorance with respect to our present life as we are with respect to any previous life? And if it would be, why should we concern ourselves with a future existence? Tucker devoted most of the third volume of *The Light of Nature Pursued* (1768), particularly in a chapter titled 'The Vision', to answering such questions. In that chapter, which is purportedly based on a dream, Tucker leaves his body to converse with departed souls, with whom he discusses his theory of the afterlife. In this conversation, Locke is his guide.

Tucker introduced his 'Vision' chapter with two others, one on the 'vehicular state', which deals with the state of existence after death, and the other on the 'Mundane soul'. So far as the vehicular state is concerned, his main idea is that personal identity, or sense of self, can be maintained by a spirit only when it is attached to some material body, organized so that it can use the body to perceive and act. He suggested that the spirit, when in a living human being, is located in the brain and has a fragile threadlike, 'vehicular' body that allows it access to different regions of the brain. When the human dies, the vehicular body becomes released from the brain and drifts off into ordinary, physical space, where it enables the spirit to interact with other spirits, in similar states. However, this vehicular state is temporary.

Once the spirit departs from its earthly body, it can no longer remember who it is. At first, it does not even know how to use its vehicular body. It has to learn how to do this from other spirits, who act as educators. The spirit's human life, and the good or evil it there performed, affects its ability to learn since it has residues or 'concretions' of earthly existence. These do not include any memories of its earthly life, which were stored in the brain itself, but only some of the previous person's acquired dispositions, the good ones helping it to learn easily in the afterlife and encouraging joy, the evil ones inhibiting its ability to learn and encouraging suffering. Only when a spirit has been in the vehicular state for some time does it finally discover who it was as an individual on earth. For this, it must wait for others to inform it of its past life, through a special form of communication available in the vehicular state. Such communication eventually provides the spirit with knowledge of both its earthly inner and outer life. Its inner life is known to other spirits by means of their having observed its outer expression, when it was connected to a body on earth.

The vehicular state is only a temporary one. Good spirits exist or will exist in this state for a shorter period than evil spirits. Once all the negative dispositions have worn themselves out, the vehicular body becomes flexible and airy. It is then released and the spirit joins the mundane soul, a kind of collective unity of all purified spirits. When this happens to an individual spirit, it *entirely loses its sense of identity* and becomes just one more spirit in the mundane soul.

The mundane soul is the collective unity of all spirits, each of which, though qualitatively identical to each of the others, has its own powers of perception and action. Such powers are the creative source for all activity in the universe.

As a host of others before him had also claimed, Tucker thought that pure matter, or *hyle*, as he called it, does not have any powers of its own, except the capacity to move as an effect of something else acting on it. In contrast to Clarke, Newton, and Berkeley, for whom God was the source of all activity in the universe except what occurs through impact, in Tucker's view, the mundane soul is responsible. He said that all organized objects and events are under the control of particular spirits.

Initially, immaterial spirits in the mundane soul are without any special identity whatsoever. Each, initially, is a perfect copy of the initial state of each of the others. Tucker realized that in thus stripping the soul of its associated mental dispositions, he thereby raised the issue of whether in the soul's persisting, what matters in survival has been preserved. In his view, it has been preserved, but for a curious reason. The soul, freed of its association with the vehicular body, 'becomes reabsorbed into the ocean from whence she sprung', which is the soul's highest good. Thus, the cycle is completed. Individual spirits begin in the mundane soul; then some of them enter into union with an earthly body; then, at bodily death, they leave their earthly bodies, but with a fragile vehicular body; finally, they shed their vehicular bodies to become reabsorbed into the mundane soul. In Tucker's view, 'the most desirable thing for Psyche ["the soul"] would be not to have been born [as a human or any other sort of organism] at all, and the next [most] desirable to have died as soon as [it was] born', before it acquired accretions (Tucker 1768–77: v. 3, 561). Yet, spirits in the mundane soul have no experiences that are uniquely their own since they are in perfect communication with each other. Some of them never become material beings. Others become anything from a plant, to an animal, to a human. But the personalities that spirits acquire as humans are materially based. Ultimately, as we have seen, the spirits shed their human personalities and are left with none of their own. Clearly, there was nothing mundane about Tucker's spirit!

In the last volume of Tucker's *The Light of Nature Pursued* (1768–77), he discussed Lucretius on personal identity and self-concern (see Introduction, n. 1) in the course of reflecting on Law's, recently published, forensic interpretation of Locke. Tucker granted to Law that his interpretation is an accurate reading of Locke's position, but he felt that this approach, whatever practical uses it may have, for instance, in convincing Christians that they ought to be concerned about their continued consciousness into the afterlife, is not adequate to determine what metaphysically constitutes personal identity. To show this, he considered the idea proposed by the anonymous writer to which Law had responded, who had proposed that 'continuation of thought' constitutes personal identity.[4] As a prelude to considering this interpretation, Tucker wrote that although 'romantic suppositions', that is hypothetical examples of impossible situations, 'I find, are not to every body's liking', the anonymous author surely 'will not be angry with me for making them, because he practices the like himself'. So:

> Let him [the anonymous author] then please to suppose a new Planet or habitable Earth created with a thousand men, who should continue to think during their abode thereon: but at the end of twenty years one half of them were annihilated, and as many new men created in their room, who should begin to think the moment the former left off. Suppose farther, that after a second twenty years the remaining half of the first men, were likewise annihilated, and succeeded by an equal number of fresh men, who should go on with their trains of thought for a third score of years. Here would be just a thousand uninterrupted continuations of thought, and no more, during the whole time: yet who will say the men of the last score were the same persons with those of the first?

Tucker then attributed to the anonymous author the view that people 'think without ceasing' and that 'it is our thinking that makes us persons; for the table which never thinks, is no person'.

> Be it so: then our thinking constitutes us persons; but what constitutes us different persons? for I am not you, nor you me. Surely not our thinking, for in that respect we are exactly the same: what else then can it be unless our substantial or numerical diversity? We may have different heights, shapes, gaits, gestures, voices, or wear different coloured cloaths, and folks may know us from one another by those marks: but these are evidences of our being different persons, not what constitutes us such. Neither in our fictitious Planet, can you ever make out a thousand continuations subsisting at one time, any otherwise than by considering them as the thoughts of so many persons, each distinguished from the rest in some other respect than that of their thinking. Thus you see the same objection actually lies against the continuation, as I had supposed lying against consciousness.
>
> (Tucker 1768–77: v. 7, 6–8)

Tucker concluded that 'the idea of person must precede that of continuation: so it is no help to tell me I may find my personality by my continuation, because I must settle my idea of personality before I can make use of the explanation'.

Soon after, Tucker turns to a discussion of Lucretius and self-concern, claiming that Lucretius took advantage of a 'prejudice among mankind' to lure young recruits to his cause 'by the promise of an indemnity for all the wickedness they might please to commit: well knowing that any specious sophisms would serve to prove his point, if he could once get them to wish it true'.

> For if the soul be nothing more than a result from the dispositions of certain material atoms in a very curious organization, whenever the

organization is broken up, there is an end of the soul, and all possibility of punishment removed. It had been objected against him, that since chance never ceases working, she might at some future time cast the same atoms together again into an arrangement precisely the same with that they stand in at present, in which case the same soul must return. He granted that the atoms would fall into their former situation . . . but he denied that this would be the same soul.

Tucker continued:

And your friend [by proposing that continuation of thinking is sufficient for personal identity] in like manner has fortified me against all alarm of a future reckoning. If your God designed me an accountable creature, he has managed very ill in making me mortal, because he will thereby put it out of his own power ever to call me to an account hereafter. What if he should work a resurrection of my atoms, and set them a thinking again? this would be a new creation, another continuation of a thought, another person, not me, nor anywise affecting me. Therefore, I will think freely and act freely, kiss the girls and put the bottle about, as long as I can: and when I can think and act no longer, then good night to you all, I shall sleep sound enough, I warrant. Why should Lucry the Second care what becomes of Lucry the Third? let the devils pinch, and scourge, and burn, till they are tired, I shall feel nothing of them. But sure he can never be so unjust as to have another boy flogged for naughty tricks played by me.

He then excused the anonymous author; and, no doubt, Law as well because of his Christian beliefs, but expressed concern about 'freethinkers' that would need more convincing in order to live a moral life. Finally, he concluded that while 'consciousness may do well enough for Mr. Locke's purpose, and that most useful one of impressing the idea of an after-reckoning upon the generality', for the purpose 'of accurately understanding our nature, I humbly conceive it necessary to place the identity of the person in that of the substance, and its essence in the faculty of perceptivity' (Ibid.: 13–17).

Even though Tucker was undaunted by metaphysical extravagance, he tried to empirically ground his bizarre speculations. In the case of humans, his immaterial spirits are little more than placeholders for unknown functions of the brain that provide unity to perceptions. They have no 'lives' of their own. All of the functions the spirits perform in a human depend on physical properties of the human. And a spirit's personality is simply that of its associated human's brain. All that is required to convert a theory like Tucker's into one like Priestley's, to be discussed in a moment, is to give matter power both to think and to unify experiences.

Although Tucker admired Hartley, he thought that Hartley's mechanistic theory was naive. But Tucker was not opposed to mechanism *per se*. However, since he could not see how matter could either think or be active entirely on its own, he posited immaterial spirits to perform these functions. But then he gave them no independent earthly life of their own. Priestley, on the other hand, adopted the mechanistic theory of Hartley and saw that if matter could think there was no need to posit anything immaterial. At about the same time, Kant saw more clearly the problems of unity of mind that bothered Tucker but never bothered Priestley. Of course, Kant also argued that metaphysical flights of fancy, such as Tucker's, are worse than useless. And Hazlitt, who held Tucker in the highest esteem, would on the basis of more naturalistic ideas, but similar concerns, anticipate much that is central to the debate in our own times over personal identity and what matters in survival.

Thomas Reid

Reid entered Marischal College, Aberdeen, when he was 12 years old. He was the student of George Turnbull, who, along with Francis Hutcheson, was one of the initiators of the Scottish Enlightenment. Turnbull accepted Berkeley's immaterialism, but was interested in applying the methods of natural science to pneumatology and moral philosophy, in addition to vision. Reid became attracted to pneumatology through Turnbull, and wholeheartedly accepted his views, including the idea that 'common sense' should be the final arbiter in all questions. However, in 1739, when Reid was introduced to Hume's *Treatise*, he abandoned his commitment to Berkeley. Apparently what most disturbed him upon reading Hume, was not that the existence of a material world was called into question (Berkeley had already done that), but the rejection of spiritual substance.

At the time of his introduction to Hume, Reid was a pastor at New Machar, a post which he held for nine years. He went from there to Aberdeen. And in 1763 he was offered the post of moral philosophy at Glasgow, replacing the retiring Adam Smith. The following year he published *An Inquiry into the Human Mind on the Principles of Common Sense* (1764). Ten years later, this book was criticized by Priestley, who as a scientific materialist argued against the authority of common sense (Priestley 1774). Reid did not respond immediately, except for an anonymously published review of Priestley's subsequent republication of Hartley's work (Priestley 1775; Wood 1995: 35–6). It seems likely, however, that Reid's next two books were, in part, a response to Priestley. In them, Reid defended common sense and tried on empirical grounds to justify believing in a distinct mental or spiritual realm, not reducible to the material, to be studied by different methods. Subsequently, many thinkers would agree with Reid on his methodological point without sharing his commitment to the immaterial soul.

Reid was an exemplary empirical methodologist. He believed strongly that Newtonian methods could be applied to the mental or spiritual world. Hume, of course, had made a similar suggestion, but Reid was more consistent than Hume in putting it into practice. One of Reid's main criticisms of Hume was that Hume's suppositions about the relations between impressions and ideas could not be justified empirically, given what was known about how the senses functioned. In the *Essays on the Intellectual Powers of Man* (1785), Reid drew the consequence, in apparent reference to Hume, that, 'if we conceive the mind to be immaterial – of which I think we have very strong proofs – we shall find it difficult to affix a meaning to [the words] *impressions made upon it*' (Reid 1785: 254).

Also in the *Essays*, Reid criticized Hume for supposing that there is nothing more to mind than a 'succession of related ideas and impressions, of which we have an intimate memory and consciousness'. Reid pointed out that on this view of mind, all agency is lost. He asked 'to be farther instructed, whether the impressions remember and are conscious of the ideas, or the ideas remember and are conscious of the impressions, or if both remember and are conscious of both? and whether the ideas remember those that come after them, as well as those that were before them?' His point was that since ideas and impressions are passive, they cannot do anything, whereas Hume implies that the 'succession of ideas and impressions not only remembers and is conscious' but also 'judges, reasons, affirms, denies', even 'eats and drinks, and is sometimes merry and sometimes sad'. Reid concluded, 'If these things can be ascribed to a succession of ideas and impressions in a consistency of common sense, I should be very glad to know what is nonsense' (Ibid.: 444).

In these criticisms, Reid, the immaterialist about the mind, criticized Hume, the immaterialist about everything, for not being able to explain, on immaterialist grounds, the difference between impressions and ideas. Here, Reid did not criticize Hume's metaphysics so much as his account of the origins of ideas. As we have seen, Reid argued that, on Hume's view, in which substance has no place, agency would have no place either. Reid thought it would be absurd to deny agency; so, substance had to be reintroduced. But even though Reid assumed that the need for substance is an argument for immaterial substance, actually, so far as his argument goes, it merely shows the need for substance of some sort. In any case, this is one of the few places in Reid's published work where his metaphysics of the soul may have made a substantive difference to the scientific account he was trying to develop.

In his first book, on *Common Sense* (1764), Reid insisted on a rigorous introspective method for the discovery of the principles by which we sense and perceive the external world.[5] Reid not only appealed to introspection but insisted that it was essential in knowing the mind. Here Reid's methodological innovations were relatively free of their metaphysical underpinning, which is partly why they could be so consequential later, to thinkers who did not share his commitment to the immaterial soul.

Reid had learned from Hume that laws of the natural world could be known only as causal regularities and only inductively. In his later works, he insisted that knowledge of mental phenomena is different. Only through introspection can we acquire direct knowledge of ourselves as agents. Since we are the agents of our actions, Reid reasoned that our actions cannot be understood in terms of mere regularities, but only as relations involving necessity. He claimed further that the mental is not directly accessible to us through physiological investigations, which could only provide material for speculation. Thus, on what he took to be empirical grounds, Reid defended a methodological dualism that is committed to a separation of mental from physical science. He believed that the study of the physical or natural world had to be kept distinct from the study of the mental and that there are no intelligible laws joining these two.

However, Reid's dualism, for all its apparent dependence on a modest empiricism, was metaphysically based. His career as a whole shows a clear attempt to defend traditional Christian beliefs about the soul and the afterlife against the skeptical onslaught of Hume and the materialism of Priestley. Although, in his published works, Reid's modesty and desire to develop an empirically based mental science kept him from often revealing his religious or metaphysical views, they nevertheless do appear there occasionally, and much more frequently in the lectures upon which his published works were based.

Perhaps most revealing of Reid's metaphysical position, is the introductory lecture to his course on 'pneumatology, ethics, and politics', recently published from hand-written manuscripts. In this lecture, he first suggests that ethics and politics depend so much on pneumatology, that they 'can not be understood nor treated scientifically' unless they are built upon it. He then described pneumatology, in a passage almost identical to that found in the later-written preface to his *Essays on the Intellectual Powers* (1785):

> All Human Knowledge is employed either about Body or Mind, about things Material or things Intellectual. The whole System of Bodies in the Universe, of which we know but a very little part, may be called the Material World; And the whole System of Minds or thinking Beings in the Universe, from the Infinite Creator to the meanest Creature endued with thought, may be called the Intellectual World. About the one or the other of these or something pertaining to them all Sciences treat, & all Arts are occupied. Those are the two great Kingdoms of Nature to which human thought is limited. Nor can the boldest flight of Imagination carry beyond their limits.
>
> (Reid 1990: 103)[6]

Reid imagined here a great divide between the sciences of nature and mind. But he also wondered if there might be a middle ground:

> Whether there be in the Universe any other kinds of being, which are neither Extended Solid and inert like Body, nor thinking &

intelligent like Mind is beyond the Reach of our Knowledge; and therefore it would be rash to determine. There is indeed a vast interval between Body & Mind; whether there may be some intermediate Substance that connects them together we know not. We have no Reason to ascribe Intelligence, or even Sensation to Plants, yet there is an active Force and Energy in them which cannot be the result of any arrangement of inert Matter. The same thing may be said of those active Powers by which animals grow & by which Matter gravitates, by which Electrical & Magnetical Bodies attract and repell each other, & by which the parts of Solid Bodies cohere. Some have conjectured that the Phenomena of the Material World which require active Force are produced by the continual operation of intelligent Beings. Others have conjectured that there may be in the Universe Beings that are active without Intelligence, which as a kind of incorporeal Machinery contrived by the supreme Wisdom perform their destined task without any Knowledge or Intention. But laying aside conjecture & all pretence to form Determinations in things beyond the reach of the human faculties we must rest in this that Body and Mind are the only kinds of Being of which we have any Knowledge or can form any Conception.

(Ibid.: 103–4)

Reid concluded that 'If there are other kinds they are not discoverable by the faculties which God hath given us', then 'with regard to us' they are 'as if they were not'. He maintained, with Berkeley but against Priestley, that there is no reason to take matter alone as having any active powers, let alone such powers as might account for life and mentality. The result of Reid's empirical strategy was to open up a vast chasm between body and mind.

Reid next turned to pneumatology, first indicating that although there may be a great variety of 'Minds or Thinking Beings Throughout this vast Universe' we cannot know them. Unlike Grove, Reid limited pneumatology to minds that are either directly accessible or whose activities can be understood through analogy with our own mind. This included Brutes and God, but excluded 'Angels', who can be known only through the 'Doctrine of Revelation' and do 'not belong to Philosophy but to theology'. Reid's pneumatology, thus, differed from Grove's in being less about 'spirits' *per se*, than about mind in manifestations accessible to empirical study (Ibid.: 104–5).

In Reid's view, the first branch of pneumatology 'treats of the human Mind, To which Wolfius has given the name of Psychologie', while 'the other treats of the Supreme Mind, and commonly goes by the name of Natural Theology'. He noted that 'as the human Mind seems to be possessed of all the Faculties which we observe in Brutes, besides some of a Superior Nature of which there is no appearance in the most sagacious Brutes; there is no Necessity for treating separately the Minds of Brutes' (Ibid.: 105).

Earlier, Christian Wolff had written two works, *Psychologia Empirica* (1738) and *Psychologia Rationalis* (1740), in which he divided psychology into two disciplines, one empirical, and one rational (or, a priori). Eventually, rational psychology fell by the wayside, partly due to the influence of Kant. By the mid-nineteenth century the term *psychology* had been generally adopted for the science of mind, displacing the term *pneumatology*. So, for instance, to Reid's statement in the preface to his *Essays on the Intellectual Powers* that 'the branch which treats of the nature and operations of minds has, by some, been called Pneumatology', Hamilton added the footnote: 'Now properly super-seded by the term *Psychology*; to which no competent objection can be made', which yields the 'convenient adjective, *psychological*' (Reid 1863: v. 1, 217). In the *Essays*, Reid does not actually characterize his own work as *pneumatology*, but says that 'some' have labelled the science that treats 'of the nature and operations of minds' pneumatology. In the lectures, he takes up the topics of Natural Theology and rational psychology, which in the *Essays* are not con-sidered. It is perhaps the different goals of the *Essays* and Reid's Lectures that caused him to be more reserved in the *Essays*.

This difference in emphasis can be seen in how Reid continued:

> We are therefore First to treat of the human Mind which is one con-stituent part of Man & the noblest part; & here we shall endeavour first to explain as distinctly as we are able the various powers and Faculties of the human Mind & then shew what Reason discovers of its nature & duration whether it be material or immaterial Whether we have reason to think that it shall perish with the Body or continue to live in some future State.
>
> (Reid 1990: 105)

This passage does not appear in the preface to the *Essays*, though the preceding and subsequent passages are included. Undoubtedly, this passage indicates that Reid's lectures included both empirical and rational psych-ology, both of which were part of typical courses on pneumatology, such as Grove's, but would be inappropriate in a book, such as Reid's *Essays*, in which the author intended to deal purely with empirical psychology.

In Reid's lectures on rational psychology (which have not yet been published), he argued against the possibility of thinking matter and in favour of a simple immaterial substance, naturally immortal, as the essence of the human mind. In his recently published papers on 'animate creation', he argued against materialism, showing in the process that he not only had read the earlier debate between Clarke and Collins but strongly sided with Clarke (Wood 1995):

> If Mr. Locke had believed that the essential Qualities of Matter and of thought are such as that both cannot subsist in the same Subject, he

certainly would have changed his Opinion. Since Mr. Locke wrote two attempts [by Clarke and Euler] have been made to prove this, by which the immateriality of thinking substances is put in a clearer Light than it was before. Dr. Samuel Clarke one of the greatest Metaphysicians of this Age, has endeavoured to shew that the divisibility of Matter is inconsistent with its being the Subject of Thought. Matter is made up of parts each of which is a distinct Substance & has its own inherent Qualities. Every Quality in the whole is compounded of parts of the same Quality inherent in some or in all the parts of the compound substance. Every part being a distinct Substance whatever is inherent in one part cannot be the same that is inherent in another part. External Denominations such as Figure or Place or Use may be common to the Whole, but no inherent Quality can. Thinking is an inherent Quality in its proper Subject, the thinking Being. To suppose one part of a thought to be in one Substance and another part of the same Thought in another Substance appears to be absurd. The Subject of Thought therefore must be one individual Substance. But no Matter nor part of Matter is one individual Substance & therefore Matter cannot be the Subject of Thought.

(Ibid.: 230–1)

Reid added:

This Argument was fully examined by Mr. Collins the most Acute of those who took to themselves the name of Freethinkers. His Objections & Dr. Clarks Answers (which appear to me very satisfying) are extant in several Replies & Duplies. of which therefore I shall say nothing more.

(Ibid.: 231)

Thus, the battle, in Reid's view, was as much religious as scientific.

In his earlier unpublished manuscript review of Priestley's book on Hartley, an edited version of which appeared anonymously in *Monthly Review*, Reid wrote of Priestley's essay on materialism:

It has been thought that Dr. Sam Clark has demonstrated the impossibility of Matter's being the Subject of Thought. But we learn from Dr. Priestley that all was labour in vain. That perception and all the mental Powers of Man are the Result of such an Organical Structure as that of the brain.... How would Epicurus? How would Hobbes? How would Collins have triumphed had they lived to see this point given up to them, even by a Christian Divine?

(Ibid.: 133)

It is the Christians versus the pagans, with Priestley in the role of a double-agent, posing as a Divine in order to sap the Christians' moral fiber from within.

In his published works, Reid tried to be more rigorously scientific. In *Essays on the Intellectual Powers*, he observed that 'In the gradual progress of man, from infancy to maturity, there is a certain order in which his faculties are unfolded. . . . The external senses appear first; memory soon follows' (Reid 1785: 339). Thus, as we saw also in the case of Hartley, by the time Reid wrote, the idea of thinking about the human mind as a developmental process had begun to take hold. Reid then distinguished between the senses and memory on the grounds that the senses 'give us information of things only as they exist in the present moment', while memory gives us 'immediate knowledge of things past'. However, in both cases, the person involved is related directly to the object in question, not indirectly through the medium of an 'idea' or any other sort of mental representation. This was part of Reid's response to what he saw as the assumptions which led to the skeptical consequences of 'the way of ideas'. Further, in Reid's view, when we are remembering some event in the past, we know immediately, and in virtue of the act of remembering itself, rather than by inference from something else, both that we are remembering and that the object of memory is in the past, that is, that we believe in the existence of the objects of memory as existing in the past. However, such knowledge, though immediate, depends on the prior development of the faculty of memory.

In what is another good illustration of Reid's interest in developmental issues, he remarked that in the case of children or people who are mentally impaired, memory may *fail* to give rise to belief in what is remembered and imagination may *give rise* to belief in what is imagined. Yet, 'in mature years, and in a sound state of mind, every man feels that he must believe what he distinctly remembers, though he can give no other reason of his belief, but that he remembers the thing distinctly; whereas, when he merely imagines a thing ever so distinctly, he has no belief of it upon that account' (Ibid.: 340). In a subsequent chapter, Reid suggested that infants, before they acquire the capacity to reflect on their own thoughts, tend to be totally absorbed in their perceptions, and may not then distinguish memory from imagination but that later they will be able to distinguish between perception, memory, and imagination.

In his account of personal identity, Reid began by noting that 'the conviction which every man has of his Identity, as far back as his memory reaches, needs no aid of philosophy to strengthen it; and no philosophy can weaken it, without first producing some degree of insanity'. Thus, 'there can be no memory of what is past without the conviction that we existed at the time remembered'. Reid continued, 'There may be good arguments to convince me that I existed before the earliest thing I can remember; but to suppose that my memory reaches a moment farther back than my belief and conviction of my existence, is a contradiction' (Ibid.: 344). Although Reid did not specifically say so, he seemed to suppose that, if we are rational, we automatically take ownership of the past thoughts, experiences, and actions that we remember. It seems, then, that Reid's continuing commitment to a reflexive account at least of memory, if not of all consciousness, may have prevented him from extending his new approach to a developmental account of the acquisition of self-concepts. In any case, Reid clearly has the view that we earlier speculated that Locke might have held: that while self-conceptions only kick in after a certain amount of psychological development, once they do kick in, they kick in as a whole, and not just piecemeal.

If a person loses conviction in the existence of the past – Reid was here thinking of what he took to be possible cases of amnesia – then 'past things are done away; and in his own belief, he only then [at that moment] begins to exist. Whatever was thought, or said, or done, or suffered before that period, may belong to some other person; but he can never impute it to himself, or take any subsequent step that supposes it to be his doing' (Ibid.). Although Reid here sounds Lockean, he does not really mean that people do not exist prior to the time of their earliest memories. Probably what he means (perhaps in implicit if only partial acknowledgement of Locke's views on appropriation) is that – subjectively, so far as the person's own phenomenological sense of who they are and what belongs to them, as part of them, is concerned, and not taking into account the corrections that people make on intellectual grounds to that subjective sense of who they are – we impute to ourselves only events that happened during periods after which we began remembering.

Reid expressed a view about unity of consciousness that Kant developed about the same time, although almost surely Reid did not know of Kant's view:

> We may observe, first of all, that this conviction ['which every man has of his identity as far back as his memory reaches'] is indispensably necessary to all exercise of reason. The operations of reason, whether in action or in speculation, are made up of successive parts. The antecedent are the foundation of the consequent, and, without the conviction that the antecedent had been seen or done by me, I could have no reason to procede to the consequent, in any speculation, or in any active project whatever.
>
> (Ibid.)

In concluding this thought, Reid remarked that 'it is evident that we must have the conviction of our own continued existence and identity, as soon as we are capable of thinking or doing anything, on the account of what we have thought, or done, or suffered before, that is, as soon as we are reasonable creatures'.

Reid then turned to an investigation of 'what is meant by identity in general, what by our own personal identity, and how we are led into that invincible belief and conviction which every man has of his own personal identity, as far as memory reaches'. He claimed that identity is too simple a concept to be defined, though 'every man of common sense has a clear and distinct notion' of identity and that it 'supposes an uninterrupted continuance of existence'. However, in the case of the concept of person, 'it is, perhaps, more difficult to ascertain with precision the meaning of Personality; but it is not necessary in the present subject: it is sufficient for our purpose to observe, that all mankind place their personality in something that cannot be divided or consist of parts. A part of the person is a manifest absurdity' (Ibid.: 344–5).

Reid continued:

> My personal identity, therefore, implies the continued existence of that indivisible thing which I call myself. Whatever this self may be, it is something which thinks, and deliberates, and resolves, and acts, and suffers. I am not thought, I am not action, I am not feeling; I am something that thinks, and acts, and suffers. My thoughts and actions, and feelings, change every moment – they have no continued, but a successive existence; but that *self* or *I*, to which they belong, is permanent, and has the same relation to all the succeeding thoughts, actions, and feelings, which I call mine.
>
> (Ibid.: 345)

The supposition here is that our notion of ourselves is of an indivisible and continued 'monad' which remains identical to itself, even though its properties constantly change.

But is this notion of ourselves as an indivisible monad 'merely a fancy without reality?' The skeptic will ask, 'What evidence have you, that there is such a permanent self which has a claim to all the thoughts, actions, and feelings, which you call yours?' Reid answers: 'remembrance'.

> I remember that, twenty years ago, I conversed with such a person; I remember several things that passed in that conversation; my memory testifies not only that this was done, but that it was done by me who now remember it. If it was done by me, I must have existed at that time, and continued to exist from that time to the present: if the identical person whom I call myself, had not a part in that conversation, my memory is fallacious – it gives a distinct and positive testimony of what is not true. Every man in his senses believes what he distinctly remembers, and everything he remembers convinces him that he existed at the time remembered.
>
> (Ibid.)

We also believe we existed at times for which we have no memories but for which we have evidence of our existence, based upon the reports of others. However, in Reid's view, in comparison with memory, such testimony provides inferior evidence of identity.

Reid asserted that 'we probably at first derive our notion of identity from that natural conviction which every man has from the dawn of reason of his own identity and continued existence'. The conviction is of the identity and continued existence of a simple, indivisible self, not of that self's operations. In Reid's view, 'the operations of our minds are all successive, and have no continued existence. But the thinking being has a continued existence; and we have an invincible belief that it remains the same when all its thoughts and operations change'. Thus, 'the identity of a person is a perfect identity' that 'admits of no degrees' (Ibid.). The identities of other things, by contrast, at least in so far as their identities can be known, whether of objects or of other persons, is imperfect. These other identities are known only through external perception of similarity, which in the absence of evidence to the contrary, can be sufficient to establish them. However, each of us has a certain knowledge, based on memory, of our own identity over time, and we willingly generalize such identity to other human beings. In the case of other material objects, however, identity is determined based on verbal agreement, since the matter out of which such objects are composed constantly changes.

From a scientific point of view, Reid's common sense epistemology and psychology of mind was in many ways an advance upon his predecessors. He took as given the world as it appears to us and tried to determine what mental faculties would give rise to our experiencing such a world. Whatever the philosophical merits of such an approach, it can have advantages scientifically. Reid's theory of perception is a case in point. It is superior to a kind of theory that could be based on a much more skeptical approach, such as Hume's. But, in other contexts, Reid too sometimes confused epistemology and psychology. Because he believed that the experience of mental unity, and the evidences of memory, reveal that we are essentially simple, unified mental beings, not decomposable like matter, he believed that he was warranted in concluding that the mind is an immaterial substance, and that body and mind must be investigated in separate sciences. Kant, in the first *Critique*, which was written close in time to Reid's *Essays*, would argue more perceptively that this sort of reliance on rational psychology yields only paralogisms of reason and is, hence, invalid. A problem with Reid's approach in such instances, is that he sometimes took as epistemological intuition what was merely psychological illusion. And he did this because he did not recognize adequately the relevance of folk-psychological and cultural influences on what appears to be solidly based in common sense. Hence, at a fundamental level his common sense philosophy sometimes became entangled with his scientific psychology.

Joseph Priestley

Priestley and Reid provide an interesting contrast. Both were Christian ministers who spent much of their careers as teachers, engaged in advancing science and writing on philosophical issues. However, Reid's scientific and

132

philosophical interests focused mainly on investigating the human mind, while Priestley's focused mainly on chemistry, electricity, and promoting materialism. In Priestley's view, the science of mind ('knowledge of *ourselves*') was not a dream but a reality, for which Hartley deserved most of the credit: 'Something was done in this field of knowledge by Descartes, very much by Mr. Locke, but most of all by Dr. Hartley'. Priestley then added, in a frenzy of hyperbole, that Hartley 'has thrown more useful light upon the theory of the mind than Newton did upon the theory of the natural world' (Priestley 1774: 2). Priestley's own interest in the science of mind was limited mainly to a critique of the philosophy of common sense, which included Reid's own first work, and to propagating a materialistic version of Hartley's associationist psychology (Priestley 1774, 1775). Priestley also wrote two philosophical works on matter, spirit, and necessarianism, in which he defended materialism pretty much as materialists today often defend it (Priestley 1777; Priestley and Price 1778). Whereas most eighteenth-century materialists viewed matter as entirely passive, in Priestley's view, it is essentially active. Priestley claimed that attraction and repulsion are responsible for all of the energetic powers of matter. Going further, his research into chemistry included investigations of photosynthesis and the role of oxygen in animal life. As such, he contributed importantly to the development of nineteenth century biochemistry.

Needless to add, in their metaphysical and religious views also, Reid and Priestley contrasted sharply. While Reid held on conservatively to the traditional belief in an immaterial soul or mind, Priestley embraced materialism, with little concern about tradition, so long as he could maintain his own liberal version of Christianity. The latter was so liberal, that many Christians, including Reid, looked on him as a pariah, while atheists tended to accept him as one of their own. Yet, Priestley, like Hartley, was a paradigm of that fusion of theologian and scientist that flourished during the Enlightenment, particularly in England. He faced the facts of science and history head on, and modified his Christianity so as to make faith consistent with reason.

Such differences between Reid and Priestley were reflected in their respective approaches to understanding the human mind. Reid, though an empiricist, assumed that the relations between mind and body could never be worked out entirely by empirical methods. Furthermore, he claimed that all hypotheses not based directly on observation of nature or of mind should be avoided, and that 'common sense' should be relied on to provide the basic truths upon which all else is built. In contrast, Priestley, impressed by the success of material science and of certain simply expressed hypotheses about the human mind, embraced a general theory based on a materialist philosophy and an associationist psychology. At the same time he criticized Reid's system for its plethora of instincts and unnecessary first principles, and for its being based on common sense rather than on science. In sum, while Reid used his inductive empiricism to resist materialism, Priestley used his more deductive scientific approach to promote it.

In Priestley's view, Reid's tendency to rely on first principles sinned against the simplicity of nature, as well as against Hartley's insights. In addition, Priestley thought advertising principles as 'instinctive' impeded inquiry into their justification. To illustrate how much Reid relied on instinctive principles, arranged in no particular order, Priestley made up a table of twelve of them, of which he remarked, 'My reader will, I suspect, imagine with me, that this catalogue of original instinctive principles is pretty large, and that when nature had gone so far in this track, but little could be wanting to accomplish all her purposes; and that, with respect to *principles*, little remained to be done by any other means'. Reid, Priestley continued, 'thinks differently' (Priestley 1774: 9). Priestley then quoted Reid as having said that since 'the original perceptions which nature gives are insufficient for the purposes of life' nature 'has made men capable of acquiring many more perceptions by habit'. Priestley says that it is his own objective 'to relieve dame nature of the unnecessary load which Dr. Reid has laid upon her, by ascribing a little more to habit, and to the necessary connections and consequences of things than he has done'. Indeed, Priestley would ascribe *a lot more* to habit, or rather to 'the association of ideas', which, in his view, is often an unconscious process. He concluded that much reliance on 'ultimate principles necessarily checks all farther inquiry, and is therefore of great disservice in philosophy'. In fact, Priestley suggests, all of Reid's instinctive principles are 'actually acquired', and 'nothing more than so many different cases of the old and well known principle of association of ideas' (Ibid.: 18–19, 22–3).

As an example of the power of habit to explain, Priestley cites the case of his own playing of the flute. He says that 'though I am no great proficient on the instrument, there are some tunes which I now very often play without ever attending to my fingers, or explicitly to the tune'.

> Now, reasoning as Dr. Reid does, I should conclude that, in this case, no skill, acquired by habit, was employed, but that my fingers were guided by some original instinctive principle; and if I had been able to do this earlier than my remembrance of any thing, I must have said that this was one of those powers, which, being latent in the mind, was called forth by proper circumstances. Whereas, I think it more natural to say, that the association between the ideas of certain sounds and the cause of certain motions of the fingers became in time so perfect, that the one introduced the other, without any attention; the intervening express volition, previous to each motion, having been gradually excluded. Facts of this kind demonstrate that the power of association is so great, and so extensive, that even whole trains and very long trains of ideas, are by this means so connected, that if the first take place, all the rest will follow of course.
>
> (Ibid.: 69)

By such means, Priestley claimed, Reid's so-called instinctive principles could be explained.

Priestley was a gradualist. He saw the differences between humans and other animals as differences of degree, rather than kind. And, he saw human infants as starting off more like other animals and only gradually learning adult human modes of thinking, including even the ability to conceptualize themselves:

> We see, then, that a child, or brute animal, is in possession of a power of pursuing pleasure and avoiding pain, and, in like manner, a power of pursuing other intermediate and different objects, in consequence of impressions made upon their minds by things external to them, without their having given any attention to the affections or operations of their minds; and indeed, consequently, without having such an idea as that of *mind* at all, or hardly of *self*. Some brute animals may possibly never advance farther than this; excepting that, their pleasurable and painful impressions being associated with a variety of particular persons and circumstances, they will necessarily acquire the rudiments of all the *passions*, as of joy and sorrow, love and hatred, gratitude and resentment, hope and fear, each of which may be as *intense*, though less *complex* than they are found in the human species.
>
> (Ibid.: liv)

In humans, though, Priestley continued, 'if time and opportunity be given for the purpose (which, for the reason assigned above, can only be obtained where there is a considerable compass of intellect, and much exercise of it) the *affections* of our ideas are as capable of being the subjects of observation as the *ideas* themselves'.

Priestley did not even mention the doctrine of the reflexive nature of consciousness, which he merely assumed is wrong, an indication of how far the science of mind had progressed since Clarke's debate with Collins. And in Priestley's supposing that brutes and children differ from adult humans in that brutes and children do not have second-order reflections, and that as a consequence their emotions are 'less complex', one can glean how far the science of mind had progressed since Hume. Finally, in Priestley's suggesting that children only gradually acquire the concept of themselves, he, in effect, invited others to explain how the notion of *self* is gradually acquired. As we shall see, his student, Hazlitt, accepted the invitation.

Priestley's rootedness in science, together with the matter of factness of his materialistic approach, was radically different from the epistemologically oriented way of ideas approach championed by Locke, Berkeley, and Hume. Although Priestley accepted 'the way of ideas', he did not think that it led to skepticism about the external world, as Reid had claimed, or, indeed, to skepticism about anything. Priestley was a realist. He did not argue for the existence of an external world, beyond simply declaring that its existence is obviously the best explanation of the fact that people report having experiences in the presence of a common stimulus.

Since realism was so unproblematic for Priestley he made a much cleaner separation between philosophy and science than Hume, in particular, had been able to do. Although Priestley did not have a lot to say about personal identity and did not even discuss fission in his main contribution to the personal identity debate (he discussed it in correspondence with Price), his understanding of related issues that fed into Hazlitt's views and that have played an important part in the personal identity debates in our own times was more subtle and clear-headed than perhaps that of any other eighteenth century thinker.

Priestley's thoughts on personal identity are primarily his attempt, in response to criticisms from more conservative Christians, to show that his materialism is compatible with the Christian idea of resurrection. He claimed, first, that 'the sentient principle *in* man' must be an extended thing. Then, to dismiss the seemingly strange hypothesis – advocated by various of the Cambridge Platonists and by Clarke – of an *extended*, and yet *immaterial* soul, he asked, 'how anything can have extension and yet be immaterial without coinciding with our idea of mere empty space', and immediately answered, 'I know not'. He, thus, concluded that 'the sentient principle in man, containing ideas which certainly have parts and are divisible and consequently must have extension, cannot be that simple, indivisible and immaterial substance that some have imagined it to be but something that has real extension and therefore may have the other properties of matter' (Priestley 1777: 163).

As follower of Hartley, Priestley thought that the sentient and thinking principle in man rather obviously must be 'a property of the nervous system or rather of the brain' (Ibid.). But he went further than Hartley in suggesting not only that the brain was necessary for human mentality, but that it was sufficient as well. In Priestley's view, it was scientifically useless to postulate an immaterial substance to account for human behavior. All of this will sound quite modern to us. However, what is truly sophisticated and innovative in Priestley's treatment of personal identity is the way he downplays the importance of personal identity per se and highlights that of the functions that belief in our own identities actually serves.

Priestley began this part of his discussion by considering an objection, which he says was made to 'the primitive Christians, as it may be at present' that 'a proper resurrection is not only, in the highest degree, improbable, but even actually impossible since, after death, the body putrefies, and the parts that composed it are dispersed, and form other bodies, which have an equal claim to the same resurrection'. He continues: 'And where, they say, can be the propriety of rewards and *punishments*, if the man that rises again be not *identically the same* with the man that acted and died?' In reply, he first makes it clear, as if just for the record, that in his opinion 'we shall be *identically the same* beings after the resurrection that we are at present'. Then, 'for the sake of those who may entertain a different opinion', he proposes to 'speculate a little upon their hypothesis' in order to show that 'it is not inconsistent with a state of future rewards and punishments, and that it supplies motives sufficient for the regulation of our conduct here, with a view to it' (Ibid.: 165). In other words, the task that Priestley sets himself is that of showing that even if after death 'resurrected selves' [our term] are not strictly identical to anyone who existed on Earth it does not make any difference since *identity is not what matters primarily in survival.* That this is Priestley's project becomes especially clear when he continues: 'And metaphysical as the subject necessarily is, I do not despair of satisfying those who will give a due attention to it, that the propriety of rewards and punishments, with our hopes and fears derived from them, do not at all depend upon *such a kind of identity* as the objection that I have stated supposes' (Ibid., emphasis added). Specifically, then, what Priestley plans to show is that neither the propriety of divine rewards and punishments nor our anticipatory hopes and fears with regard to the resurrection depends on their being resurrected persons who are strictly identical with us.

In arguing for this radical new idea, Priestley began by distinguishing between 'the identity of the man' and 'the identity of the person'. He noted that it is only the latter – personal identity – that is relevant to the present discussion. He then claimed that even if people universally and firmly came to believe that over the course of a year there was a complete change, 'though gradual and insensible', in the matter of which they were composed it 'would make no change whatever in our present conduct, or in our sense of obligation, respecting the duties of life, and the propriety of rewards and punishments; and consequently all hopes and fears, and expectations of every kind would operate exactly as before'. For, he said, 'notwithstanding the complete change of the *man*, there would be no change of what I should call the *person*'. So far as personal identity is requisite either for the propriety of rewards and punishments or for the concern that we take for our future selves, Priestley continued, endorsing Locke, 'the sameness and continuity of consciousness seems to be the only circumstance attended to by us'. Then Priestley made it clear that, in his view, whether identity per se obtains is of no great consequence:

> Admitting, therefore, that the man consists wholly of matter, as much as the river does of water, or the forest of trees, and that this matter should be wholly changed in the interval between death and the resurrection; yet, if, after this state, we shall all know one another again, and converse together as before, we shall be, *to all intents and purposes*, the same persons. Our personal identity will be *sufficiently*

preserved, and the expectation of it at present will have a proper influence on our conduct.

(Ibid.: 166–7, emphasis added)

By Priestley's use of the expressions, 'to all intents and purposes' and 'sufficiently', he here separated the questions of whether we will be identical with someone who exists in the future and of whether it matters. In other words, what Priestley is saying here is that even if the resurrected person were not strictly identical with the person on Earth, he would be close enough to being identical so that the loss of strict identity would not matter. And in considering whether strict identity does matter, he distinguished three ways in which it might: first, people's so-called self-interested concerns for their own futures; second, societal concerns that the prospect of future rewards and punishments motivate people to behave themselves; and, third, theological concerns about the propriety of divine rewards and punishments. Thus, toward the end of the eighteenth century and perhaps without inferring anything from fission examples, Priestley introduced and embraced one of the key ideas – that identity is not primarily what matters in survival – that has been central to the revolution in personal identity theory in our own times.

Following the publication of the *Disquisitions Relating to Matter and Spirit*, in which Priestley put forth this interpretation of what matters in survival, he engaged in a debate through correspondence with Richard Price, another dissenting minister, and published this correspondence the following year (Priestley and Price 1778). Price pressed Priestley on his knowledge of Clarke's views and explicitly asked him whether he has read Clarke's debate with Collins. Priestley answered that he has 'carefully read all Dr. Clarke's metaphysical works'. Then, by discussing replication, Price pursued Priestley on Priestley's interpretation of the resurrection:

> Suppose it [the soul] . . . to be merely the organization of the body; would not the change in the matter of the body make *another* body? And would not *another* body make *another* soul, though the same organization should be preserved? . . . Would not, in short, any number of living bodies be one soul, one sentient principle, supposing their organization the same?

(Ibid.: 56–9, 77–8)

Priestley answered 'that different systems of matter, organized exactly alike, must make different beings, who would feel and think exactly alike in the same circumstances. The bodies and minds of these beings would be exactly *similar*, but *numerically different*'.

When Collins was asked a question by Clarke similar to the one Price asked Priestley, he made the somewhat puzzling response that at the resurrection the fissioned descendants of a common ancestor must all be one person since

138

they all would have the same consciousness. In contrast, Priestley answered that duplicated persons must be different since they are composed of different matter, which determines a numerical difference in identity, in spite of their having similar consciousnesses. Although Price continued to ask questions about these multiple men who have the same soul, Priestley declined to discuss it further, saying: 'I professedly argue on an hypothesis that is not my own, and submit the force of the argument to the judgement of the reader'. Later, Priestley was 'happy to concur' with Price's insistence that the same matter will make the same person in the miracle of the resurrection (Ibid.: 108–9, 113, 120).

William Hazlitt

Hazlitt's first work, *An Essay on the Principles of Human Action*, was published in 1805, when he was 27 years old. It was the culmination of a kind of perspective on personal identity that began with Locke, and then was developed in various ways by Collins, Hume, Law, and Priestley. Yet, with respect to certain questions that would become important in our own times, Hazlitt reads more like one of our own contemporaries than any of his predecessors. It is not too much to say that had Hazlitt's views on personal identity received the attention they deserved, the *philosophical* discussion of personal identity may well have leaped ahead 150 years and the *psychological* discussion been significantly advanced.

Hazlitt's views did not receive the attention they deserved. Far from it. Keats's idea of the 'negative capability' of the imagination was based on a careful study of Hazlitt's *Essay*, Coleridge mentioned the *Essay* in print, but only once and briefly, and Mackintosh, in the seventh edition of the *Encyclopedia Britannica*, remarked in a footnote to his discussion of Butler that 'the very able work' done by Hazlitt in the *Essay* 'contains original views' on the nature and origin of 'the private appetites'.[7] But few others, and no mainstream philosophers, seem even to have noticed.[8] Discouraged, Hazlitt turned from metaphysics to painting, politics, and aesthetic criticism.

Recently Hazlitt's star has risen. During the last few decades his writings have been reprinted, previously unpublished correspondence has been published, and there have been several books written about him.[9] However, it is as critic and stylist, not also as personal identity theorist, that his reputation has grown. Most commentators on his thought have been reluctant even to discuss the *Essay* in detail.[10] More importantly, no mainstream personal identity theorist, so far as we know, has ever even mentioned, much less discussed, any aspect of Hazlitt's views on personal identity.[11] In sum, *as personal identity theorist*, Hazlitt, like Vico before him, is a fascinating example of what is sometimes dismissed as a romantic fiction: the original and penetrating thinker whose insights and perspectives are so far ahead of his own times that they drop through the cracks of history.

In the *Essay*, Hazlitt remarked:

> There are moments in the life of a solitary thinker which are to him what the evening of some great victory is to the conqueror and hero – milder triumphs long remembered with truer and deeper delight. And though the shouts of multitudes do not hail his success . . . , as time passes . . . [such moments] still awaken the consciousness of a spirit patient, indefatigable in the search of truth and a hope of surviving in the thoughts and minds of other men.
>
> (Hazlitt 1805: 133)

Hazlitt's moment occurred in 1794. He was 16 years old. In that moment, he thought he realized three things: that we are *naturally* connected to ourselves in the past and present, but only *imaginatively* connected to ourselves in the future; that with respect to the future, we are naturally no more self-interested than other-interested; and that for each of us, our future selves should have the same moral and prudential status as that of anyone else's future self. Whether these realizations are genuine is, of course, debatable. Some today would say that they are. What is not debatable is that when in his *Essay on the Principles of Human Action* (1805) Hazlitt explained and defended them, he sketched theoretical possibilities and drew explosive morals from them that would not again be considered seriously until our own times.

Hazlitt wrote that he was led to his central realizations by wondering 'whether it could properly be said to be an act of virtue in anyone to sacrifice his own final happiness to that of any other person or number of persons, if it were possible for the one ever to be made the price of the other?' The question arose for him as he was reading, in d'Holbach's *System of Nature*, a speech put into the mouth of a supposed atheist at the Last Judgment. Suppose, Hazlitt wondered, I could save twenty other persons by voluntarily consenting to suffer for them. 'Why', he asked, 'should I not do a generous thing, and never trouble myself about what might be the consequence to myself the Lord knows when?' On behalf of common sense, Hazlitt answered his own question:

> However insensible I may be to my own interest at any future period, yet when the time comes I shall feel differently about it. I shall then judge of it from the actual impression of the object, that is, truly and certainly; and as I shall still be conscious of my past feelings, and shall bitterly regret my own folly and insensibility, I ought, as a rational agent, to be determined now by what I shall then wish I had done, when I shall feel the consequences of my actions most deeply and sensibly. It is this continued consciousness of my own feelings which gives me an immediate interest in whatever relates to my future welfare, and makes me at all times accountable to myself for my own conduct.

Hazlitt was dissatisfied with this answer.

> I cannot . . . have a principle of active self-interest arising out of the immediate connection between my present and future self, for no such connection exists or is possible. I am what I am in spite of the future. My feelings, actions, and interests must be determined by causes already existing and acting, and are absolutely independent of the future.
>
> (Ibid: 133–5)

Where there is no 'intercommunity of feelings', he claimed, 'there can be no identity of interests' (Ibid: 139).

Hazlitt conceded that because we remember only our own past experiences and are directly 'conscious' only of our own present experiences, in relation to the past and present people are naturally self-interested.

> [Any] absolute distinction which the mind feels in comparing itself with others [is] confined to two faculties, viz., sensation, or rather consciousness, and memory. The operation of both these faculties is of a perfectly exclusive and individual nature; and so far as their operation extends (but no farther) is man a personal, or if you will, a selfish being.
>
> (Ibid: 110–11)

The reasons for this, Hazlitt insisted, are physiological. Memories depend on physical traces of prior sensations, and these traces are not communicated among individuals. Present sensations depend on the stimulation of one's nerves, and 'there is no communication between my nerves, and another's brain, by means of which he can be affected with my sensations as I am myself'. In the case of the future, however, Hazlitt stressed that people are neither 'mechanically' nor 'exclusively' connected to themselves. They cannot be, he thought, since no one's future yet exists. Instead, people are connected both to their own futures and to the futures of others by means of their faculties of anticipation. These, he claimed, unlike the faculties of memory and sensation, are a function of *imagination* and, thus, do not respect the difference between self and other:

> [Imagination] must carry me out of myself into the feeling of others by one and the same process by which I am thrown forward as it were into my future being and interested in it. I could not love myself, if I were not capable of loving others. Self-love, used in this sense, is in its fundamental principle the same with disinterested benevolence.
>
> (Ibid: 3)

In other words, Hazlitt maintained that to feel future-oriented concern for someone, one first must project oneself imaginatively into the feelings of that person, and that imagination, functioning naturally, that is, independently of its having acquired a bias through learning, projects as easily into the feelings of others as into one's own future feelings.

Hazlitt exaggerated the extent to which memory is independent of imagination and underestimated our mechanical connections to our future selves. Like everybody else in the eighteenth century, he thought of memory along Lockean lines, as the replication in the present of a past experience, coupled with the feeling that the experience replicated is of something that happened in the past. Today we know better. Memory is not just personal episodic memory, but comes in a variety of guises; and even 'veridical' episodic memories are highly reconstructive, and thus importantly the product of imaginative activity.[12] In addition, people may well be linked to their future selves in ways that Hazlitt did not recognize. For instance, Hazlitt's observation that, in 1805, his causal links to his future self had not yet happened hardly justifies his view that 'I am what I am in spite of the future'. If, as many philosophers believe, selves or persons are four-dimensional objects, only one stage of which exists in the present, then it cannot be true, in 1805, that Hazlitt *is what he is in spite of the future*, that is, that he is what he is in spite of any stages of himself that came into being after 1805. For both past and future person stages of Hazlitt are none the less person-stages of Hazlitt for being past and future.[13] The problem is that Hazlitt considered the future only from the point of view of common sense, that is, from a perspective situated within a temporal series in which 'now' is the current moment. From that common sense point of view, causal links to our future selves have *not yet* happened. However, from a timeless point of view, Hazlitt, in 1805, was causally linked both to his past and to his future.

Even so, Hazlitt was right in insisting that *at any given time* there is a crucial difference in our relations to our past and future selves. It is that we are *already* affected by past stages of ourselves and *not yet* affected by future stages of ourselves. Hence, at any given time, our imaginations play a greater role in linking current to future stages of ourselves, than they do in linking current to past stages of ourselves. Hence, even though present stages of ourselves will connect mechanically to future stages of ourselves and, from a timeless point of view, are 'already' connected, we are *not yet affected* by those connections to the future, as we are connected via memory to the past. Hence, *for the time being*, we have to rely almost exclusively on imagination to connect psychologically to our future selves.

Thus, while Hazlitt may have been wrong in regard to the causal and metaphysical dimensions of his pivotal assertion that he is what he is in spite of the future, he was right that to connect *psychologically* with our future selves, we have to rely on our imaginations in ways, and to a degree, that we do not have to rely on our imaginations to connect with our current and past selves.

He may also have been right in insisting that so far as our values are concerned, past, present, and future do not have the same status or, if they do, that they come to have it in different ways. And he saw that to understand what these different ways are, one must investigate two issues that none of his predecessors had addressed adequately: one is the role of the imagination in connecting us to the future generally and, in particular, to ourselves in the future; the other is the role of self-conceptions, in possibly masking from ourselves, in connection with self-interest, salient differences between past, present, and future.

It was in Hazlitt's account of the role of self-conceptions in our values and in our views of our own interests that he contrasts most sharply with the eighteenth century tradition of which he was the culmination. According to Hazlitt, people are naturally concerned about whether someone is pleased or suffers as a consequence of their actions. This is because 'there is something in the very idea of good, or evil, which naturally excites desire or aversion'. But, he claimed, before the acquisition of self-concepts, people are indifferent about whether those who may be pleased or suffer are themselves or others: 'a child first distinctly wills or pursues his own good . . . not because it is his but because it is good'. As a consequence, he claimed, 'what is personal or selfish in our affections' is due to 'time and habit', the rest to 'the principle of a disinterested love of good as such, or for it's own sake, without any regard to personal distinctions' (Ibid: 33–4). He thought that such thoughts provided a basis for founding morality not on self-interest, which he regarded as an 'artificial' value, but on the *natural* concern people have to seek happiness and avoid unhappiness, regardless of whose it is. He concluded triumphantly that 'we are not obliged at last to establish generosity and virtue "lean pensioners" on self-interest' (Ibid: 48–9).

More important than such possible ethical implications, a consequence of Hazlitt's emphasizing the thesis that people are mechanically related to their own presents and pasts, but only imaginatively related to their futures, and that the 'natural' uses to which they put their imaginations do not respect the difference between self and other, led him to ask a question which did not arise as starkly or in the same form for any of his predecessors. The question was: if people connect to the future through imagination, which does not respect the difference between self and other, why is the force of habit almost invariably on the side of selfish feelings? His answer involved his trying to account for the growth of selfish motives in humans by appeal to their acquisition of self-concepts. In his view, when very young children behave selfishly it is not because they like themselves better, but because they know their own wants and pleasures better. In older children and adults, he thought, it is because they have come under the control of their self-concepts, which is something that happens in three stages. First, young children acquire an idea of themselves as beings who are capable of experiencing pleasure and pain. Second, and almost 'mechanically' (since physiology insures that children remember only their own pasts), children include their own pasts in their notions of themselves. Finally, imaginatively, they include their own futures (Ibid: 34–5). The first two of these stages may have been suggested to Hazlitt by his reading of Locke. The third is original. However, even in the case of the first two, Hazlitt thought of them less as a philosopher and more as a psychologist might think of them, in terms of the acquisition of self-concepts, and whereas it was unclear whether Locke meant to distinguish developmental stages in the acquisition of self-concepts, Hazlitt clearly wanted to do so.

In the first half of the eighteenth century, the developmental psychological hypotheses that Locke saw dimly were invisible to most of his readers. As commonsensical as the idea of psychological development may seem to us today, it did not come into focus in the views of eighteenth century thinkers until mid-century. Hartley had a developmental, associational account of the mind, but he focussed on the development of the passions and never considered the acquisition of self-concepts.[14] Rousseau, in *Emile*, showed deep sensitivity to developmental concerns, but not particularly with respect to the acquisition of self-concepts. Reid, late in the century, had a developmental psychology, but because of his commitment to the immateriality of the soul and the reflexive nature of consciousness, he may actually have made an exception in the case of the idea of self. And Priestley, largely under the influence of Hartley, did think that his own developmental account could be extended to the acquisition of self-concepts, but neither stressed nor elaborated the point. Hazlitt did both.

Hazlitt thought that to progress through all three of the development stages that he distinguished in the acquisition of self-concepts, a child has to differentiate its own mental activities from those of others. In his view, this involves 'perceiving that you are and what you are from the immediate reflection of the mind on its own operations, sensations or ideas'.

> It is by comparing the knowledge that I have of my own impressions, ideas, feelings, powers, etc. with my knowledge of the same or similar impressions, ideas, etc. in others, and with the still more imperfect conception that I form of what passes in their minds when this is supposed to be essentially different from what passes in my own, that I acquire the general notion of self. If I had no idea of what passes in the minds of others, or if my ideas of their feelings and perceptions were perfect representations, i.e., mere conscious repetitions of them, all proper personal distinction would be lost either in pure self-love, or in perfect universal sympathy.
>
> (Ibid: 105–8)

Hazlitt here raised the question of how a child's formation of self-concepts is related to its development of empathy and sympathy. So far as we know,

144

no one previously had ever asked this question. As we shall see, currently developmental psychologists are preoccupied with it.

Hazlitt's genetic approach is a real advance beyond the approaches of earlier theorists, especially those who wrote in the first half of the eighteenth century. For instance, in Hume's emotional contagion model of human sympathy, humans infer from external behavior, facial expressions, and the like that others are in some particular mental state. Then, the resulting idea that humans form of another's state becomes converted in their own minds into an impression, so that now they too are in the same state, though perhaps less vivaciously. In explaining how the conversion from idea to impression occurs, Hume appealed to the *idea*'s 'proximity' in one's mind to the *impression* one has of oneself, which he said is 'so lively' that 'it is not possible to imagine that any thing can in this particular go beyond it'. But, then he added not a word of explanation about how people acquire their super-lively self-impressions.[15]

Hazlitt's approach is also more advanced than those who wrote much later in the eighteenth century. Smith, for instance, gave an unusually thorough account of the role, in sympathy, of shifts from one's own to another's point of view. Yet he never attempted to explain how people acquire their ideas of the distinction between self and other. Aside from the applications of his ideas to ethical theory, his gaze was fixed on the importance of point of view as a feature of our already formed adult minds, not on the psychogenetics of point of view in our mental development. The closest he came to discussing the mentality of children was in his explanations of how adults sympathize with 'poor wretches', children and the dead. As we have seen, in his view, in so sympathizing, adults do not simply replicate the other's state of mind in their own minds but, rather, imagine what they themselves would feel if they were reduced to the other's situation, but somehow, per impossible, were allowed to keep their own current reason and judgment. But while Smith was preoccupied with explaining how sympathy is possible, it did not occur to him to explain how the mental concepts that make it possible came to be acquired in the first place. In contrast, Hazlitt's approach is psychogenetic.

Hazlitt also wondered why young children imaginatively include only their *own* futures and not the futures of others in their ideas of self. He hypothesized that it is the 'greater liveliness and force with which I can enter into my future feelings, that in a manner identifies them with my present being'. He added that once the notion of one's own personal identity is formed, 'the mind makes use of it to strengthen its habitual propensity, by giving to personal motives a reality and absolute truth which they can never have' (Ibid: 140). This happens, he thought, because 'we have an indistinct idea of extended consciousness and a community of feelings as essential to the same thinking being'. As a consequence, he said, we assume that whatever 'interests [us] at one time must interest [us] or be capable of interesting [us] at other times' (Ibid: 10–11).

145

Hazlitt claimed that a bias in favour of ourselves in the future could never 'have gained the assent of thinking men' but for 'the force' with which a future-oriented idea of self 'habitually clings to the mind of every man, binding it as with a spell, deadening its discriminating powers, and spreading the confused associations which belong only to past and present impressions over the whole of our imaginary existence'. However, whereas a host of previous thinkers, such as Descartes, Locke, Clarke, Berkeley, and Butler, thought that people have intuitive knowledge of their own identities, Hazlitt rejected as 'wild and absurd' the idea that we have an 'absolute, metaphysical identity' with ourselves in the future, and hence that people have identities that are available to be intuited.

We have been misled, Hazlitt thought, by language: by 'a mere play of words'. In his view, both children and adults fail to look beyond the common idioms of personal identity and as a consequence routinely mistake linguistic fictions for metaphysical realities. To say that someone has a 'general interest' in whatever concerns her own future welfare 'is no more', he insisted, 'than affirming that [she] shall have an interest in that welfare, or that [she is] nominally and in certain other respects the same being who will hereafter have a real interest in it'. No amount of mere telling 'me that I have the same interest in my future sensations as if they were present, because I am the same individual', he claimed, can bridge the gulf between the 'real' mechanical connections I have to myself in the past and present and the merely verbal and imaginary connections that I have to myself in the future (Ibid: 6, 10–11, 27–9).

Assuming that people have no mechanical connections to themselves in the future, it follows, Hazlitt thought, that so far as peoples' 'real' interests are concerned, their 'selves' in the future are essentially others. So, for instance, if you have injured yourself, you may in the present suffer as a consequence. But 'the injury that I may do to my future interest will not certainly by any kind of reaction return to punish me for my neglect of my own happiness'. Rather, Hazlitt concluded, 'I am always free from the consequences of my actions. The interests of the being who acts, and of the being who suffers are never one'. So, it makes no difference 'whether [you] pursue [your] own welfare or entirely neglect it' (Ibid: 31). Your suffering in the future is only nominally your suffering.

In sum, Hazlitt gave a psychological account of how people come to identify with their future selves, from which he drew a metaphysical conclusion: that peoples' seeming identities with their future selves are illusions. He then used this metaphysical conclusion as the basis for an inference to a normative conclusion: that we have no self-interested reason to be concerned about the fate of our future selves. Whether or not Hazlitt's *conclusions* are correct, both of his *inferences* are fallacious. Psychology, all by itself, does not have such implications for metaphysics, and metaphysics, all by itself, does not have such implications for ethics. Nevertheless, Hazlitt asked questions, perhaps for the first time, that deeply interest theorists in our own times.[16]

Hazlitt's consideration of fission examples occurred in the context of his critique of the Lockean idea that one's identity extends as far as one's consciousness extends. What, Hazlitt asked, would a theorist committed to this idea say 'if that consciousness should be transferred to some other being?' How would such a person know that he or she had not been 'imposed upon by a false claim of identity?' He answered, on behalf of the Lockeans, that the idea of one's consciousness extending to someone else 'is ridiculous': a person has 'no other self than that which arises from this very consciousness'. But, he countered, after our deaths:

> this self may be multiplied in as many different beings as the Deity may think proper to endue with the same consciousness; which if it can be so renewed at will in any one instance, may clearly be so in a hundred others. Am I to regard all these as equally myself? Am I equally interested in the fate of all? Or if I must fix upon some one of them in particular as my representative and other self, how am I to be determined in my choice? Here, then, I saw an end put to my speculations about absolute self-interest and personal identity.
>
> (Ibid: 135–6)

Thus, Hazlitt saw that, hypothetically, psychological continuity might not continue in a single stream but instead might divide.

In asking the two questions: 'Am I to regard all of these [fission descendants] as equally myself? Am I equally interested in the fate of all [of these fission descendants]?', Hazlitt correctly separated the question of whether *identity* tracks psychological continuity from that of whether *self-concern* tracks it. And, in direct anticipation of what would not occur again to other philosophers until the 1960s, he concluded that because of the possibility of fission neither identity nor self-concern necessarily tracks psychological continuity. Thus, he used his theological speculations in the same spirit, and to the same effect, as philosophers in our own times have used science-fiction scenarios.

Hazlitt also used fission examples to call into question whether in cases in which there is no fission, a person's present self-interest extends to his or her self in the future. He began by asking:

> How then can this pretended unity of consciousness which is only reflected from the past, which makes me so little acquainted with the future that I cannot even tell for a moment how long it will be continued, whether it will be entirely interrupted by or renewed in me after death, and which might be multiplied in I don't know how many different beings and prolonged by complicated sufferings without my being any the wiser for it, how I say can a principle of this sort identify my present with my future interests, and make me as much a

participator in what does not at all affect me as if it were actually impressed on my senses?

Hazlitt's answer was that it cannot.

It is plain, as this conscious being may be decompounded, entirely destroyed, renewed again, or multiplied in a great number of beings, and as, whichever of these takes place, it cannot produce the least alteration in my present being – that what I am does not depend on what I am to be, and that there is no communication between my future interests and the motives by which my present conduct must be governed.

He concluded:

I cannot, therefore, have a principle of active self-interest arising out of the immediate connection between my present and future self, for no such connection exists, or is possible. . . . My personal interest in any thing must refer either to the interest excited by the actual impression of the object which cannot be felt before it exists, and can last no longer than while the impression lasts, or it may refer to the particular manner in which I am mechanically affected by the idea of my own impressions in the absence of the object. I can therefore have no proper personal interest in my future impressions . . . The only reason for my preferring my future interest to that of others, must arise from my anticipating it with greater warmth of present imagination.

(Ibid: 138–40)

With the exception of F. H. Bradley, such ideas would not be taken seriously again until the 1960s.

6

FUTURE OF THE SELF

We shall briefly summarize chapters one to five. In the late seventeenth century, virtually all philosophers subscribed to a basically Platonic conception of self. The times were ripe for that conception to be challenged. Earlier, Hobbes and Spinoza had challenged it, but not effectively. So, the task was left to Locke, who played his part as challenger remarkably effectively. Yet from the point of view of contributing to an empirical science of the self, Locke retained some old-fashioned commitments that became obstacles. One was to the idea that each of us has an intuitive knowledge of his own existence, which for Locke meant his own existence as a self. A second was to the reflexive nature of consciousness, according to which necessarily if someone is conscious of anything, then that person is also conscious that he is conscious. And, a third – about which Locke seems to have wavered – was to a static, rather than developmental, account of the acquisition of self-concepts.

Because of the first two of these commitments, Locke's critics were able to refute the simple memory-view of personal identity that they attributed to him, and as a consequence ignore his intimations about mental development. They were also able to ignore the closely related idea that the self is a fictional construct, or more accurately they were able to wave it in Locke's face as an objection to his view. So, for instance, both Clarke and Butler protested that if Locke's view were true, then since the self would be a fiction people would have no reason to value their future selves. With the sole exception of Hume (some of the time), and to a lesser degree of Law, no one was willing to embrace this seeming-consequence of Locke's view. And Hume's endorsement of the idea that the self is a fiction was against the backdrop of his global skepticism in Book 1 of the *Treatise*, according to which the whole world is a fiction.

By mid-century the empirical science of human nature was being born. Skepticism could easily be set aside because it does not give rise to a meaningful strategy for empirical research. Perhaps partly for this reason, Hume's *Treatise*, by his own admission, 'fell still born from the press'. Yet, primarily in the second book of the *Treatise*, Hume had views which, from the point of view of a nascent science of psychology, were more progressive. But he never explained the relationship between his earlier skepticism and these more scientifically progressive ideas, probably because he did not understand the relationship himself. His reticence on this issue was especially glaring in his account of the self. After roundly denouncing in Book 1 of the *Treatise* the idea that we have an impression of a 'simple and continu'd' self, in Book 2 Hume declared that we not only have some sort of impression of self but one that is more vivid and constant than any other impression we have.

Although there are intimations in Priestley of how, without rejecting the main impetus in Locke's account, one could get beyond its limitations in developing a modern account of the self, it was left to Hazlitt to bring it all together. Hazlitt rejected Locke's idea that each of us has an intuitive knowledge of our own existence as a self, as well as Locke's commitment to the reflexive nature of consciousness. Instead of these, Hazlitt embraced the idea, as had Hume, that the self is a fictional construct. But, good student of Priestley that he was, Hazlitt embraced this idea within the context of a materialistic and realistic view of the world. So, animated as Hazlitt was by ethical concerns, rather than departing altogether from the topic of self under the cloak of skepticism, he advanced the idea, which was latent in Locke and some subsequent thinkers, that people acquire their conceptions of their own selves and those of others in developmental stages. Hazlitt then not only conceded but embraced and celebrated the idea that the self is a fictional construct, since, in his view, it had the further implication that people have no special ('self-interested') reason to value their future selves. At least to his own satisfaction, and in a way that clearly anticipated the work of Derek Parfit and others in our own times, Hazlitt tried to explain how the idea that the self is a fiction, far from being destructive to theories of rationality and ethics, actually made them better. In the process, he sowed the seeds, albeit on barren ground, of a modern psychology of the acquisition of self-concepts.

Thus, ends the story that we intended to tell in the present book. Hazlitt is the last progressive figure in a more or less continuous tradition of discussion of the nature of self and personal identity that began with Locke and that took place in Britain throughout the eighteenth century. Several things broke up the continuity of this tradition. One of the major things, which we have already begun to discuss, was the increasing separation of philosophy and psychology, each of which throughout the nineteenth and increasingly into the twentieth centuries have tended to go their separate ways. Another, which only began to be felt seriously in Britain in the nineteenth century, was the influence of Kant. Nevertheless, the ideas that animated the eighteenth century British debate over self and personal identity have continued to be discussed and have even enjoyed a remarkable rebirth in our own times, both in philosophy and in psychology.

Nineteenth-century philosophy of personal identity

As we have seen, by the end of the eighteenth century, discussion of fission examples in connection with personal identity theory, as well as consideration of the thesis that personal identity is not what matters primarily in survival, had been introduced into debate. And toward the beginning of the nineteenth century both issues were developed progressively in the writings of Hazlitt. In short, early in the nineteenth century, the debate over personal identity was proceeding along a trajectory that will seem quite up to date to students of contemporary analytic personal identity theory. However, after Hazlitt the consideration of personal identity took a turn for the worse in Britain. Part of the reason for this is that major theorists, such as Thomas Brown, James Mill, and John Stuart Mill, looked back over the heads of Priestley and Hazlitt primarily to Hume, whose merits, whatever else they may have been, did not include advancing discussion of the forward-looking ideas that came to fruition only late in the century. Another part of the reason is that Kant, whose enormous influence took a while to reach Britain but then through the subsequent rise of idealism for nearly a century all but obliterated the sort of empirically based speculation over *personal identity* that had dominated eighteenth-century British philosophy, took the discussion of self and unity of consciousness into a different direction. As a consequence, a great deal that was progressive in the eighteenth and early nineteenth centuries discussion of self and personal identity dropped from sight, including many of the major themes debated by Clarke and Collins, the surprisingly modern views of Priestley and Hazlitt, and even the basic idea that fission examples are important to theories of personal identity.

In the eighteenth century, fission examples had been mentioned, albeit casually and ambiguously, in Locke and Reid, who continued to be read throughout the nineteenth and twentieth centuries. But neither Locke nor Reid had made the importance of fission examples to personal identity theory clear. Yet, even without the prod of fission examples, although perhaps not as dramatically, many of the same questions regarding the *importance* of personal identity that concerned Priestley and Hazlitt could have been provoked merely by attending to the view that personal identity consists not in the persistence of a substance but in relations among earlier and later persons (or person-stages). But, ironically, in those eighteenth- and nineteenth-century traditions that eventually evolved into analytic philosophy, there was not that much sympathy for a relational view of personal identity. Instead, the substance view, boosted in part by the way in which nineteenth-century thinkers interpreted Kant's transcendental philosophy, had a long, lingering demise.

Wherever the influence of the substance view was still felt, it tended to terminate reflection on the importance of identity. Although both of the Mills had a relational view of the self, substance views remained viable even among influential, empirically minded thinkers. For instance, in a passage reminiscent of Hazlitt and one that may have influenced Parfit, Henry Sidgwick mused, 'It must surely be admissible to ask the Egoist, "Why should I sacrifice a present pleasure for a greater one in the future? Why should I concern myself about my own future feelings any more than about the feelings of other persons?"'

He persisted: 'Grant that the Ego is merely a system of coherent phenomena, that the permanent identical "I" is not a fact but a fiction, as Hume and his followers maintain; why, then, should one part of the series of feelings into which the Ego is resolved be concerned with another part of the same series, any more than with any other series?' (Sidgwick 1874: 418). Sidgwick's question is one that Priestley answered and that Hazlitt, although he was no doubt aware of Priestley's answer, asked again and answered somewhat differently. However, Sidgwick, without the prod of fission examples and with substance accounts of identity still a respectable option, managed to set this question aside.

Even though in the last half of the nineteenth century, substance views still dominated the discussion of self and personal identity, there was one outstanding exception. F. H. Bradley had thoughts about the self that were remarkably like those of Law and Priestley, though without their commitment to materialism. Bradley claimed that personal identity is conventional, that it is best regarded as a matter of degree, and that how we think of it should be determined pragmatically, in ways that permit us to think of it differently for different purposes. He even used fission examples to criticize Locke's simple memory view of personal identity:

> If the self remembers because and according as it is *now*, might not another self be made of a quality the same and hence possessing the same past in present recollection? And if *one* could be made thus, why not also two or three? These might be made distinct at the present time, through their differing quality, and again through outward relations, and yet be like enough for each to remember the same past, and so, of course to *be* the same.
>
> (Bradley 1893: 72)

Bradley concluded from this example 'that a self is not thought to be the same because of bare memory, but only so when that memory is considered not to be deceptive'. He then claimed that it follows from this requirement that:

> Identity must depend in the end upon past experience, and not solely upon mere present thinking. And continuity in some degree, and in some unintelligible sense, is by the popular view required for personal identity. He who is risen from the dead may really be the same, though we can say nothing intelligible of his ambiguous eclipse or his phase of half-existence. But a man wholly like the first, but created fresh after the same lapse of time, we might feel was too much to be one, if not quite enough to be two. Thus it is evident that, for personal identity, some continuity is requisite, but how much no one seems to know.
>
> (Ibid.: 73)

Bradley concluded: 'If we are not satisfied with vague phrases and meaningless generalities, we soon discover that the best way is not to ask questions'.

But what if we do persist in asking questions? Then, Bradley said, we will be left with this result:

> Personal identity is mainly a matter of degree. The question has a meaning if confined to certain aspects of the self, though even here it can be made definite in each case only by the arbitrary selection of points of view. And in each case there will be a limit fixed in the end by no clear principle. But in what the *general* sameness of one self consists is a problem insoluble because it is meaningless. This question, I repeat it, is sheer nonsense until we have got some clear idea as to what the self is to stand for. If you ask me whether a man is identical in this or that respect, and for one purpose or another purpose, then, if we do not understand one another, we are on the road to an understanding. In my opinion, even then we shall reach our end only by more or less of convention and arrangement. But to seek an answer in general to the question asked at large is to pursue a chimera.
>
> (Ibid.)

After beginning like Clarke in his criticism of Locke's simple memory view, but without the immaterial soul hypothesis to fall back on, Bradley ended with a view something like that of Law or Priestley.

Elsewhere, Bradley, with fission examples still on his mind, even considered the possibility, for which Priestley had actually argued, of accounting for the resurrection on materialist grounds:

> After an interval, no matter how long, another nervous system sufficiently like our own might be developed; and in this case memory and a personal identity must arise. The event may be as improbable as you please, but I at least can find no reason for calling it impossible. And we may even go a step further still. It is conceivable that an indefinite number of such bodies should exist, not in succession merely, but all together and all at once. But, if so, we might gain a personal continuance not single but multiform, and might secure a destiny on which it would be idle to enlarge.
>
> (Ibid.: 445)

In sum, Bradley was a conventionalist about personal identity.

Among those who still believed in the reality of personal identity, it was not until the first quarter of the twentieth century that substance views were finally given the ax, on one side, by the positivists and, on the other, by the phenomenologists, particularly Heidegger, who had moved on to a social conception of the self. In the twentieth century, it is only in analytic philosophy that anything like a Lockean, atomistic, relational view has persisted. And in the analytic tradition, until the 1970s, no one again asked the sorts of questions that Priestley and Hazlitt had asked and that have become such a mainstay of late twentieth century analytic personal identity debates.

Contemporary philosophy of personal identity

In the late twentieth century, there have been three major developments in analytic personal identity theory: the intrinsic relations view of personal identity has been largely superseded by the extrinsic relations view (which is also sometimes called the closest-continuer view and the externalist view); the question of what matters in survival has returned to the forefront of theorist's concerns; and four-dimensional views of persons have challenged the traditional three-dimensional view.

According to the older *intrinsic relations view*, what determines whether a person at different times is identical is just how the two are physically and/or psychologically related to *each other*. According to more recent *extrinsic* relations views, what determines whether a person at different times is identical is not just how the two are physically and/or psychologically related to *each other* but also how they are related to *others*. For instance, in Locke's simple memory-version of the intrinsic relations view, you right now are the same person as someone who existed yesterday if you remember having experienced or having done things which that person of yesterday experienced or did. In an extrinsic relations version of Locke's simple memory-view, one would have to take into account not only whether you remember having experienced or having done things which that person of yesterday experienced or did, but also whether, in addition to you, anyone else remembers having experienced or done things which that person of yesterday experienced or did.

Fission examples are largely responsible for the recent move from an intrinsic to an extrinsic relations view. In the sort of fission examples that have been most discussed since the late 1960s, a person somehow divides into two (seemingly) *numerically* different persons, each of whom, initially, is *qualitatively* identical to the other and also to the pre-fission person from whom they both descended. For example, imagine that all information in human brains is encoded redundantly so that it is possible to separate a human's brain into two parts, leaving each half-brain fully functioning and encoded with all it needs to sustain the original person's full mental life just as (except for the elimination of underlying redundancy) his whole brain would have sustained it had his whole brain never been divided. Now suppose that in some normal, healthy human we perform a brain separation operation, removing the two fully functioning half-brains from his body, which is then immediately destroyed. Suppose, further, that we immediately implant each of these half-brains into its own, brainless body, which, except for being brainless, is otherwise qualitatively identical to the original person's body, so that two people simultaneously emerge, each of whom, except for having only half a brain, is qualitatively identical – physically and psychologically – to the original person whose brain was divided and removed and, of course, to each other.

Are these two fission-descendants the same person as each other? On an intrinsic view of personal identity, such as Locke's, they would be. Each would remember having experienced things and having performed actions that the original person experienced and performed. If, in deciding whether a person at one time and one at another are the same person, we have to consider *only* the relations between the person(s) at these two times, then it would seem that the pre-fission person might be related to each of the post-fission persons so as to have all that is required to preserve identity. But, the problem with supposing that we have to consider *only* the relations between the pre-fission person and a post-fission person is that another qualitatively identical post-fission person has an equal claim to be the original person.

Many contemporary philosophers believe that, in a fission scenario like the one just sketched, the pre-fission person – the brain donor – would cease. We shall review their reasons for thinking this shortly. In the view of these philosophers, it is more plausible to regard the pre-fission person and each of the fission-descendants as three separate persons. Philosophers who think this way accept an *extrinsic relations* view of personal identity, according to which what determines whether a person at one time and one at another are the same person is *not only* how the two are physically and/or psychologically related to *each other* (which is all that would need to be considered on an *intrinsic relations* view) but also how the two are related to *others* (in the case of our example, especially the other fission-descendant).

The fission examples that eighteenth-century philosophers considered were religion-fiction scenarios. The ones that contemporary philosophers have considered tend to be science-fiction scenarios. Both sorts of fission examples raise essentially the same issues for personal identity theory. In the eighteenth century, many philosophers supposed – rightly or wrongly – that the religion-fiction fission examples had a counterpart in real, albeit post-mortem, developments. In our own times the science-fiction examples have a counter-part in this-worldly real life.

In the late 1930s, neurosurgeons in the United States began performing an operation in which they severed the corpus callosums of severe epileptics in the hope of confining their seizures to one hemisphere of their brains, and thus reducing their severity. To the surgeons' initial surprise, the procedure was doubly successful. Often it reduced not only the severity of the seizures, but also their frequency. It also had a truly bizarre side-effect, not discovered until many years later: It created two independent centers of consciousness within the same human skull. These centres of consciousness lacked intro-spective access to each other and could be made to acquire and express information independently of each other. Most dramatically, they sometimes differed volitionally, expressing their differences using alternate sides of the same human bodies that they jointly shared. In one case, for instance, a man who had had this operation reportedly hugged his wife with one arm while he pushed her away with the other; in another, a man tried with his right hand (controlled by his left, verbal hemisphere) to hold a newspaper where he could read it, thereby blocking his view of the TV, while he tried with his left hand (controlled by his right non-verbal hemisphere) to knock the paper out of the way.[1]

Since 1970 there has been a second major development in personal identity theory. Philosophers have begun again to question whether personal identity is primarily what matters in survival; that is, they have faced the possibility that people might cease and be continued by *others* whose existences they would value as much as their own existence and in pretty much the same ways as they value their own existence. For the most part, they have revived this issue through the consideration of science-fiction examples of brain splitting and transplantation inspired by the real life cases just discussed. To see how such examples call into question the *importance* of identity, imagine, for instance, that you have a health problem that will result soon in your sudden and painless death unless you receive one or the other of two available treatments. The first is to have your brain removed and placed into the empty cranium of a body that, except for being brainless, is qualitatively identical to your own. The second is to have your brain removed, divided into functionally identical halves (each capable of sustaining your full psychology), and then to have each of these halves put into the empty cranium of a body of its own, again one that is brainless but otherwise qualitatively identical to your own.

Suppose that in the first treatment there is a 10 per cent chance that the transplantation will take and that if it takes, the survivor who wakes up in the recovery room will be physically and psychologically like you just prior to the operation except that he will know he has had the operation and will be healthy. In the second there is a 95 percent chance both transplantations will take. If both take, each of the survivors who wakes up in the recovery room will be physically and psychologically like you just prior to the operation except that each of them will know he has had the operation and each will be healthy. If the transplantation in the first treatment does not take, the would-be survivor will die painlessly on the operating table. If either transplantation in the second treatment does not take, the other will not take either, and both would-be survivors will die painlessly on the operating table. Suppose everything else about the treatments is the same and as attractive to you as possible: for instance, both treatments are painless, free of charge, and, if successful, result in survivors who recover quickly.[2]

As we have seen, many philosophers believe that in the first (non-fission) treatment, you would continue, but in the second (fission) treatment, you would cease and be replaced by others. They think that in the second treatment you would cease and be replaced because they believe, first, that identity is a transitive relationship, second, that the survivors, at least once they began to lead independent lives, are not plausibly regarded as the same people as each other and, third, that it would be arbitrary to regard just one of the survivors but not the other as you. Hence, in the view of these philosophers, it is more plausible to regard each of the survivors as a different person from each other and from you.

Assume, for the sake of argument, that this way of viewing what will happen in the two treatments is correct. Then, you would persist through the first treatment but in the second you would cease and be replaced by others. So, only by sacrificing your identity could you greatly increase the chances of someone's emerging from the operation and surviving for years who initially would be qualitatively just like you. The question is whether, in the circumstances specified, it would be worth it for you to have such an operation, that is, whether only from a point of view of what in more normal circumstances would be considered as a totally selfish (or self-regarding), it would be worth it. Many who consider examples like this one feel strongly that it would be worth it. So, for them, at least, it would seem that ceasing and being continued by others can matter as much, or almost as much, as persisting, and in pretty much the same ways. But if ceasing and being continued by others can matter as much (and in the same ways) as persisting, then identity is not what matters primarily in survival. Among philosophers who have felt this way, Derek Parfit's views have perhaps been more influential than anyone else's.[3]

Parfit has a neo-Lockean view of personal identity, but one according to which what binds the different stages of persons is not just memory, but mental relations more generally (anticipations, beliefs, intentions, character traits, and so on). In Parfit's view, unlike in Locke's, it is not necessary for each stage of us to be *directly* related to every other stage. Rather, it is enough if each stage is *indirectly* related through intermediate stages. Thus, Parfit's view is not vulnerable to the Grove–Berkeley–Reid objection to Locke's view. In Parfit's view, if C at t_3 is *directly* psychologically connected to B at t_2, but *not* to A at t_1, but B at t_2 *is* directly psychologically connected to A at t_1, then C at t_3, is *indirectly* psychologically connected to A at t_1; that may be enough to preserve personal identity. In sum, in Parfit's view, what binds us over time are psychological connections, overlapping 'like the strands in a rope' (Parfit 1984: 222).

So as to avoid the charge that his analysis of personal identity is circular, Parfit has responded to those who think that the notion of *same person* enters into the proper analysis of various psychological relations, but particularly of memory, by formulating his analyses of these psychological relations in terms of specially defined 'q-senses' of them. These specially defined 'q-senses', by definition, do not include the notion of *same person*. For instance, he has defined a notion of *quasi-memory* (or, *q-memory*), which is just like that of *memory*, except that whereas the claim someone *remembers* having experienced something may imply that the person remembers that they themselves experienced that thing, the claim that someone *q-remembers* having experiencing something implies – by definition – only that the person remembers that *someone* experienced that thing. Thus, Parfit's view in not vulnerable to the argument Butler and others used to try to show that Locke's view is circular.

To illustrate how q-memory might work, Parfit gave as an example Jane's seeming to remember Paul's experience, in Venice, of looking across water and seeing a lightening bolt fork and then strike two objects (Ibid.: 220). Parfit claimed that in seeming to remember this experience Jane might have known that she was seeming to remember an experience that Paul (and not she) had had originally, and that if Jane had known this, then she would have known, *from the inside*, part of what it was like to be Paul on that day in Venice. In other words, Jane would have known she was seeming to remember Paul's experience from the same sort of subjective, first-person point of view from which Paul actually had the experience originally and from which ordinarily Jane actually remembers only her own experiences. If one acknowledges that Parfit's hypothetical example is at least theoretically possible, as it seems we should (imagine, say, that part of Paul's brain had been surgically implanted into Jane's brain), then apparently it is possible, in analyses of personal identity, to substitute q-memory for memory and thereby avoid Butler's objection. In other words, even if simple memory analyses of personal identity are circular, it would not follow that q-memory analyses of personal identity are circular.

In 1694, when Locke proposed his same-consciousness view, most philosophers subscribed to a soul view. In 1984, when Parfit proposed the fullest version of his theory, probably most philosophers subscribed to the view that the continuity of our bodies, or of some part of our bodies, is necessary for personal persistence. Parfit, by contrast, denied that bodily continuity is necessary for personal persistence. To support this denial, he supposed, first, that while someone's brain is healthy, his body is ridden with cancer and his only hope for survival is to have his entire healthy brain transplanted intact to another healthy body. He supposed also that this procedure is perfectly safe and that the body into which the donor's brain will be transplanted is better than his current body, not only in that it is healthy but also in other respects that appeal to the donor. Parfit pointed out, surely correctly, that the donor has not lost much if he jettisons his old body and moves his brain to the better body that awaits it. Such an operation would not be as bad as staying in the old body and dying of cancer, even if the death were painless. In fact, vanity being what it is, if radical cosmetic surgery of this sort were available and safe, it is likely that many people would choose it, even if the old bodies they jettisoned were healthy. So, if physical continuity matters, Parfit concluded, it cannot be the continuity of the whole body but at most the continuity of the brain.

Parfit argued that the importance of our brains, like that of our other organs, is not intrinsic but derivative; that is, the brain's importance depends solely on the functions it serves. So, if half of our brains were functionally equivalent to the whole, for most of us the preservation of our whole brain would not matter much, and, it would seem, the continuity even of any part of the brain is not necessarily important. If some other organ, such as the liver, sustained our psychologies and our brains served the functions that this other organ now serves, then this other organ would be as important in survival as the brain now is and the brain only as important as this other organ now is. So, it would seem that if something else – anything else – could sustain our psychologies as reliably as the brain, then the brain (i.e., the physical organ that actually now functions as the brain) would have little importance in survival, even if this other thing were not any part of our bodies (Ibid.: 284–5).

A critic might object that even though the importance of an organ is derivative and based solely on its being the vehicle for preserving a person's psychology, given that it has always been that vehicle, then the preservation of that organ may matter importantly, even primarily, in survival. In other words, it is possible that even though something else might have assumed that organ's function of preserving a person's psychology and, hence, that under those imagined circumstances the organ that now serves that function would not have mattered importantly in survival, once an organ actually has served the function of preserving a person's psychology, then it may matter importantly in survival. But probably for most of us, the very organ that has actually sustained our psychologies, merely in virtue of its having sustained our psychologies, would not *thereby* matter all that importantly to us in survival.

Imagine, for instance, that competent doctors discover that you have both a brain disease and a brain abnormality. The disease has not impaired the functioning of your brain yet. But if it is untreated, it will result in your death in the near future. Because of the abnormality, there is a simple, effective, and painless cure. The abnormality is that you have two brains, the one now diseased, which is the only one that has ever functioned as a brain, and another, right beside it, lying dormant – healthy and perfectly capable of performing a whole brain's functions should the need arise, but nevertheless never yet functioning as a brain and not currently encoded with any of your psychology. There is a simple procedure the doctors can perform to switch the roles of your two brains: all of the encoded psychology on your diseased brain will be transferred to the healthy one; as it is transferred, it will be erased from your diseased brain, whereupon your healthy brain will begin to function just as the diseased one did (and would have continued to function had it been healthy and left alone).

Suppose that the procedure is as quick and as simple (and as abrupt) as flipping a switch, that it will not affect subjective psychology, and that consciousness will be continuous throughout the procedure. Indeed, suppose that you (and the person who emerges from the procedure) will not even notice any change. Once the transfer is completed, almost instantaneously, your diseased brain will become dormant and pose no further threat to your organism's physical or psychological health. In these imagined circumstances, how much would it matter to you that the brain of yours that has always sustained your psychology will no longer sustain it, while another that has never sustained it will sustain it from now on? Probably not much. The procedure would not be as bad as death. Unless the procedure caused existential anxiety, it would not even be as bad as a root canal. So much for the derivative value of the organs that have actually sustained our psychologies.

Those who are skeptical of this response might imagine that whereas the procedure described is the simplest way of disabling the threat to the organism posed by your diseased brain, it is not the only way. An alternative procedure the doctors can perform is to repair your diseased brain through a series of twenty brain operations spread over the next twenty years of your life. Each operation will cost about one-half of your annual salary (suppose that insurance does not and probably never will cover the procedure) and will require two months of hospitalization. In addition, the operations will be disfiguring. When they are finally completed, you will be healthy enough, but your life will have been seriously disrupted and your body and face will be somewhat deformed. We assume that on your scale of values, the disruption, expense, and disfigurement, while bad, are not as bad as death. (If they are as bad as death, reduce their severity to the point where they are not quite as bad as death.) So, if the first procedure is as bad as death, then the second procedure is a better choice. Which procedure would you choose? We think that many, if not, most people would choose the first procedure.[4]

Finally, a critic might object that even though the preservation of one's body might not matter in survival, it still might be necessary for personal persistence. However, in the case of many of the exotic examples under discussion in the personal identity literature, including the one just discussed, Parfit has argued that the question of whether one persists is an *empty question*. Once one knows all of the physical and psychological ways in which the earlier and later persons are related, and how the earlier person evolved (or transformed) into the later person, one knows everything there is to know about the situation that is relevant to the question of personal persistence. There is no *further fact* to know, including no further fact about whether in such circumstances one actually persists. That is, in the case of such examples, there may be no truth of the matter about whether one persists.

One of Parfit's most controversial claims emerged in connection with his discussion of his notorious 'branch line' example. He asks you to put yourself imaginatively into the place of a person on Earth who is trying to teletransport to Mars. You enter the teletransportation booth and push the button, activating the process. You succeed in producing a replica of yourself on Mars; but because the teletransporter has malfunctioned you fail to dematerialize on Earth. A few minutes later you emerge from the teletransporter and are told believably that due to the malfunctioning teletransporter your heart has been damaged and you have only two more days to live. Parfit argues that in such a case you should not be too concerned. Rather, you ought to regard your replica's persistence – now taking place on Mars – as an adequate surrogate for what might have been your own persistence on Earth (Ibid.: 200–1). While not many philosophers have followed Parfit in taking this line, explaining convincingly why one should not take it without returning to the view that identity is what matters primarily in survival has not been easy.[5]

Since 1970, the third major development in personal identity theory has been the emergence of theories according to which persons are four-dimensional objects. On the traditional three-dimensional view, a person is wholly present at a given moment, say, you are wholly present right now. Some philosophers have argued that we should replace this three-dimensional view with a four-dimensional view, according to which only time-slices or 'stages' of persons exist at short intervals of time. On this four-dimensional view, persons are aggregates of momentary person-stages, beginning with the person-stage that came into being at a person's birth and ending with the person-stage that existed when the person died, and including every person-stage between birth and death.[6]

To see one of the most important reasons why for personal identity theory it might matter which of these two views is correct, consider again any of the fission examples (except the branch-line case) discussed above. In commenting on each of those examples, it was suggested that the pre-fission person is not identical with either of his post-fission-descendants. That was a three-dimensional way of describing the situation. A four-dimensionalist would have said that what we are calling 'the pre-fission person' is really not a person but rather a person-stage and that what we are calling 'the post-fission-descendants' are also person-stages. According to a four-dimensionalist, in a fission-example the pre-fission person does not cease. Rather what happens is that the pre-fission person-stage becomes a shared person-stage. That is, two persons, whose post-fission person-stages are separate from the others overlap prior to fission and, thus, share their pre-fission person-stages.

Philosophers have used this four-dimensional way of conceptualizing what is going on in a fission example to argue that fission examples cannot be used to argue that identity is not what matters in survival. According to these philosophers, fission examples cannot be so used because in a fission example no one ceases (and, hence, identity is never traded for other benefits). Rather, what happens in a fission example is that the stages of two persons are shared stages prior to the fission, and then simply no longer shared after fission. Since, on this view, a given person-stage may be part of two or three (or potentially any number) of persons, this view is sometimes called the multiple-occupancy view of persons. Although it has its defenders, so far most personal identity theorists seem to have remained with the traditional three-dimensional view.

Why the theoretical revolution was so long in coming

Since fission examples were discussed throughout the eighteenth century why didn't the same sort of theoretical revolution that has occurred in our own time occur then, at least in the work of those who were sympathetic to a relational account of personal identity? For fission examples to have precipitated something like the post-1960s revolution in personal identity theory, it was not necessary for earlier theorists to have anticipated the development of other theories, such as the semantics of modal logic, that were not available until recently. Eighteenth-century theorists had all the theory they needed to make the moves that would not be made by theorists generally until our own times. Yet seriously questioning the importance of personal identity, which seemingly is so easily provoked by the consideration of fission examples and can arise even independently of them, apparently did not occur to anyone before Priestley and Hazlitt, or in the tradition that became analytic philosophy to anyone after them, until our own times. Why not?

An important part of the answer is that, as we have seen, there were not many influential eighteenth century theorists who were sympathetic to a relational account of personal identity: really only Locke and Hume, and Hume chose not to dirty his hands with discussion of the kinds of examples that might have led him to anticipate post-1960s developments. Collins, in the long run, was not an important philosopher and may even have set the cause of personal identity theory back by allowing himself to be upstaged by Clarke. Berkeley, Butler, Reid and Tucker were substance theorists. Law, whose account was readily available from the 1770s in Locke's collected works, was largely pragmatic about personal identity, and did not consider the kind of puzzle cases that intrigue relational theorists. And Priestley and Hazlitt had the misfortune of writing in a materialistic vein just before Kant burst onto the scene with his 'transcendental ego', which changed the topic and – whether intentionally or not – redirected nineteenth century ego-theorists toward idealism. In short, the revolution in personal identity theory that has occurred in our own times requires that thinkers go beyond the relational view of personal identity. But before they could go beyond that view, they first had to accept it. And, surprising as it may seem to us today, in the tradition that became analytic philosophy, the relational view was not generally accepted until the twentieth century, by which time fission examples, despite the brief mention of them in Locke, Reid, and Bradley had been forgotten.

Another part of the answer is that, in the eighteenth century, fission examples tended to be introduced into the debate over personal identity by soul-theorists as an *objection* to a Lockean relational view. Those, like Collins, who were sympathetic to Locke, were intent on defending a Lockean view against a threatened retreat back into what they regarded as obscurantist metaphysics. They saw fission examples as possibly motivating such a retreat. So, the context was not conducive to their seeing that fission examples, rather than an objection to a relational approach, were a way of pushing that approach to even more radical conclusions. In short, eighteenth century followers of Locke wanted to save the territory they had gained rather than push their new found advantage as far as it would take them; in the personal identity wars, they were Eisenhowers, rather than Pattons.

Finally, before many thinkers could seriously question the *importance* of personal identity in survival, the influence of Christianity had to be blunted. From the eighteenth to the twentieth centuries, most important western thinkers who took self and personal identity theory seriously were Christians and as such accepted the idea that there will be a resurrection attended by divine rewards and punishments. Few had Priestley's ability, or his motivation, to envision how those rewards and punishments might on a relational view, let alone in the absence of personal persistence, still serve the cause of divine justice.[7] Today, in the opinion of many thinkers, including some of the most influential, our bodies, or at least the physical mechanisms that underlie our consciousness, which almost all thinkers assume must exist continuously for the people whose mechanisms they are to persist, have replaced the immaterial soul as the bedrock on which our destinies, if anywhere, can rest secure. The more things change, the more they stay the same.

Nineteenth century psychology of self

In 1805, when Hazlitt published his *Essay*, what at the time was called *mental philosophy* was well on its way to spawning psychology, an empirical science that would, by the end of the century, emerge as a discipline separate from philosophy. However, the emergence of two distinct disciplines – philosophy as much moving away from psychology as the reverse – would take most of the century to achieve.[8] The same mixing of metaphysical and empirical issues that was so prevalent in the eighteenth century would continue to infect the thinking of major nineteenth century British theorists. And, while religious dogma would no longer dominate discussions of the mind, the presuppositions of an indivisible soul continued to work in the background of many discussions of the ego, even among many progressive thinkers.

Consider, for example, the work of Thomas Brown, James Mill and John Stuart Mill on self and personal identity. In 1820, Brown's *Lectures on the Philosophy of the Human Mind* were much more psychological than philosophical, though he believed that mental philosophy had implications for epistemology (Brown 1820). Nevertheless, for the most part he studied phenomena of mind from a realist perspective. When he dealt with the issue of personal identity, which he preferred to call *mental identity*, he was interested in analysing how we come to suppose that the self that remembers is the same one that is remembered. Viewing all conscious mental states as 'feeling', or experiential, states of various kinds, he suggested that 'the belief of our mental identity' is 'founded on an essential principle of our constitution', in consequence of which, 'it is *impossible* for us to consider *our* successive feelings, without regarding them as truly *our* successive feelings', that is, as 'states, or affections of one thinking substance' (Ibid.: v. 1, 133). From such intuitions of the substantial identity underlying *successive* (that is, proximate) experiences, one readily goes on to view more distant remembered experiences as one's own as well, thus conceiving of an identical self underlying the stream of conscious experiences.

James Mill built on Brown's observations, but tried to reduce all mental phenomena to associations. When Mill considered the problem of identity, he, first, dealt with the notion of identity of objects, which he accounted for in terms of associated resemblances over time. In the case of persons, he supposed that necessarily when one remembers having some experience, one believes that it was oneself who had it. In such cases of memory, he maintained, 'the Evidence' of one's own existence, and 'the Belief' in it 'are not different things, but the same thing' (Mill 1829: v. 2, 168). In the case of times that one does not remember, but times when one nevertheless believes one existed, one relies on verbal evidence from others, which is itself based on observations that others have made of one's bodily and psychological continuity and resemblances among person stages. In Mill's quite naturalistic view, the self can be observed by other people. He, thus, focussed less on mental identity, than on a body-based personal identity. His son John Stuart, would later find inconsistencies in his father's view (Ibid.: 174).

Brown and James Mill were predominately psychological in their theories, and for that reason, their thinking has been appreciated subsequently more by psychologists than by philosophers. For instance, William James applauded Brown's discussions of connectedness in the stream of consciousness, and quoted Brown in his famous chapter on the 'stream of thought', in *Principles of Psychology*' (James 1890: 248, 276–7). Likewise, psychologists at the end of the nineteenth century regarded James Mill's associative psychology as an important advance on Hartley's approach. By contrast, they tended to consider John Stuart Mill's psychology, which has been greatly appreciated by early twentieth century analytical philosophers, as too philosophical.[9]

John Stuart Mill's 'psychology' was primarily epistemology. By 1865, when he wrote his *Examination of Sir William Hamilton's Philosophy*, it had been thirty-five years since his father's book was first published, and much had changed in the relations between philosophy and psychology (Mill 1865). Kantian philosophy had come to Britain, and Hamilton had tried unsuccessfully to integrate it with the Scottish common sense approach. In 1856, James Ferrier, who opposed Hamilton as much as John Stuart Mill later would, published his *Institutes of Metaphysic*, in which he made a disciplinary distinction between metaphysics and psychology, declaring that metaphysics belonged to philosophy, and had to be purified of all naturalistic reasoning (Ferrier 1856). Ferrier, an apostate of the Scottish school, saw metaphysics as composed of 'Epistemology' and 'Ontology', thus introducing the term 'epistemology' into the English language. He viciously attacked Reid, declaring him philosophically incompetent and rejected as failed epistemology the naturalistic and psychological approach to the mind that Reid had tried so hard to promote.[10]

John Stuart Mill would follow a similar line in criticizing Reid's intuitionism. In place of intuition, Mill thought that his own phenomenalist project, which he called the *psychological theory*, was a kind of foundational psychology; but it was psychology in the sense in which Hume's main focus in Book 1 of the *Treatise* was psychology. In Mill's view, the external world is a 'permanent possibilities of sensation', and other minds are inferred to exist based on an analogy with one's own case, which Mill presumed one knows directly. Like objects in the external world, Mill supposed that minds too are just actual and possible sensations. Since the ego or self is not given in experience, accounting for self-knowledge was a problem for his theory. He responded that self-knowledge must be based on an intuitive belief in our own continued existence that comes with our ability to remember past states of mind as our own. Mill's view would later influence Russell and other twentieth century sense-data theorists (Mill 1865: 225–64).

There were real psychological theories of the self beginning to emerge in the nineteenth century, which were developmental as well as empirical, but they were not emerging in Britain. British theorists, having brushed aside or in most cases never even heard of Hazlitt's developmental psychology, were still torturing themselves over grounds for personal identity, rather than considering how a concept of self is actually acquired. In Germany, shortly after Hazlitt wrote the *Essay*, J. Herbart, the successor at Konigsberg to Kant, wrote several works that were primarily psychological, including his *Textbook of Psychology* (1813) and *Psychology as a Science* (1824–5), in which he advocated, based in part on his general theory of how concepts or ideas emerge out of experience, that one acquires in developmental stages the concept of self.[11] In his view, initially the idea comes from one's experience of one's bodily activities, which provides us with information about ourselves as well as about objects in the world with which we interact. Eventually, we form an organized idea of our own body as our self. But then, as we become more thoughtful, and relate past to present thoughts, we come to identify more with our ideas than our bodies and thereby develop a notion of an ego or subject of our thoughts. We then generalize this as an abstract ego, or identical subject of experience, that persists throughout our lives.

Meanwhile, in France, Maine de Biran, following the leads of Destutt deTracy and P. J. G. Cabanis, also formulated a developmental account of self.[12] De Biran's focus was on the active or voluntary self, which we first notice in experiencing the resistance of the world to our desires. The continuity of voluntary or effortful experience provides us with the ground for our concept of ourselves extended over time. In the main, subsequent nineteenth century accounts of the development of the self that had a psychological orientation

165

would build on the insights of Herbart and de Biran more than on those of the British tradition.

Toward the end of the nineteenth century, theories of dissociation of personality were also introduced. Dissociation was a phenomenon made salient to scientists when Anton Mesmer, in the eighteenth century, demonstrated what was later called *hypnotism*. But it took a while for the empirical nature of the phenomenon to come under experimental control. During most of the nineteenth century, dissociative phenomena, such as hypnotism, were not investigated scientifically. Cases of dual consciousness were reported by medical authorities, but they remained mysterious incidents open to religious and other outmoded explanations. Toward the end of the century, a number of cases of dissociative phenomena, including dual and multiple personality, were investigated by scientifically oriented doctors, and the relationship between hypnosis and some of these other dissociative states was recognized. Some theorists hypthesized relations between dissociative phenomena and brain activity, without yet having a detailed understanding of that connection. The basic idea of these scientists was that various dissociations involving personality might be due to lack of normal integration of brain activity.

One of the earlier scientific psychologists to take a brain-oriented view of dissociation of personality was Theodule Ribot, the 'father' of the French school of psychopathology. In *Diseases of Personality*, Ribot was not hesitant to contrast his scientific view of the phenomenon of personality with a traditional metaphysical view:

> By 'person' in psychological language we understand generally the individual, as clearly conscious of itself, and acting accordingly: it is the highest form of individuality. To explain this attribute, which it reserves exclusively for man, metaphysical psychology is satisfied with the hypothesis of the ego, absolutely one, simple, and identical. Unfortunately, however this is only an illusive clearness and a semblance of a solution. Unless we attribute to this ego a supernatural origin, it will be necessary to explain how it is born, and from what lower form it proceeds. Accordingly, experimental psychology must propound the problem differently, and treat it by different methods.
>
> (Ribot 1891: 1)

He went on to contrast the two hypotheses generated by these two psychologies: 'the one, a very old hypothesis, which regards consciousness as the fundamental property of the "soul" or "mind", as that which constitutes its essence', the other, 'a very recent theory, which regards it as a simple phenomenon, superadded to the brain', an 'event having its own conditions of existence, appearing and disappearing according to circumstance' (Ibid.: 3–4). He pointed out that although the first hypothesis has 'held sway for centuries' it cannot explain the 'unconscious life of the mind', whereas the second 'expresses the unconscious in physiological terms'. He took this to be a virtue of the second hypothesis since, in his view, 'nervous activity is far more extensive than psychic activity'.

Ribot claimed that every conscious episode is a complex event that is 'superadded' to 'a particular state of the nervous system', and that 'all manifestations of psychic life, sensations, desires, feelings, volitions, memories, reasonings, inventions, etc., may be alternately conscious and unconscious' (Ibid.: 5–6). As he put it, consciousness is just a 'perfection' of physiological conditions, though one that needs to be explained in terms of its concrete conditions of appearance. He pointed out that the alternative hypothesis, that the soul's essence is thinking and that it 'is impossible that consciousness should not exist even when not a trace of it is left in memory', begs the question (Ibid.: 8). Thus, his empiricism began on the same grounds as Locke's, but pushed much further the hypothesis of thinking matter; and proposed to investigate directly the physiological conditions of the 'superaddition' of consciousness.

Ribot goes through numerous cases of diseases of personality including physical ones, such as the 'double monsters' (the Hungarian twins), that were parodied in *Scriblerus*, as well as psychological cases of multiple personality. He said that the former provides evidence of the physical basis of personality, while the latter suggests that the ego is merely a synthesis of conscious states of the organism.[13] Toward the end of his book, he said that 'the organism and the brain, as its highest representation, constitute the real personality, containing in itself all that we have been and the possibilities of all that we shall be'. In the brain, 'the whole individual character is inscribed', together 'with all its active and passive aptitudes, sympathies, and antipathies; its genius, talents, or stupidity; its virtues, vices, torpor, or activity'. 'What emerges and reaches consciousness', he said, 'is little compared with what lies buried below, albeit still active. Conscious personality is never more than a feeble portion of physical personality'.

Turning, then, to consideration of the ego, Ribot continued, 'The unity of the ego, in a psychological sense, is, accordingly, the cohesion, during a given period, of a certain number of distinct states of consciousness, accompanied by others less distinct, and by a multitude of physiological states which, though not accompanied by consciousness like the others, yet operate as powerfully as they if not more so'. He concluded that 'Unity means co-ordination' and that consciousness being subordinate to the organism, 'the problem of the unity of the ego is, in its ultimate form, a biological problem'. So, 'to biology belongs the task of explaining, if it can, the genesis of organisms and the solidarity of their component parts'. 'Psychological interpretation', he concluded, 'can only follow in its wake' (Ibid.:154–6). Ribot appealed to the theory of evolution to support his view that biology is the ultimate ground upon which psychology – even human personality – is built.

The importance of social existence for a genetic psychology of self was not recognized until late in the century, in the work of James Mark Baldwin, an American experimental psychologist. Baldwin had been a student of James McCosh, the last member, and historian, of the Scottish school. Among psychologists, Baldwin is generally regarded as the first developmental psychologist of self. His wide-ranging genetic psychology had an enormous influence on subsequent developmentalists, particularly on Piaget. According to Baldwin, in *History of Psychology*, the discovery of social influence on the origins of the ego depended in part on the rise in evolutionary thinking, and in part on the anti-individualistic, collectivist orientation that emerged in the latter part of the nineteenth century (Baldwin 1913).

Baldwin and his friend, Josiah Royce, the American philosopher, apparently recognized the social origins of the self at about the same time, publishing their ideas in the mid-1890s in different works. Royce, in his original paper on the topic, pointed out that his goal is to provide an explanation for the variations in self-consciousness that are found empirically, in particular, in abnormal psychology, rather than consider 'the philosophical aspects of the problem of self-consciousness [which] belong altogether elsewhere' (Royce 1894:169). What he noted about the abnormalities of self-consciousness is that they typically involve patients' estimations of their relations with others, that is, they are *'maladies of social consciousness'*. For evidence of abnormal variations in self-consciousness, he referred to Ribot's book on *Diseases of Personality*, but proposed that these variations have their origins in social consciousness.

In *The World and the Individual*, Royce described, in words reminiscent of Hazlitt but probably inspired by Hegel, what he took to be a fundamental fact thought to be at the root of the social origin of self-consciousness: 'Were no difference observed between the contents which constitute the observed presence of my neighbor, and the contents which constitute my own life in the same moment, then my sense of my neighbor's presence, and my idea of myself, would blend in my consciousness, and there would be so far neither Alter nor Ego observed' (Royce 1901: 263). Earlier Royce had written:

> Self-conscious functions are all of them, in their finite, human and primary aspect, social functions, due to habits of social intercourse. They involve the presentation of some contrast between Ego and non-Ego. This psychological contrast is primarily that between the subject's own conscious act, idea, intent, or other experience, and an experience which is regarded by him as representing the state of another's mind.
>
> (Royce 1894: 196)

Although self-consciousness begins only in social relations to others, Royce argued that eventually it includes other aspects of the physical world. 'By means of habits gradually acquired, this contrast [between self and other] early comes to be extended to include that between one's inner states and the represented realities that make up the physical world' (Ibid.). Hence, in contrast to Herbart and de Biran, it is not the opposition of the world that makes us self-conscious, but originally, it is our relations with other animate beings, in particular human beings, by which we become aware of ourselves. This, then, generalizes to our other relations with the world.

The fundamental principle of Baldwin's theory was that imitation or mimicry was the foundation of social life and the origin of the infant's understanding of the category *person*. In the latter part of the eighteenth century, this principle had been suggested in theories about the role of mimicry in sympathetic imagination. Adam Smith, in particular, likened imagination to mimicry, and connected both to sympathy and through it to social phenomena. Later on, Dugald Stewart, Reid's student, who replaced Smith at Edinburgh, would recognize what he called sympathetic imitation as an important social phenomenon. He even postulated that such mimicry was especially powerful in childhood, and as such, at the very foundations of social life.[14] However, with the possible exception of Hazlitt, what none of the eighteenth- or early nineteenth-century philosophers or psychologists recognized was how these phenomena were connected to the development of the infant's acquired knowledge of ego and alter as persons, with minds. These thinkers were caught up in an individualistic perspective. Understanding one's own mind, either came immediately in experience through reflexive self-knowledge, or was acquired prior to acquiring knowledge of the minds of others. But, by the end of the century James Baldwin and Josiah Royce were able to go beyond this.

Baldwin, in particular, had an especially clear grip on the concept of mental development. In contrasting the old-fashioned soul view ('a fixed substance, with fixed attributes'), he said that it was as if 'knowledge of the soul was immediate in consciousness, and adequate'. 'The mind was best understood where best or most fully manifested; its higher "faculties" even when not in operation, were still there, but asleep'. It was, he said, as if soul-theorists assumed that 'the man is father of the child'. 'If the adult consciousness shows the presence of principles not observable in the child consciousness, we must suppose, nevertheless, that they are really present in the child consciousness beyond the reach of our observation'. The proper procedure ('the genetic idea'), Baldwin claimed, is precisely the opposite of this.

> Instead of a fixed substance, we have the conception of a growing, developing activity. Functional psychology succeeds faculty psychology. Instead of beginning with the most elaborate exhibition of this growth and development, we shall find most instruction in the simplest activity that is at the same time the same activity. Development is a process of involution as well as evolution, and the

elements come to be hidden under the forms of complexity which they build up.

(Baldwin 1894: 2–3)

Instead of the traditional approach, he claimed, we must try to explain adult behavior on the basis of 'faculties' available also to the child, and then, if that fails, trace the development of those faculties in the process of maturation:

> Are there principles in the adult consciousness which do not appear in the child consciousness, then the adult consciousness must, if possible, be interpreted by principles present in the child consciousness; and when this is not possible, the conditions under which later principles take their rise and get their development must still be adequately explored.
>
> (Ibid.: 3)

No one in the eighteenth century had such a clear grasp of the notion of mental development. No one, even today, has a clearer grasp.

In Baldwin's theory of the origins of self-consciousness, the child first becomes aware of others as persons, rather than of itself. This, Baldwin calls 'the projective phase'. Subsequently, the child becomes aware of its own 'subjective' activity. In this phase, self-awareness comes about through mimicry of others, but this time through the volition involved in trying to imitate. In the next, 'ejective phase', the child comes to understand what others feel by 'ejecting' his own inner states onto them: 'The subjective becomes *ejective*; that is, other people's bodies, says the child to himself, have experiences *in them* such as mine has. They also have *me's*'. In this third phase, Baldwin concludes, 'the social self is born' (Ibid.: 335–8). In sum, as the infant develops it goes through various stages in acquiring a subjective understanding of mind, all of which involve some form of mimicry and, eventually, differentiation of self and other.

In *History of Psychology*, Baldwin, rather than presenting his own particular view of the matter, generalizes the basic principles of his social–psychological approach to self-consciousness:

> In the personal self, the social is individualized. . . . A constant give-and-take process – a 'social dialectic' – is found between the individual and his social fellows. By this process the materials of self-hood are absorbed and assimilated. The 'self' is a gradually forming nucleus in the mind; a mass of feeling, effort, and knowledge. It grows in feeling by contagion, in knowledge by imitation, in will by opposition and obedience. The outline of the individual gradually appears, and every stage it shows the pattern of the social situation in

170

which it becomes constantly a more and more adequate and competent unit.

He continued:

> The consciousness of the self, thus developed, carries with it that of the 'alter'-selves, the other 'socii', who are also determinations of the same social matter. The bond, therefore, that binds the members of the group together is reflected in the self-consciousness of each member.... When the self has become a conscious and active person, we may say that the mental individual as such is born. But the individual remains part of the whole out of which he has arisen, a whole that is collective in character and of which he is a specification.
>
> (Baldwin 1913: 108–9)

Since Baldwin, this collectivist vision of the origins of self consciousness, which was beyond the scope of eighteenth- and early nineteenth-century thinkers, has in the twentieth century come to dominate the psychology of the self. While in the twentieth century most analytic *philosophers*, in accounting for personal identity, have maintained an individualistic agenda, *psychologists* have found the origins and identity of the individual self only within a shared social reality.

Contemporary psychology of self

Psychologists in our own times who are interested in the origins of self-consciousness have tried, like Baldwin, to connect an evolutionary and developmental approach. Moreover, they have worked under the supposition that knowing one's own mind as such, is related to knowing that others also have minds. Two papers published in the 1970s were important in focusing attention on this topic. Nicholas Humphrey proposed that human intelligence evolved primarily as social intelligence, and that our capacity to become conscious of our own mental states served the function of allowing us to understand the mental states of others. He suggested that by having access to our mental states, we could use our own minds to simulate the minds of others, imagining what we would feel and do in their situations. Such simulation could also help us anticipate our own reactions to imagined situations that do not currently exist but which might occur. Thus, we could not only understand and anticipate the actions and reactions of others, but we could understand and anticipate our own reactions to various possible future events (Humphrey 1976).

Within a year of Humphrey's article, Premack and Woodruff published a paper titled, 'Do chimpanzees have a theory of mind?' It was known at the time that chimpanzees could recognize themselves in a mirror, although almost all other organisms with the exception of humans could not do so (soon it was learned that orang-utans, but not gorillas, are able to recognize themselves). It was also known that infants could not recognize themselves in mirrors until they are 18 months old. But self-recognition, although it can be taken to imply knowledge of oneself as an independent being, does not imply either that one is reflexively aware of one's own mind or that one is aware that other similar beings also have minds. The Premack and Woodruff paper attempted to provide evidence that chimpanzees have theoretical under-standing of the contents of other individuals' minds, which could reflect on their understanding of minds as such – including their own (Premack and Woodruff 1978). In commentaries on the original article and elsewhere, Premack and Woodruff's conclusions have been hotly debated. It is still in doubt whether chimps appreciate mental states, whether of themselves or others. Nevertheless, a burgeoning area of research in comparative and developmental psychology has been spawned.[15]

Although the debate over whether any other organisms really have the capacity to understand mental phenomena as such still rages, in the case of humans the developmental story is fairly clear. In certain important respects, this story connects to some of the discoveries made during the eighteenth and nineteenth century that we considered. The developmentalists have tried to trace the origins of consciousness of self and other from infancy. They have discovered that almost at birth the infant is sensitive to the difference between humans and inanimate objects. There is also evidence that infants have the ability to recognize and contagiously mimic both emotional and other facial expressions. Thus, are laid the foundations of the 'social self', one that participates in feelings and activities with other beings of the same species. This does not yet imply any reflective awareness of such participation and, as we shall see, such awareness does not appear until much later.

The infant also becomes aware of its 'ecological self' early on, in a kind of self-knowledge that distinguishes its boundaries from the world within which it acts.[16] This would be the kind of self-information recognized by Herbart and de Biran, in which the infant becomes aware of its body parts and how it can manipulate and control them in ways it cannot do with respect to other objects.

Theorists have supposed, in addition, that during the first year of life as the infant acquires greater knowledge of its body, it also becomes better able to appreciate parallels between its own body and the bodies of others. So by mid-year the infant is beginning, purposely, to imitate the bodily movements of others. Yet, it also continues contagiously to mimic emotional expressions. Toward the end of the first year, the infant is able to participate with others in shared activities, and can, through attending to the emotional expressions of others, become aware of the meaning of these expressions with respect to other objects. Yet, at this time, infants are still not aware of distinctions between their own mental attitudes toward objects and those of other individuals with whom they interact. They merely enter into and share the attitudes with significant others. It is only at the beginning of the second year of life that the infant becomes increasingly aware of self and other as separate individuals with possibly different attitudes toward the same objects or events (Barresi and Moore 1996).

From our perspective, one of the interesting phenomena that occurs during this period are the infant's sympathetic responses to others' emotional expressions. In humans, but not lower animals, emotional contagion is typically a stage on the way toward understanding the point of view of another and sympathizing with it. As Hoffman, in particular, has shown, there is in humans, from the age of about 10 to 18 months, a gradual development of its understanding of the sources of its contagiously acquired emotions (Hoffman 1977). For instance, typically an infant of 10 months responds to the distress (e.g., crying) of another by becoming distressed itself, as a consequence of which it consoles only itself while ignoring the other. Later, apparently realizing that it shares a common emotion with the other, intermittently it consoles the other as well as itself. Eventually, the infant may no longer cry, but apparently recognizing that it is the other who is sad simply tries to console the other. Subsequently the normal child's sympathetic responses show an increasing sensitivity to the needs of others, not merely by consoling them, but by responding more specifically to their mental states and motivations based on a better appreciation of their points of view.

This is one, among several phenomena, including mirror self-recognition, which indicate that the 18-month- to 2-year-old child has begun to differentiate between self and other, and to acquire an appreciation of certain mental states of self and other as existing concurrently, yet as different from each other. At this time, the child is also acquiring mastery in language, which greatly facilitates its communicating about mental states. Even so, most researchers are convinced that 2-year-olds do not yet have what researchers call a (representational) theory of mind. The child at this time is competent in dealing with perceptually available mental states in self and other, but is not yet able to represent mental states that may have existed in the past or will exist in the future, but are not currently present. Nor at this stage are children able to deal with mental states, such as belief, that misrepresent current states of affairs. Since Premack and Woodruff's paper, theorists have called the possession of such capacities the possession of a theory of mind.[17] In the classic study by Wimmer and Perner, published in 1983, it was shown that not until children are 4 years old are they capable of representing correctly another's false belief (Wimmer and Perner 1983). Three-year-olds merely assume that the other knows what they themselves know, even when this could not be the case, say, because the other was not available to acquire the knowledge.

The discovery that 4-year-olds, but not 3-year-olds, were capable of representing false belief sparked an enormous amount of research on what came to be known as the age-4 transition, and important other findings were made. For instance, it was discovered that besides understanding false belief as it applied to another's mind, the child was also acquiring the ability to distinguish appearance from reality, as well as that different people might from their own points of view see things differently. But the child also learned more about its own mental states at this time. At this age it is first able to remember its own past beliefs that were false, as well as to remember previous desires that had changed. It also acquires an understanding of itself as extended in time, but as transforming through time and, more generally, it acquires an autobiographical self. There is also evidence that, at this time, the child first begins to deal with a future self, whose motives differ from its own current motives.[18]

Collectively these findings suggest that the child becomes generally conscious of its own mental states – past, present, and future – at the same time as it becomes able to represent abstractly (as opposed to perceive) the mental states of others. In other words, the child at this time becomes conscious of her own mind, as well as of the minds of others, and comes to form a belief in the existence of mind or, at least, in the existence of private, representational mental states that can differ among individuals and within an individual over time. At this time, the child thus acquires both a 'private self' and an 'extended self'. In effect, it is only at this late date in development that the child acquires reflexive consciousness, in the eighteenth century meaning of that term. Thus, only after the child turns 4 can they begin to form a concept of personal identity or self as a mind (or consciousness) that persists over time. And it is apparently a necessary condition for the child to form a concept of its own mind as such, that it be able to conceive that other individuals also have minds. Apparently, without the distinction between mental states in self and other (or between present, past, and future mental states of itself), the child would form no notion of mental states as states of mind at all. These findings in the developmental psychology of self also suggest that reflexive consciousness, far from being an intrinsic property of mind, may only be a theoretical construct, and that the mind itself may be a fiction, that is, a theory that children in Western culture acquire in order to explain human behavior.

What price self-knowledge?

As our survey reveals, the history of theorizing in the west about self and personal identity is a story of increasing fragmentation. Repeatedly what began as one question has become two, and then eventually even more. And the rate at which old questions have spawned new ones has accelerated. In classical Greece, in the hands of Plato, the more or less empirical question of whether selves survive bodily death gave birth to the primarily philosophical question of personal identity. That philosophical question is the question of what it is that makes us the same people from moment to moment, day to day, and so on. Arguably, before the empirical question can be answered, the philosophical one has to be answered. Over time, the number and complexity of competing answers to the philosophical question has continued to grow, with no signs that the process is slowing down, and with no theoretical convergence in sight.

From Plato until Locke, substance accounts of the nature of personal identity carried the day. But such seeming theoretical unanimity masks the reality that throughout late antiquity and into the Middle Ages different sorts of competing substance accounts were continually being proposed. Some of these highlighted the distinction between the immaterial soul and matter, others stressed their integration as matter and form, and so on. Once Locke proposed a relational account of personal identity, discussion of these earlier alternatives slowed down, but it never vanished completely and to this day, the competition between these alternatives has never been resolved.

Initially, the relational alternative to the traditional substance views was just Locke's simple memory theory, which was a mentalistic version of the relations account that highlighted just one element of minds. But eventually other sorts of mentalistic-relations accounts have been proposed, as well as competing bodily-relations accounts, in which different sorts of bodily relations have been stressed. Some, for instance, have focused on the importance of the continuous existence of the organic brain, others on just certain parts of the organic brain, still others merely on a material brain, whether organic or not, still others on some other sort of bodily continuity.

All of these mentalistic- and bodily-relations views were just variations on what in time came to be recognized as an internal relations view. In our own times, all internal relational views, of whatever sort, in addition to competing with each other have had to compete with external relations views. Among external relation theorists, three-dimensionalists about persons have had to contend continually with the objections of four-dimensionalists, and vice versa; and so it goes on. It is difficult even for anyone to follow just this strand of the evolving tradition of answers to the philosophical question of identity. But it is not just this strand that matters or just the answers to the traditional question that continually move on. The *question* itself has moved on.

As we have seen, as early as Lucretius the philosophical question of personal identity has had to share the limelight with the question of what matters primarily in survival. Until recently the two questions were not often thought of as two. Even so, both were there continuing to exercise an influence on the way theorists thought about self and personal identity. In the aftermath of Locke's new theory, the two questions began to take on a life of their own, and then in our own times have been reborn, increasingly becoming two separate traditions of inquiry.

While all of this was going on, beginning in the eighteenth century a science of mind, with new empirical approaches and agendas, slowly separated itself from traditionally philosophical concerns and made its appearance. Soon, what began in the early eighteenth century as different approaches to the same questions (see, for instance, Butler's discussion of alternative ways to approach the same questions about human nature) soon evolved into different approaches to what began to be seen by the theorists involved as related but distinct concerns. And throughout the nineteenth and into the twentieth century, as psychology separated from philosophy and consolidated its status as a separate discipline, questions, answers, and approaches – in each discipline – continued to multiply. Today, few philosophers of personal identity know much about related developments in the contemporary psychology of self and identity, and few psychologists know much about related developments in philosophy. Beyond that, few philosophers or psychologists know much about related developments in separate traditions even within their own disciplines. For instance, few philosophers who are engaged in the analytic consideration of these issues know much about related work being done in phenomenological traditions. And an analogous situation exists among psychologists; few who have been trained in experimental research know much about related work being done in phenomenological traditions.

The problem posed by researchers working in isolation from others who are working on similar problems is not so much due to arrogance or lack of interest, though there is plenty of both to go around. The more fundamental problem is simply lack of time. There is too much to know, even in one's own little niche, to leave time for plumbing the depths of other traditions and approaches. And this problem is going to get worse – one would like to add, 'before it gets better', except for the certainty that it never is going to get better. It is just going to get worse. No doubt, eventually it is going to get so much worse that current perplexity at what to do about it will some day be looked back upon nostalgically as quaint.

Toward the beginning of the eighteenth century, many important thinkers of the time faced a kind of existential crisis concerning the self. It was due to the emergence as a question of what previously it had seemed could not possibly be a question – whether we even exist as selves that persist. What previously would have been a laughably improbable answer to that question had suddenly become plausible. Today our sense of crisis has a different cause. What is threatening now is not an unwelcome answer but a dawning awareness that there may be no basic overarching questions to which there could be even unwelcome answers. For instance, if there is less of a sense of crisis now about the reality of the self, it is not so much because we have gotten used to unwelcome answers, or even countered them with more welcome ones, as it is that even what previously had seemed like a single, central question about the reality of the self has become hopelessly variegated. It evolved into a syndrome of related questions that are so technical that none but the carefully initiated can even wade into the project of investigating them without soon drowning in a sea of symbols, technical distinctions, and empirical results.

Where will it all end? In our admittedly speculative view, today's hand-wringing about the problem of fragmentation and the still lingering hope for eventual reintegration will be replaced by the recognition that the multi-faceted threads of debate and theorizing are never going to be gathered together and woven into a single fabric. We have passed from an era in which the chief source of concern was unwelcome answers and both the hope and fear of new knowledge, to one in which the chief source of concern is lack of any comprehensive questions, let alone answers, and the certainty of continually increasing, albeit fragmenting additions to our knowledge. In short, there is nothing to do about fragmentation, except perhaps to get over the feeling that there is anything that needs to be done about it. We have come a long way since Plato. The crucial turn came during the eighteenth century, when knowledge became secularized. Enlightenment thinkers, in effect, made a pact with the devil. They set in motion a process that has culminated, beyond their wildest dreams, in knowledge if not of the self *per se*, then at least of human nature and of the rest of the natural world. In exchange, they relinquished their souls.

NOTES

1   The translations of Lucretius in the passages quoted are due to R. E. Latham. Other scholars translate these crucial passages differently. In William H. D. Rouse, for instance, Lucretius wrote, 'Even if time shall gather together our matter after death and bring it back again as it is now placed, and if once more the light of life shall be given to us, yet it would not matter one bit to us that even this had been done, when the recollection of ourselves has once been broken asunder' (Lucretius 1924: 255). In H. A. J. Munro's translation, the same passage reads, 'And if time should gather up our matter after our death and put it once more into the position in which it now is, and the light of life be given to us again, this result even would concern us not at all, when the chain of our self-consciousness has once been snapped asunder' (Lucretius 1940: 131).

Even though the word *repetentia*, which Latham translated as *identity* is trans-lated by Rouse as *recollection of ourselves* and by Munro as *self-consciousness*, the point of Lucretius' reflections remains basically the same. It is that one's body and spirit, including one's memories, must be united and exist *continuously* into a future about which it is rational for one to feel egoistic concern. Once this conti-nuity is broken, as it is at bodily death, then rational egoistic concern is no longer possible. A natural way to express this point is that once this continuity is broken, then rational egoistic concern is no longer possible because *we* no longer exist.

In the eighteenth century, Lucretius was studied by virtually every British thinker. So, whatever he may have meant in the passages here under discussion, to assess his influence on subsequent accounts of self and personal identity, it is necessary to consider what others took him to mean. Abraham Tucker, writing toward the end of the eighteenth century, took Lucretius to be making a point not just about memory and self-concern, but about identity and self-concern. According to Tucker, Lucretius was forced to consider the objection that 'the atoms, some thousands of years hence, after infinite tumblings and tossings about, would fall into their former situation, from whence a thinking, feeling soul must necessarily result: but he denied that this would be the same soul. Just as when a company of dancers assemble together and dance for 6 hours, the whole is one ball: but if they leave off at the end of 3 hours, and a fortnight afterwards a second party is proposed whereon they meet to dance for 3 hours again, this is a ball too, but another ball distinct from the former. So the soul, which is but a dance of atoms, cannot be the same . . . [and] therefore, whatever wretched fortune may befal it, we, that is, our present souls, have no concern therein' (Tucker 1805, v. 7: 11–12).

2 For instance, in a later section of the same *Ennead* from which the previous remarks were taken, Plotinus wrote that when 'a single coition and a single sperm suffice to a twin birth or in the animal order to a litter; there is a splitting and diverging of the seed, every divergent part being obviously a whole: surely no honest mind can fail to gather that a thing in which part is identical with whole has a nature which transcends quantity, and must of necessity be without quantity: only so could it remain identical when quantity is flitched from it, only by being indifferent to amount or extension, by being in essence something apart. Thus, the Soul and the Reason – Principles – are without quantity' (Plotinus 1952: 194). It would take us too far afield to pursue the question of how this passage should be interpreted. However, it clearly suggests how Plotinus would have responded to the possibility of a person's fissioning into two apparently separate persons, neither of which is conscious of the other's internal mental states in the same 'first person' way in which the other is conscious of them. What it suggests is that Plotinus would have thought that both of these apparently separate persons (that is, the fission-descendants) would actually be the same person as the pre-fission person and as each other. Plotinus may or may not have entertained this idea. As we shall see in Chapter 2, Locke's disciple, Anthony Collins explicitly endorsed it.

3 When he died, Locke did not have a copy of Plotinus in his library, so, the suggestion that he read Plotinus in the original is speculative. Locke did, however, own copies of the main works of Cudworth, More, and Smith, who quoted profusely from Plotinus. It is also known that, in 1682, at about the time Locke wrote his first journal entry on the role of conscious memory in identity, he read Smith's *Discourse on Immortality*, and also read Cudworth shortly thereafter, well before he wrote the 1683 journal entry which gives his first definition of personal identity. See Aaron and Gibb 1936: 121–3; Ayers 1991; Marshall 1994.

4 For more on this and related passages, see Sutton (1998: 72–3).

5 Leibniz would have been included in those who set the stage, if he had published his *Discourse on Metaphysics* (section 34), which was written in 1686 and sent to Arnauld. In this work, Leibniz's reflections on personal identity are remarkably similar to Locke's own private Journal notes on the issue, written several years earlier. For instance, in comparing the human soul to animal souls, Leibniz wrote, 'But the intelligent soul, knowing what it is – having the ability to utter the word "I", a word so full of meaning – does not merely remain and subsist metaphysically, which it does to a greater degree than the others, but also remains the same morally, and constitutes the same person. For it is memory or the knowledge of this self that renders it capable of punishment or reward'. As we shall see, Leibniz's focus on the relationship between recollective memory of past actions and capacity for reward and punishment is echoed perfectly in Locke's account. Leibniz continues: 'Thus the immortality required in morality and religion does not consist merely in this perpetual subsistence common to all substances, for without the memory of what one has been, there would be nothing desirable about it'. Again, the focus is similar to Locke, in that 'forensic' concerns involving this life as well as any future life do not depend on mere substance, but on memory. But Leibniz continues with a passage more reminiscent of Lucretius (who may have been his source) than of arguments that Locke would use: 'Suppose that some person all of a sudden becomes the king of China, but only on the condition that he forgets what he has been, as if he were born anew; practically, or as far as the effects could be perceived, wouldn't that be the same as if he were annihilated and a king of China created at the same instant in his place? That is something this individual would have no reason to

desire' (Leibniz 1989: 65–6). Like Lucretius, Leibniz supposes that without memory, even a reconstituted 'self' would not really be oneself, at least with respect to self-concern, and that this would be so even if the reconstituted self were a continuation (or reconstitution) of one's substance. For more on Leibniz's views on self-concern, see Bobro 1998.

6 Locke was interested in the topic of the Trinity, and owned several critiques of Sherlock's views, published before the second edition of Locke's *Essay*. He also owned the 1694 edition of Sherlock's book. In correspondence, in 1690, one of Locke's friends in Holland commented on Sherlock's book in a letter written to Locke (De Beer 1979, v. 4: 145). It hardly seems possible that Locke could have failed to have read Sherlock's book shortly after it came out. Furthermore, as Ayers (1991, v. 2: 257, 323) has suggested, it seems that Locke borrowed some language, if not ideas, from Sherlock's work. See also Wedeking (1990), on the relationship between Sherlock and Locke.

1 PERSONAL IDENTITY

1 Locke structured his larger account of identity around two fundamental assumptions: that two things of the same kind cannot exist in the same place at the same time; and that one thing cannot have two beginnings of existence. He made two additional assumptions, which are less clear: that there are only three basic kinds of substance: God, finite intelligences, and bodies; and that the identity conditions for a substance or mode depend on the *idea* of that substance or mode. The first of these two latter assumptions is unclear because it is not obvious what Locke understood by two or his three basic kinds of substance, 'finite intelligence' and 'body'. He surely thought that angels are finite intelligences. However, angels are immaterial and, hence, not composed of any more basic parts which may themselves be substances. What about humans and persons? Locke admitted that, for all we know, humans may be wholly material. By implication, he seems to have admitted that persons too may be wholly material. But, then, are humans and/or persons also finite intelligences? A reason for thinking that, in Locke's view, humans and persons may not be genuine substances and, hence, may not qualify as finite intelligences, is that humans and persons may be composed of material atoms, which Locke clearly did regard as genuine substances. Another reason for thinking that humans and persons may not be genuine substances is that it would help explain why in remarking that 'if *Person*, *Man*, and *Substance* are three Names standing for three different *Ideas*', it is 'one thing to be the same *Substance*, another the same *Man*, and a third the same *Person*', Locke *contrasted* Substance, Man, and Person (Locke, 1975, II.xxvii.7; 332).

In the case of the second assumption, it is unclear whether Locke subscribed to what has come to be known as an absolute or a relative conception of identity. On an absolute conception, the relation of identity which obtains between things is always the same even though the kind of things between which it obtains may vary. Thus, we mean the same thing in saying of a chair or a person that exists today that it (or a stage of it which exists today) is the same chair or person that existed yesterday, even if chairs and persons are different kinds of things. On a relative conception, by contrast, there is a different kind of identity corresponding to each different kind of thing. And relative-identity theorists reject the identity of indiscernables – the principle that if two things are identical, then they have all of the same properties. Instead, relative-identity theorists maintain that it is possible for two things to be identical under one description but not under another. Commentators differ about which view of identity it is most plausible to ascribe to Locke (see Uzgalis 1990). For our purposes, it will not matter whether

Locke subscribed to an absolute or a relative conception of identity.

2 The futility of seventeenth-century debates involving the soul can be seen by considering the titles of some of the 'psychological theses' defended at Harvard University during the seventeenth century: *one body does not have a plurality of souls*; *the soul is wholly in the entire body and in every part of it*; *the soul has its most natural seat in the body*; *the soul is unaffected by the body*; *the functioning of the soul depends on the body*; *life is the union of form and substance*; *no soul consists of the form of the animate being*; *the destruction of the soul entails that of the composite*; and, somewhat surprisingly – *the rational soul is divisible*. (Roback 1964: 31–2).

3 At this time, Aristotelian psychology was actually quite a bit more diverse than we have indicated. For an excellent account, see Hatfield 1995.

4 Ayers 1991: v. 2, ch. 18, nicely explains why in this respect Locke's account is inadequate.

5 Sergeant 1697: ref. 14, sec. 12; Clarke 1738: v. III, 787.

6 This is something that Locke's early critics often had trouble grasping. Edward Stillingfleet, for instance, asked, 'From whence comes *Self-consciousness in different times and places* to make up this *Idea* of a Person? Whether it be true or false, I am not now to enquire, but how it comes into this *Idea* of a Person? Hath *the common use of our Language appropriated it to this Sense*? If not, this seems to be a meer Arbitrary Idea; and may as well be denied as affirmed'. Stillingfleet 1698: 59; quoted in Fox 1988: 40.

7 Part of the problem is that commentators have radically different views about what Locke meant by *substance*; compare, for instance, the excellent but radically conflicting discussions of this question in Ayers (1991: v. 2, pt. I), and McCann (1994). But even were it clear what Locke meant by substance, there are still profound difficulties in determining what Locke took to be the substantial status of both humans and persons. On this latter question, compare, for instance, Atherton (1983), Alston and Bennett (1988), Bolton (1994), and Lowe (1995).

8 See also Locke 1975: II.xxvii.10; 336, II.xxvii.25; 345–6.

9 See also Ibid.: II.i.20; 116; II.i.22; 117; II.xi.8; 158; III.iii.7; 411, etc.

10 Compare Ayers 1991: v. 2, 266–7.

11 Uzgalis 1990.

12 See, e.g., Alston and Bennett 1988; Bolton 1994; Lowe 1995.

13 See also Locke 1975: III.vi.27; 455.

14 See, e.g., Ashcroft 1969, who stresses Locke's preoccupation with theological concerns. Ashcroft is roundly criticized by Ayers (1991: v. 1, 123). In our view, the truth about this aspect of Locke's thought lies somewhere between the accounts of Ashcroft and Ayers.

2 FISSION

1 See, e.g., Wiggins 1967; Parfit 1971, 1984; Shoemaker 1970, 1984; Perry 1972, 1976, 1978; Lewis 1976, 1983; Nozick 1981; Brennan 1988; White 1989; Sosa 1990; Rovane 1990; Unger 1991; Hirsh 1991; Baillie 1993; Hanley 1993; Doepke 1996; Martin 1995, 1998.

2 That fission examples were discussed throughout the eighteenth century will come as a surprise to many contemporary students of personal identity theory. It will even come as a surprise to some who are also students of eighteenth century philosophy. Paul Helm, for instance, argues that neither Locke nor eighteenth century 'Lockeans' would acknowledge the relevance of fission examples as objections to Locke's theory of personal identity since they were interested only in factual and not also in conceptual objections to his account (Helm 1977).

3 See Fox (1988: Chs. 3–4).

4 Alexander Pope et al., *Memoirs Of the Extraordinary Life, Works, and Discoveries of Martinus Scriblerus* (1966). At the time, George Berkeley was a good friend of Arbuthnot and so may well have read *Scriblerus* and probably at least knew of its contents. In the nineteeth century, Thomas Brown, in his influential *Lectures on the Philosophy of the Human Mind* (1820), quotes approvingly from *Scriblerus*, v. 1, 118–19, v. 2, 489–70.

5 For instance, Thomas Brown, Reid's leading successor early in the nineteenth century and an important influence on James Mill, John Stuart Mill, and William James, wrote, 'Although the constant state of flux of the corporeal particles furnishes no argument against the identity of the principle which feels and thinks, if feeling and thought be states of a substance, that is, essentially distinct from these changing particles, the unity and identity of this principle, amid all the corpuscular changes, – if it can truly be proved to be identical, – furnishes a very strong argument, in disproof of those systems which consider thought and feeling as the result of material organization. Indeed, the attempts which have been seriously made by materialists to obviate this difficulty, involve, in every respect, as much absurdity, though certainly not so much pleasantry, at least not so much *intentional* pleasantry, as the demonstrations which the Society of Freethinkers communicated to Martinus Scriblerus . . . The arguments which they are represented as urging in this admirable letter, ludicrous as they may seem, are truly as strong, at least, as those of which they are the parody; and, indeed, in this case, where both are so like, a very little occasional change of expression is all which is necessary to convert the grave ratiocination into the parody, and the parody into the grave ratiocination' (1820: v. I, 118–19).

6 See Ducharme (1986) on Clarke's anticipations of Butler's arguments.

7 Curiously, Burthogge, in the book in which he described the Siamese twins, previously mentioned, had made the same basic criticism against Sherlock's account of the 'numerical oneness' of the self being constituted in consciousness. Ironically, Burthogge's book was dedicated to Locke, who was about to publish his own theory of personal identity, to which many critics, to this day, think the same criticism applies. Burthogge writes: 'A Being (and even a Cogitative Being as Being) must be conceived to *be*, before it can be conceived to *Act*; so again, it must be conceived to act, that is to *Think* to *Reason*, to *Love*, to *Hate* . . . for some moment of Reason *Before* it can be conceived to be *Conscious* of these its actings. Now for that *Moment* of Reason, in which a Spirit is conceived *in Being*, without being conceived to be acting, and in which it is conceived *Acting* before it becomes *Conscious* of its actings, in that precedent moment, (which speaks *Order*, not *Duration*,) it must be conceived to be *one with it self*, and numerically different from every thing besides; and therefore that it is *so*, cannot arise from self-consciousness, or its being conscious of its own actings'. (Burthogge 1694: 272–3).

3 THE SELF AS SOUL

1 Hatfield (1994, 1995, 1997) has shown that researchers in France and Germany, as well as in England, contributed importantly to the development of a scientific psychology in the eighteenth century. This early empirical psychology was a collective vision of individuals with radically different metaphysical presuppositions; and it was continuous, rather than discontinuous, with the later development in the late nineteenth century of a more experimental psychology.

2 See, e.g., Yolton 1983.

3 Late in the eighteenth century, traditionalists were still arguing over whether animals had immaterial, immortal souls and, why, if they did have souls, they behaved as they did. As reported in the article on Brutes in the third edition of

the *Encyclopedia Britannica* (1797), Father Bougeant proposed that brutes were really the temporary residence of devils, until the last judgment. As to why they do not consistently exhibit that intelligence that they have essentially in their nature, Father Bougeant wrote: 'I discover the reason for this: it is because, in beasts as well as in ourselves, the operations of the mind are dependent on the material organs of the machine to which it is united; and those organs being grosser and less perfect than in us, it follows, that the knowledge and thoughts, and the other spiritual operations of the beasts, must of course be less perfect than ours'. He continues: 'And if these proud spirits know their own dismal state, what an humiliation must it be to them to see themselves reduced to the conditions of beasts! But whether, they know it or no, so shameful a degradation is still, with regard to them, the primary effect of the divine vengeance I just mentioned; it is an anticipation of hell' (vol. III, p.740)

4 See also Clarke 1738: 785, 790.

5 Compare ibid.: 802 (Collins).

6 It can readily be seen how Hume was guided by Shaftesbury's overall argument, particularly in Hume's treatment of personal identity. Their arguments are parallel: both dismiss the attempts of subtle reason to reach conclusions about simple identity; both are concerned less with proving a real substantial identity, than becoming clear that even an assumed and fictional identity will be 'sufficient ground for a moralist' (see Mijuskovic 1971, 1974, who makes this point).

7 Numerals in parentheses in our ensuing text are to numbered items in Berkeley 1948.

8 In a letter dated, 25 November, 1729, written to the American philosopher, Samuel Johnson, Berkeley writes: 'As to the second part of my treatise concerning the principles of human knowledge, the fact is that I had made a considerable progress in it, but the manuscript was lost about fourteen years ago during my travels in Italy; and I never had the leisure since to do so disagreeable a thing as writing twice on the same subject'. (Berkeley 1965: 228). This report, combined with another made by his brother that some manuscripts were lost off a ship on the way to Naples, combine to suggest that this particular manuscript was lost at sea along with the others.

9 Reid, making a somewhat different use of the metaphor of an abyss, writes: 'Thus we see that Des Cartes and Locke take the road that leads to scepticism, without knowing the end of it; but they stop short for want of light to carry them further. Berkeley, frighted at the appearance of the dreadful abyss, starts aside and avoids it. But the author of the "Treatise of Human Nature", more daring and intrepid, without turning aside to the right hand or to the left, like Virgil's Alecto, shoots directly into the gulf'. (Reid 1764: 7.iii; 207–8).

10 The history of pneumatology as a discipline has, to our knowledge, not yet been written, but several sources have provided us with some indication of the transformations in the use of the term. See, in particular, Fiering 1981, and Stewart 1990.

11 In discussing Grove's views on compassion, N. S. Fiering wrote: 'Ten years before Frances Hutcheson set out to refute Bernard Mandeville's renewal of cynicism and psychological pessimism, irresistible compassion was already being cited as proof of the real existence of unadulterated altruism'. Thus, in the *Spectator* . . . , a dissenting minister, Henry Grove, who went on later to become a moderately distinguished lecturer on moral philosophy, presented an argument for the irreducibility of kind and benevolent propensities to humankind: "[The] Contriver of human nature hath wisely furnished it with two principles of action, self-love and benevolence; designed one of them to render men wakeful to his own personal interest, and the other to dispose him for giving his utmost

assistance to all engaged in the same pursuit". Man is led to "pursue the general happiness" through his reason, according to Grove, for he sees that this is the way "to procure and establish" his own happiness. Yet, if besides this consideration, there were not a natural instinct, prompting me to desire the welfare and satisfaction of others, self-love, in defiance of the admonitions of reason, would quickly run all things into a state of war and confusion. But we are happily saved from this Hobbesian nightmare by "inclinations which anticipate our reason, and like a bias draw the mind strongly towards" social ends. As part of the evidence for this thesis, Grove adduces the following observation: "The pity which arises on sight of persons in distress, and the satisfaction of mind which is the consequence of having removed them into a happier state, are instead of a thousand arguments to prove such a thing as a *disinterested benevolence*" (Fiering 1976: 202–3; emphasis added). The remarks just quoted from Grove continue as follows: 'Did pity proceed from a reflection we make upon our liableness to the same ill accidents we see befal others, it were nothing to the present purpose; but this is assigning an artificial cause of a natural passion, and can by no means be admitted as a tolerable account of it, because children and persons most thoughtless about their own condition, and incapable of entering into the prospects of futurity, feel the most violent touches of compassion'. (*The Spectator*, #588, Wed., Sept 1, 1714). In a footnote, Fiering says, 'This is the earliest use of the term "disinterested benevolence" that I have seen' (1976: 203).

12 Grove, *c.* 1720; see note 15.
13 Grove seems, here, to be referring to Locke's section in the *Essay* on the 'Division of the Sciences' where he includes 'Spirits' as part of 'natural Philosophy' and then Locke goes on to write: 'The end of [natural Philosophy], is bare speculative Truth, and whatsoever can afford the Mind of Man any such, falls under this branch, whether it be God himself, Angels, Spirits, Bodies, or any of their Affections, as Number, and Figure, etc.' (Locke 1975: (IV.xxi.2; 720).
14 268 ms. pp on the human soul, compared to 32 on angels and 25 on God.
15 Because Grove taught his pneumatology course into the 1730s, it is conceivable that he read Berkeley's *Alciphron* (1732/1837) before generating his own similar example. However, this seems extremely unlikely as the undated lecture notes refer to a large number of works, all of which were published before 1720.
16 Butler's first biographer writes (in the second, revised, edition), apparently based on direct information from Secker, another minister and Butler's closest friend: 'Whilst our Author continued preacher at the Rolls Chapel, he divided his time between his duty in town and country; but when he quitted the Rolls, he resided during seven years wholly at Stanhope, in the conscientious discharge of every obligation appertaining to a good parish priest. This retirement, however, was too solitary for his disposition, which had in it a natural cast of gloominess. And though his reclusive hours were by no means lost, either to private improvement or public utility, yet he felt at times, very painfully, the want of that select society of friends to which he had been accustomed, and which could inspire him with the greatest cheerfulness. Mr Secker, therefore, who knew this, was extremely anxious to draw him out into a more active and conspicuous scene, and omitted no opportunity of expressing this desire to such as he thought capable of promoting it' (Butler 1736: 68).

4 HUMAN NATURE

1 George Turnbull, who published his *Principles of Moral Philosophy* (1740) at about the same time as Hume published the *Treatise*, also advocated a science of human nature, using Newton and Bacon as models. However, for Turnbull, the

sciences of nature and of human beings would be co-ordinate sciences using similar methods on different objects. Reid, Turnbull's student, would follow a similar course, rather than Hume's foundational approach. But despite his scientific intentions, Turnbull, like Hume, also mixed philosophy with psychology. In Turnbull's case, it was a mixing of a priori considerations about the final ends of human nature with empirical investigation of human faculties. Nevertheless, because of Turnbull's scientific intentions, as expressed in his teaching and works, he had an enormous influence on subsequent developments in Scottish philosophy, especially at Aberdeen, and is thought, more than Hutcheson, to be the father of the Scottish Enlightenment (See McCosh 1875; Wood 1990).

2   Noxon (1973) proposes that the unified and foundational science of human nature that Hume tried to achieve in the *Treatise*, failed, and that Hume knew it failed even before he finished it. This applies especially to Book I, Part IV, where his analytical skepticism overwhelmed his constructive psychological goals. Nevertheless, Noxon believes that for the most part, Hume's philosophical skepticism did not interfere with his constructive psychology. Furthermore, Noxon claims that Hume realized that the *Treatise* was confusing because of the intermixture of philosophy and psychology and, so, in his subsequent works tried to keep the focus on one or the other. For example, in Hume's skeptical, *Enquiry on Human Understanding* (1748), he only briefly mentions constructive associative principles and, in his *An Enquiry Concerning the Principles of Morals* (1751) he pursues more constructive goals. Biro (1993), on the other hand, maintains that in the *Treatise,* and even in his discussion of self and personal identity, Hume pursues constructive goals in ways that have many similarities to current cognitive science.

3   Perhaps Hume was not completely dismissive of intuition as a source of knowledge, as we have suggested (see, e.g., *Treatise*, I.iii.i). For present purposes, the issue is not important.

4   Some recently have argued that Hume was importantly influenced by the debate between Clarke and Collins, and partly because of it was particularly anxious in the *Treatise* to refute Clarke's views on the self. See Russell 1988, 1995, and McIntyre 1994.

5   On the importance of imagination in accounts of sympathy in the latter part of the eighteenth century, see Bate (1945), Radner (1979), Engell (1981), and Bromwich (1983).

6   Mercer, for instance, in the context of a generally unsympathetic portrayal of Smith's account, stresses that 'Smith's most serious confusion stems from his failure to clarify whether sympathy involves imagining what one would feel if one were in the other's situation or whether it involves imagining oneself as the other person' (Mercer 1972: 86).

7   Compare the 'physics exam example' in Parfit (1984: 246–7).

8   On dissociation, see Hacking 1995. On the child's acquisition of a theory of mind, see our discussion of contemporary developments in psychology in Chapter 6.

9   Law himself recognized, with some amazement, the change in context. As his biography in the 1797 edition of *Encyclopedia Britannica* notes, 'There was nothing in his elevation to his bishopric which he spoke of with more pleasure, than its being a proof that decent freedom of inquiry was not discouraged' (Vol. IX, p. 736).

5 THE SELF AS MIND

1   Willey aptly describes Hartley as an instance of 'that peculiarly English phenomenon, the holy alliance between science and religion', and places him in a 'succession of English physico-theologians' that includes Bacon, Boyle, Locke, Newton, and Priestley (Willey 1940:133).

2 For an extensive and extremely erudite discussion of seventeenth- and eighteenth-century views on the relationship between the physiology of memory and sense of self, see Sutton (1998).

3 Compare Frankfurt (1971).

4 [Anonymous], 1769, as cited by Tucker (1768–77: v. 7, 4).

5 Although unnoted in the nineteenth century for his contribution to scientific method, more recently Reid has been recognized as the first scientific intro-spectionist, setting a model that in the latter part of the nineteenth century would be developed into an experimental introspectionism (Robinson 1976).

6 Compare Reid (1785: v. I, 216).

7 Coleridge 1817: 187; Mackintosh 1830: 133; Bate 1966: 239f; Bromwich 1983: 374. Hazlitt had sent Mackintosh a copy of his *Essay* when Mackintosh was in India. He later wrote of Mackintosh's grasp of his main idea that 'the way in which he spoke of that dry, tough, metaphysical choke-pear showed the dearth of intellectual intercourse in which he lived, and the craving in his mind after those studies which had once been his pride, and to which he still turned for conso-lation in his remote solitude' (Hazlitt 1825: 177).

8 The case of J. S. Mill is particularly intriguing. Although his theorizing about personal identity was strongly influenced by the Lockean tradition through Hume, Hartley, and his father, James Mill, he was an original thinker not constrained entirely by this tradition. The 'mental crisis' that he describes in his auto-biography, which began in 1826, led him to investigate aspects of the imagination not appreciated by prior theorizers in this tradition. For instance, Mill began to appreciate the poetic imagination, particularly through the works of Wordsworth and Coleridge, as well as to consider the philosophical contributions of Cole-ridge. Although the evidence is meager, it seems that Hazlitt, himself, may have contributed to Mill's intellectual crisis: In *The Spirit of the Age* (1825) Hazlitt criticized Bentham's calculative reason and lack of imagination (followed in 1826 by Hazlitt's essay, 'Reason and Imagination'). The young Mill was to take up this issue as his own for awhile, though later to return to a more conservative defense of Bentham. But Mill wrote about Coleridge's views as a complement to his (Mill's) essay on Bentham. To judge from Mill's autobiography, it seems that completing these two essays was the termination of his crisis. Long before, in 1831, Mill published his own, 'The Spirit of the Age', a series of newspaper articles (Mill 1986). Yet, if one looks for citations of Hazlitt in Mill's works, there is hardly a mention of him and certainly no mention of Hazlitt's *Essay*. Probably Mill never read it.

9 See, e.g., Hazlitt 1967; Bonner and Lahey 1972; Kinnaird 1978; Mahoney 1978; Bromwich 1983; Jones 1989.

10 Howe, an early and influential biographer of Hazlitt, called it 'a book by a meta-physician for metaphysicians' and added that 'the few words we may say of it here' concern only 'its relation to Hazlitt's other works and to his character' (Howe 1947: 76). More recently, Jones (1989) begins his account of Hazlitt's life and thought with Hazlitt's marriage, in 1808, three years after the publication of the *Essay*! Among those who have considered the *Essay* in detail, Kinnaird had as his professed aim to write 'a biography of [Hazlitt's] mind', but he does not mention Hazlitt's discussion of fission examples. He does, though, have inter-esting things to say about Hazlitt's contribution to the psychology of self-concepts, especially that for Hazlitt the sense of self is 'always in some mode or degree *intersubjective*, as existing and acting only in tension with real or imagined otherness' (Kinnaird 1978: 24–30, 58). Bromwich, in his excellent study, does mention Hazlitt's consideration of fission examples but only briefly and in a footnote (Bromwich 1983: 418, n. 32).

11 Philosophers, even those who have noticed Hazlitt's early *Essay*, have had little to say about his views on personal identity. For instance, Noxon, in discussing sympathetically Hazlitt's ethical views, briefly sketches Hazlitt's account of personal identity but fails to appreciate its importance (Noxon 1963). And Schneewind, in his well-regarded study of Sidgwick's ethics, mentions that 'Hazlitt in his early days wrote philosophical essays in one of which he put forward some original and interesting objections to egoism', but then Schneewind says no more about it (Schneewind 1977: 148).

12 In recent years there has been a re-emergence of interest in episodic memory along the lines of Locke's notion of memory involving a recollective process of having been there, but this kind of memory has been compared to two other kinds. Tulving began with a distinction between 'episodic memory' and 'semantic memory' but later added 'procedural memory' to his scheme. In his most recent publications, he speaks of the 'autonoetic' process, or self-referring aspect, of episodic memory, which contrasts with the 'noetic' process, or 'knowing that', without self-reference, which applies to semantic memories, and the 'anoetic process', or knowing how, which applies to procedural knowledge. See Tulving 1985; Wheeler, Stuss, and Tulving 1997. The role of imagination in reconstruction of memories has been well known to psychologists from the time of the seminal work on this issue by Bartlett (1932).

13 See, for instance, Lewis (1976, 1983), on persons as four-dimensional objects.

14 The closest that Hartley came to suggesting a developmental account of the acquisition of self-concepts was in connection with his discussion of memory in children. For instance, he says, 'Children often misrepresent past and future Facts; their Memories are fallacious; their Discourse incoherent; their Affections and Actions disproportionate to the Value of the Things desired and pursued; and the connecting Consciousness is in them as yet imperfect' (Hartley 1749: v. 1, 391).

15 One might wish to suggest that Hume's Book 1 discussion of personal identity just is his account of how one forms a concept of self, and that this is intended as a true developmental account. But, in addition to the mixed motives – both philosophical and psychological – involved in the account, which make this attribution speculative, there is the further difficulty that Hume does not distinguish developmental stages. Hence, his account, which is not much richer as a developmental account than Locke's, is either not meant to be developmental at all or else is only minimally developmental.

16 The real issue, hotly debated in our own times, is whether the metaphysics of persons has normative implications. See, e.g., Parfit 1984: Pt. 3; Korsgaard 1996; and Schechtman 1996.

6 FUTURE OF THE SELF

1 For discussion of both the medical and philosophical aspects of these cases, see Sperry 1968; Nagel 1979; Parfit 1987; Puccetti 1989 (all four are reprinted in Kolak and Martin (1991: 55–88).

2 This example is based on one presented by Shoemaker (1984: 119).

3 Parfit's views may be found in Parfit (1971, 1976, and especially 1984). Other important work since 1970 that would have been discussed in a more complete survey includes: Shoemaker 1970; Perry 1972, 1976, 1978; Nozick 1981; Shoemaker and Swinburne 1984; Nagel 1986; Sosa 1990; Unger 1991; Korsgaard 1996; Schechtman 1996; Martin 1998.

4 For more on this example, see Martin (1998: 80–5). If the reader is not entirely convinced, reflecting on the following analogy will help. During most of the eighteenth century – not to mention earlier – it was taken as a 'basic fact' of

'folk metaphysics' that 'what mattered for survival' was to persist as the same 'unchanging and identical' immaterial substance. No material substance could perform this function because the body was constantly changing and, hence, did not preserve identity. Now, in the twentieth century, a 'basic fact' of 'folk metaphysics' is that 'what matters for survival' is to persist as the same continuing brain/body, even though the matter of the brain and body is constantly changing. What will 'matter for survival' in a century or two? We suggest that by then people will be used to all sorts of transformations in self and identification that we can hardly imagine at the present time. The example in the text represents only the tip of the iceberg: many additional transformations of 'self' may well become accepted as part of the 'folk metaphysics' of the future.

5 For more on this, see Martin (1998: Chs. 5 and 6).

6 David Lewis is the philosopher most responsible for the rise of four-dimensional views of person, especially in Lewis (1976), but see also Lewis (1983).

7 Even, in our own times, well-regarded philosophers have expressed doubts about whether in the absence of personal persistence, such a theological view can be worked out; see, e.g., Ayers 1991: v. 2, 272.

8 See Kusch 1995; Reed 1997.

9 For instance, compare Boring (1950: 219–33) with Passmore (1957).

10 'With vastly good intentions, and very excellent abilities for everything except philosophy, he had no speculative genius whatever – positively an anti-speculative turn of mind, which, with a mixture of shrewdness and *naivete* altogether incomparable, he was pleased to term *common sense*' (Ferrier 1856: 494).

11 See Herbart (1813, 1824–5), and Stout (1888), for Herbart's views on self.

12 See Hallie (1959) for a discussion of de Biran's views on personal identity and on his genetic psychology of self.

13 It would take us too far afield to discuss all aspects of Ribot's fascinating work. But we must quote a remark of his which refers, in part, to the Hungarian twins whose 'organ of generation', recall, was shared: 'Even where the personalities [of the two headed individuals] are most distinct, there exists an interpenetration of organs and functions such that each cannot be itself except on condition of being more or less the other, and of being conscious of the fact' (Ribot 1891: 42). Also, within the context of the organic basis of personality, Ribot discusses the hypothetical possibility that two individuals might be identical in all respects: 'If, by an impossible hypothesis, two men were so created that their two organisms were constitutionally identical; that their hereditary influences were rigorously alike; if, by a still greater impossibility, both received at the same instant the same physical and moral impressions, there would be no other difference between them than of their position in space' (p. 49). While not exactly a case of fission, this example does indicate how a late nineteenth century materialist conceives of duplicates with respect to the concept of personality.

14 Stewart 1829: v. 3, 108–61.

15 See Barresi and Moore (1996), for a review of this literature.

16 Neisser (1988), formulated the concepts of the ecological and social selves, as well as the private self and the extended self, which will be discussed momentarily.

17 One of the criticisms that was put forward in commentaries by the philosophers Bennett (1978), Dennett (1978), and Harman (1978), against the evidence presented in Premack and Woodruff (1978), was that there was no sign that the chimps could represent false beliefs.

18 See Barresi and Moore (1996) for a review of most of these findings. On the future self, see Thompson, Barresi and Moore (1997), Moore, Barresi and Thompson (1998), and Barresi (2001).

BIBLIOGRAPHY

Aaron, R. I. and Gibb, J. (eds) (1936) *An Early Draft of Locke's Essay Together with Excerpts from his Journals*, Oxford: Clarendon Press.

Alston, W. and Bennett, J. (1988) 'Locke on people and substances', *Philosophical Review* 97: 25–46.

Anonymous (1769) *An Essay on Personal Identity*, London.

—— (1806) 'Review of William Hazlitt's *An Essay on the Principles of Human Action*', *British Critic* xxxviii: 536–48.

—— (1835) 'Hazlitt's first essay', *Monthly Repository* ix: 480–85.

Ashcroft, R. (1969) 'Faith and knowledge in Locke's philosophy', in J. Yolton (ed.) *John Locke: Problems and Perspectives*, Cambridge: Cambridge University Press.

Atherton, M. (1983) 'Locke's theory of personal identity', *Midwest Studies in Philosophy*, 8: 273–93.

Ayers, M. (1991) *Locke*, vol. I, II, London: Routledge.

Baillie, J. (1993) *Problems in Personal Identity,* New York: Paragon.

Baldwin, J.M. (1894/1898) *Mental Development in the Child and the Race*, New York: Macmillan.

—— (1913) *History of Psychology: A Sketch and an Interpretation*, vol. I, II, London: Watts & Co.

Barresi, J. (2001) 'Extending self-consciousness into the future', in C. Moore and K. Lemmon (eds) *The Self in Time: Developmental Perspectives* (141–161), Hillsdale, NJ: Erlbaum.

Barresi, J. and Martin, R. (2003) 'Self-concern from Priestley to Hazlitt', *The British Journal for the History of Philosophy* 11: 499–507.

Barresi, J. and Moore, C. (1996) 'Intentional relations and social understanding', *Behavioral and Brain Sciences* 19: 107–54.

Bartlett, F. C. (1932) *Remembering*, Cambridge: Cambridge University Press.

Bate, W. J. (1945) 'The sympathetic imagination in eighteenth-century British thought', *ELH* 12: 144–66.

—— (1966) *John Keats*, New York: Oxford University Press.

Behan, D. P. (1979) 'Locke on persons and personal identity', *Canadian Journal of Philosophy* 9: 53–75.

Berkeley, G. (1837) *The Works of George Berkeley, Bishop of Coyne*, London: Charles Daley Publisher.

—— (1709/1948) 'An essay towards a new theory of vision', in A. A. Luce and T. E. Jessop (eds) *The Works of George Berkeley*, vol. I (1–139), London: Thomas Nelson and Sons Ltd.

189

—— (1710/1965) 'A treatise concerning the principles of human knowledge', in C. M. Turbayne (ed.) *Principles, Dialogues, and Philosophical Correspondence* (1–101), Indianapolis: Bobbs-Merrill Company, Inc.

—— (1732/1837) 'Alciphron: or the minute philosopher', in *The Works of George Berkeley, Bishop of Coyne* (117–240), London: Charles Daley Publisher.

—— (1733/1948) 'The theory of vision, or visual language shewing the immediate presence and providence of a diety vindicated and explained', in A. A. Luce and T. E. Jessop (eds) *The Works of George Berkeley*, vol. I (241–279), London: Thomas Nelson and Sons Ltd.

—— (1948) *Philosophical Commentaries*, in A. A. Luce and T. E. Jessop (eds) *The Works of George Berkeley*, vol. I (1–139), London: Thomas Nelson and Sons Ltd.

—— (1965) *Principles, Dialogues, and Philosophical Correspondence*, Indianapolis: Bobbs-Merrill Company, Inc.

Biro, J. (1993) 'Hume's new science of mind', in D. F. Norton (ed.) *The Cambridge Companion to Hume*, Cambridge: Cambridge University Press.

Bobro, M. (1998) 'Prudence and the concern to survive in Leibniz's doctrine of immortality', *History of Philosophy Quarterly* 15: 303–22.

Bolton, M. (1994) 'Locke on identity: the scheme of simple and compound things', in K. F. Barber and J. K. Gracia (eds) *Individuation and Identity in Early Modern Philosophy: Descartes to Kant*, Albany: State University of New York Press.

Boring, E. (1950) *A History of Experimental Psychology*, New York: Appleton-Century-Crofts, Inc.

Bradley, F. H. (1893/1897/1978) *Appearance and Reality: A Metaphysical Essay*, Oxford: Oxford University Press.

Brennan, A. (1988) *Conditions of Identity*, Oxford: Clarendon Press.

Brett, G. S. (1921) *History of Psychology, vol. II: Medieval & Early Modern Period*, London: George Allen & Unwin Ltd.

Bromwich, D. (1983) *Hazlitt: The Mind of a Critic*, Oxford: Oxford University Press.

Brown, R. (1970) *Between Hume and Mill: An Anthology of British Philosophy 1749–1843*, New York: The Modern Library.

Brown, T. (1820/1828) *Lectures on the Philosophy of the Human Mind*, vol. I, II, Boston: Glazier & Co.

Burthogge, R. (1694/1976) *An Essay Upon Reason and the Nature of Spirits*, reprinted at New York: Garland Publishing, Inc.

Butler, J. (1726/1729/1897) 'Sermons on Human Nature', in L. A. Selby-Bigge (ed.) *British Moralists*, vol. I, Oxford: Clarendon Press.

—— (1736/1852) *The Analogy of Religion, Natural and Revealed*, London: Henry G. Bohn.

Clarke, S. (1738/1928) *The Works of Samuel Clarke*, vols I–IV, reprinted at New York: Garland Publishing, Inc.

Coleridge, S. T. (1817/1972) *Lay Sermons*, Cambridge: Routledge and Kegan Paul.

Cook, J. (ed.) (1991) *William Hazlitt: Selected Writings*, New York: Oxford University Press.

De Beer, R. S. (1979) *The Correspondence of John Locke*, vols I–VIII, Oxford: Clarendon Press.

Dennett, D. C. (1978) 'Beliefs about beliefs', *Behavioral and Brain Sciences* 1: 568–70.

Descartes, R. (1984) *The Philosophical Writings of Descartes*, vols I–II, J. Cottingham, R. Stoothoff, and D. Murdoch (trans.), Cambridge: Cambridge University Press.

Doddridge, P. (1763) *A Course of Lectures on the Principle Subjects in Pneumatology, Ethics, and Divinity: with References to the most Considerable Authors on each Subject*, S. Clark (ed.), London: J. Buckland et al.

Doepke, F. C. (1996) *The Kinds of Things: A Theory of Personal Identity Based on Transcendental Argument*, Chicago: Open Court.

Ducharme, H. (1986) 'Personal identity in Samuel Clarke', *Journal of the History of Philosophy* 24: 359–83.

Encyclopedia Britannica (1797) 3rd edn, in eighteen volumes, Edinburgh: A. Bell and C. MacFarquhar.

Engell, J. (1981) *The Creative Imagination: Enlightenment to Romanticism*, Cambridge, MA: Harvard University Press.

Erickson, R. A. (1965) 'Situations of identity in *The Memoirs of Martinus Scriblerus*', *Modern Language Quarterly* 26: 388–400.

Ferrier, J. F. (1856) *Institutes of Metaphysic: The Theory of Knowing and Being*, Edinburgh: William Blackwood and Sons.

Fiering, N. S. (1976) 'Irresistible compassion: an aspect of eighteenth-century sympathy and humanitarianism', *Journal of the History of Ideas* 37: 195–218.

—— (1981) *Moral Philosophy at Seventeenth-Century Harvard: A Discipline in Transition*, Chapel Hill: University of North Carolina Press.

Fox, C. (1988) *Locke and the Scriblerians*, Berkeley: University of California Press.

Frankfurt, H. (1971) 'Freedom of the will and the concept of a person', *Journal of Philosophy* 47: 5–20.

Fraser, A. C. (1898) *Thomas Reid*, Edinburgh: Oliphant, Anderson & Ferrier.

Grove, H. (*c.* 1720) *A System of Pneumatology In A Series of Lectures by the late Rev: d Mr. Henry Grove*. From the library of W. Davies, Magd. College, Oxford, 1786 (Huntington Manuscript HM46326 – hand copied and bound).

Hacking, I. (1995) *Rewriting the Soul: Multiple Personality and the Sciences of Memory*, Princeton: Princeton University Press.

Hallie, P. P. (1959) *Maine de Biran: Reformer of Empiricism 1766–1824*, Cambridge, MA: Harvard University Press.

Harman, G. (1978) 'Studying the chimpanzee's theory of mind', *Behavioral and Brain Sciences* 1: 576–7.

Hanley, R. (1993) 'On valuing radical transformation', *Pacific Philosophical Quarterly* 74: 209–20.

Harris, P. L. (1989) *Children and Emotion*, Oxford: Basil Blackwell.

Hartley, D. (1749/1966) *Observations on Man, His Frame, His Duty, and His Expectations* (two vols in one), reprinted with an introduction by T. L. Huguelet, Gainesville, Fl: Scholars' Facsimiles & Reprints.

Hatfield, G. (1994) 'Psychology as a natural science in the eighteenth century', *Synthese* 115: 375–91.

—— (1995) 'Remaking the science of mind: psychology as a natural science', in C. Fox, R. Porter and R. Wokler (eds) *Inventing Human Science: Eighteenth-century Domains*, Berkeley: University of California Press.

—— (1997) 'Wundt and psychology as science: Disciplinary transformations', *Perspectives on Science* 5: 349–82.

Hazlitt, W. (1805/1969) *An Essay on the Principles of Human Action and some Remarks on the Systems of Hartley and Helvetius,* reprinted, with an introduction by J. R. Nabholtz, Gainesville, Fl: Scholars' Facsimiles & Reprints.

—— (1825/1906/1983) *The Spirit of the Age, Or, Contemporary Portraits,* New York: Clearing House Publishers.

—— (1826/1970) 'On reason and imagination', in J. R. Nabholtz (ed.) *Hazlitt: Selected Essays*, (1–17), New York: Appleton-Century-Crofts.

—— (1828) 'Self-love and benevolence', *The New Monthly Magazine*, Oct. and Dec. issues. Reprinted, in part, in Cook (1991).

—— (1835/1990) *Essay on the Principles of Human Action and some Remarks on the Systems of Hartley and Helvetius and on Abstract Ideas*, reprinted, with an introduction by J. V. Price, Bristol: Thoemmes Antiquarian Books Ltd.

—— (1839/1902) 'My first acquaintance with poets', in *Winterslow: Essays and Characters Written There* (1–23), London: Henry Frowde.

—— (1967) *The Complete Works of William Hazlitt*, 22 vols, P. P. Howe (ed.), New York: AMS Press, Inc.

Helm, P. (1977) 'John Locke's puzzle cases about personal identity', *The Locke Newsletter* 8: 43–68.

Herbart, J. F. (1813/1850–2) *Lehrbuch zur Psychologie*, in *Sammtliche Werke*, Leibzig: G. Hartenstein.

—— (1824–5/1850–2) *Psychologie als Wissenschaft, neu gegrundet auf Erfahrung, Metaphysica und Mathematik*, in *Sammtliche Werke*, Leibzig: G. Hartenstein.

Hirsh, E. (1991) 'Divided minds', *The Philosophical Review* 100: 3–30.

Hobbes, T. (1656/1839) *Elements of Philosophy: First Section, Concerning Body*, in W. Molesworth (ed.) *The English Works of Thomas Hobbes*, vol. 1, London: J. Bohn.

Hoffman, M. L. (1977) 'Empathy, its development and prosocial implications', in C. B. Keasey (ed.) *Nebraska Symposium on Motivation*, vol. 25, *Social Cognitive Development*, Lincoln: University of Nebraska Press.

Howe, P. P. (1947/1972) *The Life of William Hazlitt*, Westport, CT: Greenwood Press.

Hume, D. (1739/1888) *Treatise of Human Nature*, L. A. Selby-Bigge (ed.) Oxford: Clarendon Press.

—— (1748/1939) *An Inquiry Concerning Human Understanding*, in E. A. Burtt (ed.) *The English Philosophers from Bacon to Mill*, (585–689), New York: The Modern Library.

—— (1751/1957) *An Inquiry Concerning the Principles of Morals*, C. W. Hendel (ed.), Indianapolis: The Bobbs-Merrill Company, Inc.

Humphrey, N. (1976/84) 'The social function of intellect', in *Consciousness Regained: Chapters in the Development of Mind*, Oxford: Oxford University Press.

James, W. (1890/1918) *The Principles of Psychology*, vols I, II, New York: Henry Holt and Co.

Jones, S. (1989) *Hazlitt: A Life,* Oxford: Oxford University Press.

King, W. (1731/1978) *An Essay on the Origin of Evil,* ed. E. Law, reprinted in New York: Garland Press.

Kinnaird, J. (1978) *William Hazlitt: Critic of Power*, New York: Columbia University Press.

Kolak, D. and Martin, R. (eds) (1991) *Self and Identity*, New York: Macmillan.

—— (1999) *The Experience of Philosophy*, 4th edn, Belmont, CA: Wadsworth.

Korsgaard, C. (1996) *Creating the Kingdom of Ends*, New York: Cambridge University Press.

Kuehn, M. (1987) *Scottish Common Sense in Germany, 1768–1800: A Contribution to the History of Critical Philosophy*, Kingston: McGill-Queen's University Press.

Kusch, M. (1995) *Psychologism: A Case Study in the Sociology of Philosophical Knowledge*, London: Routledge.

Laudan, L. L. (1970) 'Thomas Reid and the Newtonian turn of British methodological thought', in R. E. Butts and J. W. Davis (eds) *The Methodological Heritage of Newton*, Toronto: University of Toronto Press.

Law, E. (1759) *Considerations on the Theory of Religion*: in three parts, 4th edn, London: L. Davis and C. Reymers.

—— (1769/1815) *A Defence of Mr. Locke's Opinion concerning Personal Identity*, in John Locke, *An Essay concerning Human Understanding*, Vols. I–III, Edinburgh: Doif & Stirling, vol. 3, pp. 145–68.

Lehrer, K. (1989) *Thomas Reid*, London: Routledge.

Leibniz, G. W. (1765/1896) *New Essays Concerning Human Understanding*, A. G. Langley (trans.), New York: Macmillan.

—— (1989) *Philosophical Essays*, R. Ariew and D. Garber (ed. and trans.), Indianapolis: Hackett Publishing Co.

Lewis, D. (1976) 'Survival and identity', in A. O. Rorty (ed.), *The Identities of Persons*, Berkeley: University of California Press.

—— (1983) 'Postscripts to "Survival and identity"', *Philosophical Papers*, vol. I, New York: Oxford University Press.

Locke, J. (1690/1694/1975) *An Essay Concerning Human Understanding* P. H. Nidditch (ed.), Oxford: Clarendon Press.

—— (1823/1963) *The Works of John Locke*, ten vols., London: Thomas Tegg, reprinted in Germany: Scientia Verlag Aalan.

Lowe, E. J. (1995) *Locke on Human Understanding*, London: Routledge.

Lucretius (1951) *De Rerum Natura*, R. E. Latham (trans.), Harmondsworth: Penguin.

—— (1942/1961) *De Rerum Natura*, W. H. D. Rouse (trans.), Cambridge, MA: Harvard University Press.

—— (1940) *De Rerum Natura*, H. A. J. Munro (trans.), in Whitney J. Oates (ed.) *The Stoic and Epicurean Philosophers*, 69–219, New York: The Modern Library.

Mackintosh, Sir J. (1830/1847) *Dissertation on the Progress of Ethical Philosophy, Chiefly during the Seventeenth and Eighteenth Centuries*, in the 7th edn of the *Encyclopedia Britannica*, reprinted in *Miscellaneous Works of the Right Honourable Sir James Mackintosh* (94–198), Philadelphia: Carey and Hart.

Mahoney, J. L. (1978) *The Logic of Passion: The Literary Criticism of William Hazlitt*, Salzburg: Institut fur Anglistik und Amerikanistik, Universitat Salzburg.

Marshall, J. (1994) *John Locke: Resistance, Religion and Responsibility*, Cambridge: Cambridge University Press.

Martin, C. B., and Deutscher, M. (1966) 'Remembering', *The Philosophical Review* 75: 161–97.

Martin, R. (1995) 'Fission rejuvenation', *Philosophical Studies* 72: 17–40.

—— (1998) *Self-Concern: An Experiential Approach to What Matters in Survival*, New York: Cambridge University Press.

—— (1999) 'Personal identity from Plato to Parfit', in D. Kolak and R. Martin (eds) *The Experience of Philosophy*, 4th edn (142–60), Belmont, CA: Wadsworth.

—— (2000) 'Locke's psychology of personal identity', *Journal of the History of Philosophy* 38: 41–61.

Martin, R. and Barresi, J. (1995) 'Hazlitt on the future of the self', *Journal of the History of Ideas* 56: 463–81.

193

Martin, R., Barresi, J. and Giovannelli, A. (1998) 'Fission examples in the eighteenth and early nineteenth century personal identity debate', *History of Philosophy Quarterly* 7: 323–48.

McCann, E. (1994) 'Locke's philosophy of body', in V. Chappell (ed.) *The Cambridge Companion to Locke* (56–88), Cambridge: Cambridge University Press.

McCosh, J. (1875) *The Scottish Philosophy, Biographical, Expository, Critical, From Hutcheson to Hamilton*, New York: R. Carter and Brothers.

McIntyre, J. (1994) 'Hume: second Newton of the moral sciences', *Hume Studies* 20: 3–18.

Mercer, P. (1972) *Sympathy and Ethics: a Study of the Relationship between Sympathy and Morality with special reference to Hume's Treatise*, Oxford: Clarendon Press.

Mijuskovic, B. (1971) 'Hume and Shaftesbury on the self', *Philosophical Quarterly* 21: 324–36.

—— (1974) *The Achilles of Rationalist Arguments: the Simplicity, Unity, and Identity of Thought and Soul from the Cambridge Platonists to Kant: a Study in the History of an Argument*, The Hague: Martinus Nijhoff.

Mill, J. (1829/69) *Analysis of the Human Mind*, 2 vols., A. Bain, A. Findlater, and G. Grote (eds), with additional notes by J. S. Mill, London: Longman's Green Reader and Dyer.

Mill, J. S. (1865/1878) *An Examination of Sir William Hamilton's Philosophy*, London: Longman's Green Reader and Dyer.

—— (1986) 'Newspaper Writings: December 1822–July 1831', in *Collected Works*, vol. 1, A. P. Robson and J. M. Robson (eds),Toronto: University of Toronto Press.

Moore, C., Barresi, J. and Thompson, C. (1998) 'The cognitive basis of prosocial behavior', *Social Development* 7: 198–218.

Nagel, T. (1979) 'Brain bisection and the unity of consciousness', in *Mortal Questions*, Cambridge: Cambridge University Press.

—— (1986) *The View from Nowhere*, New York: Oxford University Press.

Neisser, U. (1988) 'Five kinds of self-knowledge', *Philosophical Psychology* 1: 37–59.

Noonon, H. (1989) *Personal Identity*, London: Routledge.

Norton, D. F. (ed.) (1993) *The Cambridge Companion to Hume*, Cambridge: Cambridge University Press.

Noxon, J. (1963) 'Hazlitt as moral philosopher', *Ethics* 73: 279–83.

—— (1973) *Hume's Philosophical Development: a Study of his Methods*, Oxford: Clarendon Press.

Nozick, R. (1981) *Philosophical Explanations*, Cambridge: Harvard University Press.

O'Connor, T. (1994) 'Thomas Reid on free agency', *Journal of the History of Philosophy* 32: 605–22.

Paley, W. (1785/1856) 'Principles of moral and political philosophy', in *Paley's Works*, London: Henry G. Bohn.

Parfit, D. (1971) 'Personal identity', *The Philosophical Review* 80: 3–27.

—— (1976) 'Lewis, Perry, and what matters', in A. O. Rorty (ed.) *The Identities of Persons*, Berkeley: University of California Press.

—— (1984) *Reasons and Persons*, Oxford: Clarendon Press.

—— (1987) 'Divided minds and the nature of persons', in C. Blakemore and S. Greenfield (eds) *Mindwaves*, Oxford: Basil Blackwell.

Passmore, J. (1957/80) *A Hundred Years of Philosophy*, New York: Penguin Books Ltd.

Penelhum, T. M. (1975) 'Hume's theory of self revisited', *Dialogue* 14: 389–409.

—— (1976a) 'The self in Hume's philosophy', in K. R. Merrill and R. W. Shahan (eds) *David Hume: Many-sided Genius*, Norman: University of Oklahoma Press.

—— (1976b) 'Self-identity and self-regard', in A. O. Rorty (ed.) *The Identities of Persons*, Berkeley: University of California Press.

Perner, J. (1991) *Understanding the Representational Mind*, Cambridge: MIT Press/ Bradford Books.

Perry, J. (1972) 'Can the self divide?', *Journal of Philosophy* 69: 463–88.

—— (1976) 'The Importance of being identical', in A. O. Rorty (ed.) *The Identities of Persons*, Berkeley: University of California Press.

—— (1978) *A Dialogue on Personal Identity and Immortality*, Indianapolis: Hackett.

Perronet, V. (1738/1991) *A Second Vindication of Mr. Locke*, London: Fletcher Gyles, reprinted at Bristol: Thoemmes Press.

Plato (1954) *Phaedo*, in *The Last Days of Socrates*, Harmondsworth, Middlesex: Penguin Books Ltd.

Plotinus (1952) *The Six Enneads*, S. MacKenna (trans), Chicago: Encyclopedia Britannica, Inc.

Pope, A., Arbuthnot, J., Swift, J., Gay, J., Parnell, T. and Harley, R. (1950/1966) *Memoirs of the Extraordinary Life, Works, and Discoveries of Martinus Scriblerus*, C. Kerby-Miller (ed.), New York: Russell and Russell.

Premack, D. and Woodruff, G. (1978) 'Do chimpanzees have a theory of mind?' *Behavioral and Brain Sciences* 1: 516–26.

Priestley, J. (1774/1978) *An Examination of Dr. Reid's Inquiry into the Human Mind on the Principles of Common Sense, Dr. Beattie's Essay on the Nature and Immutability of Truth, and Dr. Oswald's Appeal to Common Sense on the Behalf of Religion*, London: J. Johnson, reprinted at New York: Garland Publishing Inc.

—— (1775/1973) *Hartley's Theory of the Human Mind, on the Principles of Association of Ideas; with Essays Relating to the Subject of It*, London: J. Johnson, reprinted at New York: AMS Press, Inc.

—— (1777/1976) *Disquisitions Relating to Matter and Spirit and the Doctrine of Philosophical Necessity Illustrated*, reprinted at New York: Garland Publishing, Inc.

Priestley, J. and Price, R. (1778/1977) *A Free Discussion of the Doctrines of Materialism, and Philosophical Necessity, In a Correspondence Between Dr. Price and Dr. Priestley*, reprinted at Millwood, New York: Kraus Reprint Co.

Puccetti, R. (1989) 'Two brains, two minds? Wigan's theory of mental duality', *British Journal for the Philosophy of Science* 40: 137–44.

Radner, J. B. (1979) 'The art of sympathy in eighteenth-century British moral thought', in R. Runte (ed.) *Studies in Eighteenth-century Culture*, vol. 9, Madison: University of Wisconsin Press.

Rand, B. (1900) *The life, unpublished letters and philosophical regimen of Anthony, Earl of Shaftesbury*, New York: The Macmillan Co.

Reed, E. S. (1997) *From Soul to Mind: the Emergence of Psychology from Erasmus Darwin to William James*, New Haven: Yale University Press.

Reid, T. (1764/1967) 'An inquiry into the human mind on the principles of common sense', in Hamilton, W. (ed.) *Philosophical Works of Thomas Reid*, vol. I (93–211), reprinted Hildesheim: Georg Olms.

—— (1785/1967) 'Essay on the intellectual powers of man', in Hamilton, W. (ed.) *Philosophical Works of Thomas Reid*, vol. I (213–508), reprinted Hildesheim: Georg Olms.

—— (1990) *Practical Ethics: Being Lectures and Papers on Natural Reiligion, Self-Government, Natural Jurisprudence, and the Law of Nations*, ed. from manuscripts with an introduction and commentary by K. Haarkonssen, Princeton: Princeton University Press.

Ribot, T. (1891/1906/1997) *Diseases of Personality*, reprinted in D. N. Robinson (ed.) *Significant Contributions to the History of Psychology, 1750–1920, Series C: Medical Psychology, Vol. 1: T. A. Ribot*, Washington: University Publications of America, Inc.

Roback, A. A. (1964) *A History of American Psychology*, New York: Collier Books.

Robinson, D. (1976) 'Thomas Reid's *Gestalt* psychology', in Barker, S. and Beauchamp, T. L. (eds) *Thomas Reid: Critical Interpretations*, Philadelphia: Philosophical Monographs.

Rorty, A. O. (ed.) (1976) *The Identities of Persons*, Berkeley: University of California Press.

—— (1990) ' "Pride produces the idea of self": Hume on moral agency', *Australasian Journal of Philosophy*, 68: 255–69.

Rovane, C. (1990) 'Branching self-consciousness', *The Philosophical Review*, 99: 355–95.

Royce, J. (1894/1964) 'Some observations on the anomalies of self-consciousness', in *Studies of Good and Evil* (169–97), Hamden, CT: Archon Books.

—— (1901/1913) *The World and the Individual: Second Series, Nature, Man, and the Moral Order*, New York: Macmillan Company.

Russell, P. (1988) 'Skepticism and natural religion in Hume's *Treatise*', *Journal of the History of Ideas*, 49: 247–65.

—— (1995) 'Hume's *Treatise* and the Clarke–Collins controversy', *Hume Studies* 21: 95–115.

Scheler, M. (1954) *The Nature of Sympathy*, P. Heath (trans.), London: Routledge & Kegan Paul.

Schechtman, M. (1996) *The Constitution of Selves*, Ithaca: Cornell University Press.

Schneewind, J. B. (1977) *Sidgwick's Ethics and Victorian Moral Philosophy*, Oxford: Oxford University Press.

Sergeant, J. (1697/1984) *Solid Philosophy Asserted, against the Fancies of the Ideists*, reprinted at New York: Garland Publishing, Inc.

Shaftesbury, A., Earl of (1711/1964) *Characteristics of Men, Manners, Opinion, Times*, vols I–II, J. M. Robertson (ed), Indianpolis: Bobbs-Merrill Company, Inc.

Sherlock, W. (1690) *A Vindication of the Doctrine of the Holy and Ever Blessed TRINITY and the Incarnation of The Son of God. Occasioned by the Brief Notes on the Creed of St. Athanasius, and the Brief History of the Unitarians, or Socinians, and containing an Answer to both*, Imprimatur, Jun.9.1690, London: W. Roger.

Shoemaker, S. (1970) 'Persons and their pasts', *American Philosophical Quarterly*, 7: 269–85.

—— (1984) 'Personal identity. A materialist account', in S. Shoemaker and R. Swinburne (eds), *Personal Identity*, Oxford: Basil Blackwell.

Shoemaker, S. and Swinburne, R. (eds) (1984) *Personal Identity*, Oxford: Basil Blackwell.

Sidgwick, H. (1874/1907/1962) *The Methods of Ethics*, 7th edn, Chicago: The University of Chicago Press.

Sikes, H. M., Bonner, W. H. and Lahey, G. (1972) *The Letters of William Hazlitt*, New York: New York University Press.

Smith, A. (1759/1984) *The Theory of Moral Sentiments*, D. D. Raphael and A. L. MacFie (eds), Indianapolis: Liberty Fund.

—— (1776/1937) *Wealth of Nations*, E. Cannan (ed.), New York: Modern Library.

Sperry, R. W. (1968) 'Hemisphere disconnection and unity in conscious experience', *American Psychologist*, 23: 723–33.

Spinoza, B. De (*c.*1675/1955) *Chief Works*, R. H. M. Elwes (ed. and trans.) New York: Dover.

Sosa, E. (1990) 'Surviving matters', *Nous* 24: 305–30.

Stewart, D. (1829) *The Works of Dugald Stewart*, vols I–VII, Cambridge: Hilliard and Brown.

Stewart, M. A. (ed.) (1990) *Studies in the Philosophy of the Scottish Enlightenment*, Oxford: Clarendon Press.

Stillingfleet, Edward, Lord Bishop of Worchester (1697) *A discourse in Vindication of the Doctrine of the Trinity: With an Answer to the Late Socinian Objections Against it from Scripture, Antiquity, and Reason And A Preface concerning the different Explications of the Trinity, and the Tendency of the present Socinian Controversies* (2nd edn), London: Henry Mortlock.

—— (1698) *The Bishop of Worchester's Answer to Mr. Locke's Second Letter, Wherein his Notion of Ideas is prov'd to be Inconsistent with it self And with the Articles of Christian Faith*, London.

Stout, G. F. (1888/1930) 'The Herbartian psychology', in *Studies in Philosophy and Psychology*, (1–50), London: Macmillan and Company.

Sutton, J. (1998) *Philosophy and Memory Traces: Descartes to Connectionism*, Cambridge: Cambridge University Press.

Thiel, U. (1979) 'Locke's concept of person', in R. Brandt (ed.) *John Locke: Symposium Wolfenbuttel 1979,* Berlin: de Gruyter.

Thompson, C., Barresi, J. and Moore, C. (1997) 'The development of future-oriented prudence and altruism in preschoolers', *Cognitive Development,* 12: 199–212.

Toland, J. (1696/1978) *Christianity Not Mysterious,* reprinted at New York: Garland Publishing.

Trawick III, L. M. (1963) 'Sources of Hazlitt's "metaphysical discovery"', *Philological Quarterly*, 42: 277–82.

Trotter (Cockburn), C. (1702/1751) 'A defence of the Essay of Human Understanding, written by Mr. Lock', in T. Birch (ed.) *The Works of Mrs Catharine Cockburn*, London: J. and P. Knapton.

—— (1726/1751) 'A letter to Dr. Hodsworth, in vindication of Mr. Locke', in T. Birch (ed.) *The Works of Mrs Catharine Cockburn*, London: J. and P. Knapton.

Tucker, A. [Pseudonym – Edward Search (1763a/1990) *Freewill, Foreknowledge, Fate: A Fragment*, London: R. & J. Dosdley, reprinted at Bristol: Thoemmes Antiquarian Books.

—— (1763b/1984) *Man in Quest of Himself: Or a Defence of the Individuality of Human Mind, or Self*, reprinted in S. Parr (ed.) *Metaphysical Tracts by English Philosophers of the Eighteenth Century*, reprinted: Hildesheim, Germany: Geog Olmes Verlag.

—— (1768–77/1805/1997) *The Light of Nature Pursued*, Vols I–VII, reprinted at New York: Garland Publishing.

Tulving, E. (1985) 'Memory and consciousness', *Canadian Psychology* 26: 1–12.

Turnbull, G. (1740) *The Principles of Moral Philosophy*, London: John Noon.

Unger, P. (1991) *Identity, Consciousness, and Value*, New York: Oxford University Press.

Uzgalis, W. (1990) 'Relative identity and Locke's principle of individuation', *History of Philosophy Quarterly*, 7: 283–97.

Vico, G. B. (1744/1986) *The New Science of Giambattista Vico: Unabridged Translation of the Third Edition* T. G. Bergin and M. H. Frisch (eds and trans.), Ithaca: Cornell University Press.

Watts, I. (1789) *Relique Juveniles: Miscellaneous thoughts in prose and Verse on Natural, Moral, and Divine Subjects, Written Chiefly in Younger Years*, London: J. Brickland.

Wedeking, G. (1990) 'Locke on personal identity and the Trinity controversy of the 1690's', *Dialogue*, XXIX: 163–88.

Wheeler, M. A., Stuss, D. T. and Tulving, E. (1997) 'Toward a theory of episodic memory: The frontal lobes and autonoetic consciousness', *Psychological Bulletin*, 121: 331–54.

White, S. (1989) 'Metapsychological relativism and the self', *The Journal of Philosophy*, 86: 298–323.

Wiggins, D. (1967) *Identity and Spatio-Temporal Continuity*, Oxford: Basil Blackwell.

Willey, B. (1940/1967) *The Eighteenth Century Background: Studies on the Idea of Nature in the Thought of the Period*, London: Penguin Books.

Wimmer, H. and Perner, J. (1983) 'Beliefs about beliefs: Representations and constraining function of wrong beliefs in young children's understanding of deception', *Cognition*, 13: 103–28.

Wolff, C. (1738) *Psychologia Empirica*, Frankurt and Leipzig: Officina Libraria Rengeriana.

—— (1740) *Psychologia Rationalis*, Frankfurt and Leipzig: Officina Libraria Rengeriana.

Wood, P. (1990) 'Science and the pursuit of virtue in the Aberdeen Enlightenment', in M. A. Stewart (ed.) *Studies in the Philosophy of the Scottish Enlightenment*, Oxford: Clarendon Press.

—— (1995) *Thomas Reid on the Animate Creation: Papers Relating to the Life Sciences*, Edinburgh: Edinburgh University Press.

Yolton, J. W. (1983) *Thinking Matter: Materialism in Eighteenth-Century Britain*, Minneapolis: University of Minnesota Press.

INDEX

Printed in Great Britain
by Amazon